AF779747

BUILDING YOUR ARK

Your Personal Survival Guide To The Year 2000 Crisis

by *Lia Marie Danks*

GARY NORTH SAYS:

"I think this is the best introductory guide for Y2K personal preparation plans on the market."

* * * * * * * * * *

"Building Your Ark" is available in two forms:
Electronic, downloadable version or
printed, spiral-bound workbook

Visit our Website at **www.yourark.com**
for further information about "Building Your Ark"
and ordering instructions, or order from:

DAL Enterprises, P.O. Box 17, West Fork, AR 72774,
or call: **888-240-9074**

Dealer prices available on request.

THE ACTION CHECKLIST - *Your **step-by-step personal guide** to Y2K preparedness. Use this checklist to get organized, shop for all your preparedness needs, and track your progress. For easy reference, pages are keyed to the related chapters.*

PREFACE

(Why You MUST Read This Book In The Next 72 Hours!)

Even the most cursory review of the thousands of Y2K sites on the Internet will reveal that there is an enormous variety of beliefs about the impact of the Y2K computer crisis. Opinions range all the way from "It's the end of the world as we know it", to "It's no big deal, just a minor inconvenience", and just about anything you can imagine in-between! And even the media is getting into the act with a growing number of reports about various congressional committee hearings and other events relative to the Y2K. For instance, CNN began their programming year on Jan. 1, 1999, with a series about the Year 2000 crisis. Most of the experts widely disagree about the consequences of this looming crisis, but everyone agrees on one crucial fact: ***THE YEAR 2000 IS COMING SOON, and no one can stop it!*** More and more people are becoming aware that no matter how hard we work to prevent it, something unavoidable is going to happen at the end of the century with the world's computers, and the machinery they operate. But no one as yet has any really concrete idea what that will be, or what the repercussions will be to our society or to ourselves as individuals.

No matter what your personal, religious or political agenda, you probably have a very strong interest in staying healthy, and alive, and reasonably comfortable, and in seeing that your loved ones do, too! So as you read through all the hype and hyperbole, the doom-and-gloom reports, it's time to begin thinking about what you can do for yourself and your family in the event that some of our vital infrastructures go down. The main problem most of us face is knowing how and where to begin our preparations. This book was created out of my own efforts to deal with the Y2K, and to share them with others.

I'm no stranger to crisis situations: Growing up in a coastal Texas town, I lived through many hurricanes, and I remember that it was fun and exciting for the kids, but quite difficult for the adults, coping with power outages, and water in the living room, and empty shelves at the grocery store. Also, my husband and I survived a very severe winter storm in Chicago some years ago, and saw how people, especially the elderly, struggled just to get food and stay warm. We have also lived simply in the country for nearly two decades, heating with wood, using composting toilets, and producing much of our own food, and have made it through some extended winter storms and power outages. But in these cases, and in the recent worldwide weather disasters, because the problem is usually confined to a regional area, there is always some non-local government agency or disaster service that can be depended on to ship in supplies and provide other necessary assistance.

However, in the Y2K scenario, ***the problem will be national and even worldwide in scope!*** So who will we call on for rescue if everyone else is in the same boat? If utilities, food and fuel deliveries, medical care, communications, and other vital services are in difficulty or down nationwide and worldwide, even for a short time, all of the people and organizations that we normally rely on for disaster assistance will be having the same problems that we are! ***So who will help the helpers?***

It's a scary thought, and one nobody seems to want to address...When they finally realize the vast scope of this problem, most people feel so helpless that they simply shut down and try not to think about it. ***But we must think about how we will take care of ourselves and our loved ones, because in this case, there will likely be nowhere else to turn. It's up to us...*** Since even the most optimistic computer gurus are saying that we're in for some difficulty, and since we can't rely on the usual disaster organizations to be available, making preparations for our own health and safety would seem to be a prudent course. But where and how to begin?

> ***"Start by doing what's necessary, then what's possible, and suddenly you are doing the impossible."*** St. Francis of Assisi

You have insurance for your life, your home and your auto, don't you? Then a good place to start is to begin setting up some "insurance" for the Y2K, in the form of a store of basic necessities that you and your family will need in order to weather the crisis. There are many emergency and survival manuals in print, but most are geared to random natural disasters or wilderness survival, and to very long-term storage preparations. Much of their advice is good, *but some will not be applicable in this crisis,* since we know when it will happen, and where we probably will be located. Most of us will not be trying to escape a disaster area and won't need a lot of the portable emergency supplies featured in many catalogs. And some of this can get very expensive! This workbook, however, provides you with a detailed, do-able, affordable, **Y2K-SPECIFIC PROGRAM** to follow, so that you will be able to meet the potential problems head on, in your own environment, instead of putting them off and hoping they will go away.

> ***"A perfect method for adding drama to life is to wait until the deadline looms large."*** Alyce P. Cornyn-Selby "Procrastinator's Success Kit"

The Boy Scout motto is right...be prepared! Wouldn't you agree that it is easier to make preparations ahead of time, when there are no shortages or other problems, than it is to do so in the middle of an emergency situation? So why not put away some easily obtained supplies now, while you can afford the time and money, *and while they're available*? In the worst/best case scenario, if nothing much happens with the Y2K, and life continues as usual, you can just eat up the extra food (or donate it to charity), drink up the extra water, and sell the other equipment to campers and hikers, (or use it yourself). No big deal. And...if you purchase food and other supplies now, when prices are low, you will have made a wise investment, because prices are sure go up after the Y2K, no matter how uneventful it is.

But time is becoming a critical factor. *Many companies that provide survival supplies are already months behind in filling orders.* And it's unlikely that some manufacturers will ever be able to meet the increasing demand for their products. So **YOU MUST GET STARTED ON YOUR Y2K PREPARATIONS IMMEDIATELY!** Many experts feel that we don't have until the actual January 1, 2000 date to prepare, but that we only have a few months before things could start to unravel. Many government fiscal years will begin early in 1999, and extend into the year 2000, and their problems could show up as soon as their fiscal year begins. Here are several dates to watch:

December, 1998: This date has been set by most major computer users for their programmers to have their systems compliant and ready for testing, as it is expected that this will take up most of the year 1999. Testing the newly corrected programs can be time-consuming, and is considered to be a critical 40% of the compliance procedure. Any company that is not ready to *test* their systems by this date can be considered seriously behind in their Y2K compliance.

March 31, 1999: This is the deadline that the U.S. Office of Management and Budget has set for for all government agencies to begin implementation of their supposedly compliant computer programs. As of the fifth quarterly report, the OMB reported that, "Six agencies have identified systems that are either behind schedule or that will miss the 3/31/99 implementation deadline."

July 1, 1999: In the U.S., forty-six of the fifty states begin their fiscal year 2000. Since many of the states are known to be behind in their compliance efforts, this could be the beginning of problems at the local level.

August 31, 1999: The Global Positioning System (GPS) is the multi-satellite system that controls the reception of all navigation information for everything from campers to trucks, to trains, to the movements of armed services. Most importantly, it is used to co ordinate power generators in the electrical grid that are too far away for conventional coordination. It is keyed to a date function that will roll over to zero in September, 1999. Because these satellites are controlled by embedded microchips that we are unable to check for compliance, as of now, no one can accurately predict what will happen with the GPS system.

September, 1999: Some programmers are concerned about the "99" problem: Many computer programs have an "end code" that tells the computer when it has come to the end of a job, and this is often a date-like code such as 9/9/99 or 99/99/99. Many computers are programmed to do a recap, a summary, a delete, or an erasure of the material containing this code. This function could be triggered by the "99" at the end of date codes, or by a date such as Sept. 9, 1999 (9/9/99). Some feel that this is an unlikely occurance, but it could happen, and many vital records could be lost.

October 1, 1999: The Federal Government starts their fiscal year 2000. It's possible that any government agencies that are not yet compliant could experience serious disruption of their functions and services.

Any of these dates could be the beginning of some degree of confusion or chaos in our data processing systems. And because they are all deeply interrelated, one problem can easily lead to another, and another...So it's easy to see that we probably don't have an entire year from January, 1999, to begin our preparations!

Considering the wide-spread uncertainties concerning the functioning of our modern technological infrastructure, you may not want to wait until the last minute to begin your personal preparations! When you weigh the the effort, time and expense of "building your Ark", against the possible life-threatening effects of not being prepared, the advantages are clear. Fortunately, the **"BUILDING YOUR ARK"** workbook solves the biggest problem for most people - ***time***. You don't have to spend hours reading, studying, and searching for preparedness information and sources of supply. I've taken many months to coordinate all this for you in one easy-to-use manual, and even created a step-by-step ***ACTION CHECKLIST***, so you can begin your preparations right away. All you have to do is read the workbook, and follow directions. There's no easier way to insure that you and yours will pass through the Y2K with a minimum of trouble!

A FEW WORDS ABOUT THE UPCOMING Y2K CHANGES...

"The problem with discussing the subject of change is that everyone changes the subject!" Anonymous

Obviously, the underlying theme of this entire book is change, because if only some of the events outlined in the preceeding chapter do come to pass, things could change radically for all of us. And it won't matter a bit whether we like it or not; we will have to adapt to the demands of the times and the realities of our personal situations.

Studies have shown that people forced to make these changes under unexpected emergency conditions, such as weather disasters and social unrest, almost always suffer varying degrees of psychological stress and even physical illness. So it seems that it would be best for us to begin initiating a series of small, planned, lifestyle changes well before the necessity to do so arises. This way, we can begin to simplify our lives in positive ways, and still keep many decisions under our control.

WHERE TO BEGIN

"Change starts when somebody sees the next step." Wm. Drayton in "Esquire"

There are many things that you can do to begin positive change...and most of them would be good to do under any circumstances: For instance, simplify your diet, which most health care practitioners say is good for us anyway! If you don't already have an exercise program, start one now, in order to be in top shape when the time comes. Cultivate a group of friends and neighbors with whom you can share necessities and activities. Get your personal finances in order. Study about health and first aid. And of course, begin to stock up on basic supplies. We'll cover all of these in later chapters. The extent to which you prepare will be according to how severe you believe the crisis will be, and that is something only you can decide. But, everyone really needs just a few basic things to survive - shelter, water, food, health supplies, and sanitation facilities, so we'll give these the most attention. Once we have them secured, we can go on to other concerns such as safety, personal finance, transportation, communication, etc...

THINK MANUAL

When gathering supplies and equipment, think "manual". Remember that a little over a century ago, almost all of the things that we take for granted in our modern society were not in existence, yet people managed to survive in reasonable comfort, spending most of their time manually caring for their basic needs. So think 1900 instead of 2000! Don't worry about how you will pass the time during the crisis: If there are no utilities, even for just a little while, there are many things that you will have to do by hand that will take more time than you realize. Preparing food, cleaning up afterwards, keeping warm, washing clothes, and dealing with sanitation and personal hygiene can use up a lot of energy and most of the daylight hours. You probably won't even miss the TV!

In any emergency, tools and practical equipment become scarce and very valuable. We'll discuss many of these indoor appliances in the text, but necessary outdoor equipment will vary widely depending on your living arrangements. So take an inventory of all the outdoor tools and equipment that you think you will need to replace the electric or gas-powered ones that you're currently using - such as a hand saw, a drill, garden tools, wheelbarrow, etc. A list of these is in the ***ACTION CHECKLIST,*** and you can expand it to suit your needs. Many can be obtained at flea markets and garage sales at very low cost.

ADDICTIONS

A word on a sensitive subject: if you are currently ingesting any addictive substance, from nicotine and caffeine to alcohol or drugs, you may want to try to deal with it before the Y2K. There is probably nothing more uncomfortable than being forced to quit an addictive habit under emergency conditions! You might think you can stock up enough of the substance, but what would happen if supplies are exhausted and you couldn't obtain any more? What would you do to get it? You'll have enough to deal with without going "cold turkey" from an addictive habit!

Just a suggestion to make things easier...

THE DATE IS KNOWN

The good news is that since we know the date of this probable "disaster", we can prepare for it much more deliberately. For instance, you can choose an optimal setting if you don't wish to stay home during this time. Perhaps you have family or close friends who live in suburban or rural locations with whom you could arrange an extended vacation and could pool resources. Or,if you live in a suburban or rural area and have room, you can invite family and close friends to join you. You can bring the elderly or those needing special care to your location. Don't limit your creativity: perhaps church and summer camps can be activated, and groups can plan to spend this time together. This will take some planning, but could have many advantages. The possiblities are endless.

As mentioned in the Preface, problems could begin as early as spring of 1999, as that is when the various state governments' fiscal years begin, and their computing will then have to include the year 2000. So plan to have most of your preparations finished as quickly as possible.

TRAVEL

Hotels all over the world are booked full with holiday travelers for the big Millennium celebration, and if you are one of those planning a trip, you might want to reconsider. It probably would not be a good idea to be traveling during the actual week of the Y2K. You could get stranded in a foreign location with no way to return home for some time. Even the government is suggesting that no one be on an airplane over the New Year's weekend. Most airlines will probably not schedule flights. And what if you left children, pets or other dependents behind? *How would they manage if you couldn't get home?* It's worth considering.

A DRY RUN

One of the most helpful things you can do during the time before the Y2K is to conduct a dry run to test your equipment and skills. You don't want to wait until the time is upon us to find that some equipment doesn't work, or that you have forgotten to stock a crucial item. Take a weekend and really pretend that all utilities and outside communications are down. Test both your supplies, equipment, and your reactions to the situation. If you have children, you can frame this as a "home camping trip" and make it as fun as possible. You might want to conduct it during cold weather in order to closely duplicate the probable conditions. If you live in a warm climate, then you can do it anytime. But don't wait until the last minute to find out that you've forgotten something critical.

THE REAL WORST CASE SCENARIO

If you decide on a location and travel to it, or stay home, stock up on necessities, and hunker down to wait things out - and nothing happens - the worst thing is that you've spent some money and time getting prepared. And your ego will probably be a bit bruised as the naysayers take this opportunity to laugh at you. But the real worst case scenario is not to have prepared at all and suddenly find that it's too late, *that you are responsible for a lot of suffering for yourself and your loved ones, and that there's nothing you can do about it.* When you weigh the options, being prepared seems to make a lot of sense.

> ***"When we have provided against cold, hunger, and thirst, all the rest is but vanity and excess."*** Seneca

SHELTER

Unlike major weather disasters, the Y2K problem probably won't cause any physical damage at first, so you are not likely to be driven out of your home. You can probably count on having some kind of shelter available, but how comfortable and safe will it be? You should take an inventory of your shelter, and what you will need to heat it during the winter months and to keep it safe and secure. Because the severest part of this crisis could occur during the winter in the northern hemisphere, keeping warm will be a priority for most people. However, if you live in the southern hemisphere, keeping cool will likely be your greatest need. You will also need to provide lighting, some means of cooking food, and the fuel for both activities. Knowing how to do this safely is important.

WATER

Assuming there will be enough air to breathe, the next most important thing is water. You can't live very long without it. And you quickly can become very ill and even die of waterborne diseases. It's crucial that you know what kind of water purification you will need for different water sources, and that there is a difference between a water *filter* and a water *purifier*. It's also important to know what kind of chemical purifiers treat the different waterborne pathogens. So if the public utilities go down for any length of time, you'll need to assure yourself of an ample supply of clean water, or the means to get it.

FOOD

Unlike people in many third world countries, most of us are used to eating at least three meals a day. It doesn't take very long to run out of food if you have a family with big appetites! Fortunately, this is the one area that gives you a lot of latitude to experiment and innovate. You can get by quite well on much less than you're acustomed to, and it's a good idea to begin planning some dietary changes well before you're forced to do so. It doesn't have to be boring or leave you feeling deprived. I'll show you how to eat well and enjoy delicious, nutritious meals for very little time, effort, and money.

HEALTH & SANITATION

Obviously, this manual is not for those in special conditions, such as hospitals, prisons, etc. This is for those people who have a choice in the way that they manage their lifestyle, and the freedom to change it. And one of the biggest areas of concern is that of health. If you've been putting off any health care at all, now's the time to see to it. Don't wait until the last minute to get yourself in the best possible shape. Getting through the crisis period will be hard on even the healthiest people. Don't leave yourself vulnerable in this area. And dealing with sanitation is a major problem even in normal times, and one that most people don't want to think about. So don't forget to make preparations for waste disposal.

OTHER AREAS

Information about how to deal with the problems with finances, self defense, transportation, and communications are also important, but these won't be your absolute survival priority in a severe crisis, unless you live in an area that has a history of violence and unrest. Some of these issues are both very personal and individual, and you will have to decide how important they are to you. There is a lot of information available from other sources about these subjects, but later chapters address these and offer helpful suggestions.

NO FEAR...

Getting through the crisis ahead is going to take a change of attitude more than anything else. So don't fear or resist change; it's inevitable, anyway. And probably the easiest attitude to adopt is one of curiosity, openness, and willingness to accept it, such as: "Change is coming...what is it likely to be, and how can I adapt to it with the least amount of effort and stress?" This attitude will leave you relaxed, alert, and hopefully, prepared for anything.

It can be done. Buying this book was the first step. Putting the plan into action is the next. So let's get started on your plan...

YOUR PLAN

"The best way to predict the future is to create it." Peter F. Drucker

First of all, this is a workbook; it is not meant as an in-depth analysis of the Year 2000 problem. I'm assuming that if you've bought the book, you are somewhat aware of the pending problem with the world's computers, and are therefore interested in providing for yourself and your family during the upcoming crisis period. Most of Chapter One is devoted to a brief discussion of the expected Year 2000 crisis, (Y2K, as it is abbreviated). We then move on to more practical advice. If you are connected to the Internet, you can easily access the enormous number of sites covering the Y2K via any search engine (*or Appendix B - Internet Links*), and obtain as much information as you desire.

The main focus of this workbook is to spur you to take action and begin your own Y2K preparations! In reading it, I hope you will be as surprised and pleased as I was at the enormous variety of supplies and specialized equipment available for emergencies. Please take the time to learn as much as you can about what's appropriate for your individual situation before you begin to order and stock up on equipment and supplies.

YOUR CHOICE...

As with any book of this kind, the ideas presented herein are my own - I've done the research for you, and I've also distilled the knowledge I've gained from many years' experience in this field. The lifestyle might not be how you would want to live all the time, but following these suggestions can get you through this emergency with a minimum of hassle. Know that everything in this book is optional: Even though I will give many suggestions, *you will have to make the final assessment of how you use the information and how much preparation you think is appropriate.*

The ***ACTION CHECKLIST*** in the Appendix contains a detailed listing of all suggested supplies and equipment, and space for you to add your own items as you personalize the list. If you live in an area where you can find most of the suggested products, you might want to consider purchasing supplies locally to save time and money, and make returns easier. But you will probably have to order some prepared storage food and certain specialty items from online or printed catalogs.

HOW LONG TO PREPARE FOR

"Wisdom consists of the anticipation of consequences" Norman Cousins

The question of how long to prepare for is a hard one to answer. Some experts who are survivalists think that planning for a year or longer is necessary. Other experts think that there will be just a day or two of inconvenience. The truth probably lies somewhere in-between. If you can afford to do so, *laying in at least a six month supply of food, medicine, heating fuel and water would be prudent.* You definitely don't want to run out of water, so store as much of that as you possibly can. Simply take the recommended per-person amounts of food and water for the time you choose, and multiply by the number of people you will have to provide for. And if you can plan to grow a garden of any size in the spring, it would help ease the problem of a fresh food supply *(see Chapter 6 - Food Production).* Whatever the length and severity of the Y2K problem, the more people who have extra supplies to rely on, the greater the relief on our infrastructure as it tries to put itself back together.

It would also be wise to put aside extra food and supplies in case you have to share with others. You might consider storing items that have been used in the past for barter during times of war. It's not pleasant to contemplate, but it might become necessary if shortages continue for a time. Currently, (according to CNN), most of the Russian people are surviving on barter, as their money continues to devalue and their fragile economic situation grows worse. Many will face starvation over the winter of '99 if they don't receive massive shipments of food and fuel from outside sources. These people never believed that this could happen to them, but it did...and we might do well to take a lesson from them. *(Barter is discussed in Chapter 13 - Personal Safety.)*

HOW TO USE THIS BOOK

The workbook is divided into several sections to make it easier to use: since it's written for a wide audience living in varied situations, when appropriate I've divided some chapters into three areas - Urban, Suburban, and Rural. Each of these locations will have their own advantages and disadvantages, both in the preparation and actual crisis stages, which we'll discuss.

* **"Urban"** denotes those persons living in apartments, condos, dormitories, high-rises and other multi-family dwellings with no useful land.
* **"Suburban"** denotes those living on property with any small amount of useful land.
* **"Rural"** is for those living in unincorporated areas, with several acres of land available.

By using these categories, you can further tailor your preparations to your local situation. If you are on a strict budget, those items that should be obtained by everyone will be starred (*) in the ***ACTION CHECKLIST,*** and you will know to start your preparations by obtaining them first. There are several Appendices with lists of useful information, such as sources for catalogs of supplies and information, food and nutrition, links to other sites, and more.

Be aware that getting ready for a crisis of this magnitude may take some time and thought, even with this workbook and the ***ACTION CHECKLIST***. You may have to reschedule your time to accomodate this. Here's some suggestions for getting started:

1) **BEGIN BUILDING YOUR ARK:**

a) Many people skip around in a book, but your most efficient way to begin is by reading each chapter as they are presented in the book, as they are arranged in order of the most crucial areas to consider. As you read, mark any products that you think you'll need.

b) Make notes of any ideas that occur to you as you study this information, total up the approximate cost of your chosen supplies, and make a budget for their purchase over the time you have left to prepare *(plan to be finished by summer of '99 or earlier, if at all possible).*

c) Prioritize your purchases to take advantage of dwindling supplies in several areas (this will be discussed in the appropriate chapters), and seasonal availability of some foods and other items.

d) Decide where you will be located when the expected problems arise, and if you will have to travel to a different location from your home. (This can determine how and where you store your supplies.)

e) If you decide to join with others to share space and expenses, make any necessary arrangements and agreements now. This can determine what and how much of the recommended supplies that you will need to purchase yourself, and what can be shared with your group.

2) **ORDER CATALOGS** - Note the catalogs offering the products you will need, (the catalog code is abbreviated at the left margin of each product listing) ***and order them right away***, as it can take several weeks to get them. Addresses and phone numbers are listed in Appendix D - Catalogs. Order most of the general merchandise catalogs for a good comparison on prices.

3) **WORK WITH THE *ACTION CHECKLIST*:**

a) Study the ***ACTION CHECKLIST***, personalize it, and add any items you have thought of while reading the book, in order to adapt the plan to your needs.

b) When the catalogs arrive, read them carefully, compare the prices with your local list, and decide what you'll purchase locally and what by catalog order.

c) Then go back to the ***ACTION CHECKLIST*** and note on it where you'll purchase each item.

4) **BEFORE THE CATALOGS ARRIVE**

a) Purchase any books mentioned in the text that you want to study during this time, if you can obtain them from your local bookstore or online. Otherwise, you can order them from the catalogs when they arrive *(books are listed by subject, within the text of each chapter).* Much of the information in these books will allow you to make an informed decision about your Y2K supplies purchases. Also access the online Websites listed in *Appendix B - Links*, for much useful, free information.

b) Go shopping for local prices on the items you plan to buy. Take the ***ACTION CHECKLIST*** with you and record the prices you find on it. Don't buy anything yet, until you compare these prices with those in the catalogs (unless money is no object).

c) Possible local sources for supplies:

* Sporting goods and outdoor camping supply stores.

* Farm supply, hardware, and home-supply department stores.
* Discount "dollar" stores for good prices on many small items.
* Don't forget local natural food stores for herbs and other specialty food items (which they can usually order if they don't carry them).
* Wholesale natural food warehouses *(listed in Appendix A - Food),* will deliver orders on a wide variety of bulk food items. If necessary, get with others to make a bulk order.
* Talk to your grocer to see if he will order cases of products for you.
* Shop flea markets and attend garage sales to pick up some great bargains, but don't depend on this method to obtain the priority items.

d) Keep a detailed record of your food and household supply purchases for at least two weeks to get an idea of how much to store and what your family's specific needs are *(more information on this can be found in Appendix A - Food).*

5) **STORAGE SPACE** - Another thing to do while waiting for the catalogs to arrive is to locate and prepare a storage space for the extra supplies you'll be stocking:

a) Clean out a closet normally used for out-of season items and clothing. Pack these in away in boxes or under-the-bed containers.
b) Clean out a storeroom, basement, or garage, and install any needed shelving. Be sure that any area with an outside entrance can be securely locked.
c) Use an extra bedroom, a laundry room, the space under a stairwell, or even the corner of a larger room for storage.
d) Locate a safe place to store your fuel supplies, well away from any dwelling, but easily accessesd without driving, that can also be locked. (This can involve putting up a small storage building.) If you find that your local regulations don't allow for fuel storage, you may have to get a friend in a rural area to store it for you.
e) If you suspect that you'll need to get permission to store fuel or make any alterations to your living space, take care of this before you order any items, as this can determine what supplies you stock.

6) **OBTAIN YOUR SUPPLIES:**

a) Begin ordering all priority items from the catalogs. *Do this first, as some suppliers could run out of certain critical products very soon, and many food storage companies are already experiencing shortages and delays in shipping.*
b) Take the ***ACTION CHECKLIST*** with you when you shop, and begin making any local purchases. Take advantage of sales and specials to stock up on household items.
c) Some items can be purchased via the "buddy" system - every time

you go to the store, simply buy an extra item or two, and add it to your storage inventory. This allows you to spread the expense out over time. Keep a running tally of these items.

d) Cross off each item on the ***ACTION CHECKLIST*** as you buy or receive it, and note the date. (This will help you keep on schedule.)

7) **INVENTORY** - If you have supplies stored in several locations around your home or property, you might want to keep an inventory list showing where everything is located. And keep this list in a safe and hidden place!

8) **SHARE** - Encourage your friends and family to get this workbook and ***ACTION CHECKLIST*** and follow your lead. The more people who are prepared, the easier it will be for everyone, and the less you'll have to supply for them! Don't think they won't come knocking at your door when they run out of water and food....

9) **RELAX** - and enjoy the feeling of being ready for whatever comes!

You can use the information in this book in any way that you please; the above are just suggestions to keep you on track to complete the important project of preparing your Ark.

DISCLAIMER

The information in this book is not meant as personal, dietary, medical, or financial advice, and in no case should you take any actions based on it without consulting your chosen lawyer, doctor or health care professional. Nor will I be responsible for any injuries sustained from the use of any products recommended in this publication. It's up to you to learn how to safely use any equipment that you purchase. Please take all advised safety precautions.

The sources for equipment and supplies in this book are those that I have found over the years to be useful. *However, I claim no responsibility for the performance of any of the businesses listed, or of their products, nor is any guarantee implied*...in other words, "Caveat Emptor"! Let the buyer beware!

INPUT

I will continue to be open to further input that can add to the information in this book. Simply contact me via mail (see address on order form at back of book), or email with your contribution (see the email form on our Members Update Page at our Website at **www.yourark.com**). The free Update Page is in the Member Section on the Website for all customers to access, and I will include new information as it becomes available. I have written this book as a service...if it helps even one family weather the coming crisis, then my purpose has been fulfilled. And if you find this workbook useful, ***please recommend it to family and friends ...you may be able to help them prepare, also.*** I am offering it first on the Internet because I feel that there is no time to wait; ***we need to get our preparations started right away !*** A printed version also is now available *(see page 2 for ordering information).* So if you know of anyone who is not connected to the Internet, please help them obtain a copy. Word-of-mouth recommendation speaks louder than any advertising, so thanks in advance for spreading the word!

BUILDING YOUR ARK FOR THE YEAR 2000
Chapter 1

"It wasn't raining when Noah built the Ark".....Anonymous

The above well-known quote implies that there is wisdom not only in planning ahead for an emergency, but also in taking definite action on those plans. I'm writing this book because, in my opinion, it's 'way past time for us to get busy.

"Doing what?", you ask...

Well, for starters, ***getting ready to deal with what could possibly be the single greatest disruption of life that the world has experienced since the advent of modern technology.***

Sounds dramatic, doesn't it?

It is, and it's something that is coming - inevitably. The date is fixed and our deadline (as of this writing, 1/99) is exactly 12 months away, and probably less than that *(see the Preface).* And time is something that no one knows how to extend, no matter how hard we try. So... what is this awful deadline?

It's something that you've already heard about from the Internet, the news, or other sources - it's the Year 2000 Computer Problem, Y2K...the Millennium Bug.

"Oh," you say, "that's just a problem with the computer-geek community...they're working on it...things will get fixed in time, they always do."

Oh, really....?

The truth is, recent polls (late1998), have shown that almost 70% of the people outside the computer world, or below the level of corporate management in business, don't yet have a clue about what's really going on. *That's very dangerous, because you or your family's well being or lives could be at stake.* According to computer experts and others who've investigated the situation, *there is no possibility that all of the problems will be fixed in time (see the Quotes and Questions page on our Website at* **www.yourark.com***).* It's certain that there will be some disruptions in our lives at the turn of the century. The only question is, will they be minor blips, or will they rip apart the fabric of our society?

On June 25, 1998, in Senate hearings on Government Computer Security, Lt. General Kenneth Minihan, Director of the NSA said, "The Year 2000 is the El Nino of the Digital Age."

As recently as June, 1998, Alan Greenspan, head of the Federal Reserve, questioned in an interview on CNN about the impact of the Year 2000 computer crisis, stated that he didn't think anyone really knew what the extent of the problem would be. If someone this highly connected to economic and government circles doesn't know *(or isn't saying)* what to expect from the Y2K problem, then we have cause to worry...

THE BAD NEWS FIRST...

As in most things, there's some good news and some bad news. Let's look at the bad news first:

Over the past century, we've developed an interconnected, electronically-based civilization that is more complex and more dangerously fragile than anything the world has known before. In less than fifty years, computers have become the basic operating systems in virtually every aspect of modern life. And now, facing the end of this century, we find that many aspects of our complex culture operate in large part without direct human intervention, and instead depend almost completely on powerful systems of computerized machinery. These systems connect our world in innumerable ways that the average person can't imagine, certainly can't operate, and usually never even notices. But they've provided us with a level of luxury and comfort that none of us are eager to relinquish, so we continue to use them, ignoring how dependent we are on them to provide us with the basic necessities of life. In fact, almost everything that we take for granted as part of modern life, such as banking, entertainment, the media, travel, education, utilities, food production, medicine, social services, manufacturing, commerce, you-name-it, relies on computers.

But all that may change drastically by the year 2000, because a great many of our computers (and microchips) are simply going to quit doing what they normally do because of a small mistake made half a century ago...

THE PROBLEM

If you want to go into the technical details of the so-called Millennium Bug there are thousands of sites on the Internet that you can explore *(see Appendix B - Internet Links)*. It's enough to know that it's going to happen because of a very simple mistake. About fifty years ago, before the advent of the personal computer (PC), the first programmers working on the early mainframe computer systems tried to save some time and money. Some savings! It never occurred to them that any of these mainframes would still be up and running half a century later, so they took a shortcut and programmed the computers to access dates according to a two-digit code, instead of a four-digit code. In other words, the year date in all computations would be recognized as 49, or 98, instead of 1949, or 1998.

Now this works as long as we're in the same century, but what happens when it all rolls over into the year 2000? The computers don't know about this new century (they have a distressing tendency to do what you tell them to do, not what you want them to do...), and they think it's 1900, not 2000!

This can wreak complete havoc with date-sensitive records of any kind, because the computer then won't recognize any data entered after the year 1900! The data still may be stored in its memory, but the computer doesn't know how to access it. It will think that you aren't even born yet, and won't print your paycheck; or it may figure you were born in 1859 instead of 1959, and now owe well over century's worth of interest on your loans... It's possible that the bank will lose access to your records, as will insurance companies, the IRS, the Social Security System, and most other government institutions. Businesses will not be able to access their customers' data for orders or deliveries, or obtain supplies from their vendors, and will have to shut down operations, and on and on...And the computers that control our nation's utility grids, basic communications, and industrial machinery, may also malfunction, with disastrous results. In June, 1998, it was reported on CNN that *eight out of the ten major utility suppliers reviewed by a Senate committee weren't expected to be Y2K compliant.* Senator Bob Bennett (R-Utah), who released the results of the special committee, said that he was worried *"about the very real prospects of power shortages as a consequence of the Millennial date change."*

SO FIX IT...

So just fix it, you say? Well, if it were only that simple...

You see, in order to remedy the problem, you have to go in and change each separate date code, searching for them in one of the many languages in which they were programmed. Most of these old computer languages, including COBOL, are deader than Latin, and almost no one knows how to use them now. But supposing you *could* find a good COBOL programmer: he would still have to figure out the individual access codes that the original programmers used in order to locate the essential information. And if he can accomplish this, then he has to sort through literally millions of lines of code to find and correct the errors... and this takes time - LOTS of time. It's been estimated that we should have started on this project well over a decade ago, in order to stand any chance of finishing before the end of the century. It's also been estimated that we will need around *600,000 programmers* worldwide who are literate in COBOL and the other arcane computer languages to complete the job! Know of any? Many of the programmers who once knew these languages have gone on to other things, and many, in spite of the enormous salaries offered, are refusing to work under the pressures of the Y2K project. So just finding enough skilled people for the job is a major part of the problem.

And then, there's the testing, to see if all the code changes - often millions of them in any one system - will work. This can take longer than correcting the errors, and use up at least half of any computer's operating capacity. How many mainframe computers that are still running our largest institutions have this kind of extra capacity and time available? Almost none. And it's a known fact that whenever you make any changes in a program, there is a certain percentage of *new* errors introduced, which then have to be located, remedied, tested, and so on...

So even the briefest investigation of this situation quickly reveals that *very few of our vital infrastructure institutions can realistically be expected to be Y2K compliant in time.* And this could cause major systems-wide crashes, because the real problem is that unless all computers within any linked system (think international banking or the stock exchanges) are Y2K compliant, then *they can't interface and function with the compliant computers in that system.* So even one or two laggard computers can cripple the functioning of an entire national or international business or industry!

As recently as May 20, 1998, in reporting on the failure of the pager system due to a fault in a satellite, ABC news said, "*A failure in one part of the system radiates outward, and can bring the entire system down.*" They estimated that it would take about a month to repair the damage. This was inconvenient, but what if it had been a system vital to national health or security?

Unfortunately, many different aspects of modern life are now so interdependent that it's virtually impossible to untangle them. For instance, the food industry depends on the rail and trucking industry for delivery of their products. The trucking industry, in turn, depends on computers for routing and invoicing, and upon the gasoline industry for fuel. The gas stations depend on trucks to deliver that fuel, on electricity to pump it, and on computers for scheduling and invoicing, and so on in a circular dance of dependency! *If any part of this cycle falters, the entire system can break down entirely.* How and where do you start repair efforts in a system this complex once it breaks down?

And never mind the cost to business and industry of becoming Y2K compliant... some estimates are in the *trillions* of dollars! Ned Potter, on ABC World News Tonight, 11/11/98 reported that U.S. and European firms alone will have to spend over $850 *billion* just upgrading their computer systems (that's equal to half the economy of Germany). And this number has jumped 20% in just the last six months! This is money that will not produce any profits, but is spent only to avoid disaster. Some companies simply can't afford to make the necessary Y2K changes, but unfortunately, none of them can afford not to. Many businesses are expected to go under due to the expense, and there are already several mergers that are attributed to the pressures of Y2K. The legal ramifications and costs of all this also are staggering and far too extensive to go into here.

PERSONAL COMPUTERS

So why not just switch everything over to PCs, you ask? Because unless they were manufactured in the past two years and tested, a very large percentage of them will revert to 1980 or 1984 date codes! *Don't assume that because you have bought a recent model PC, that it has been tested for the Y2K problem.* Many haven't been, so don't rely on them to keep your business or home running as usual. They **all** will have to be tested and made compliant before the Y2K. And transferring the functions of the large mainframe computers onto the smaller PC systems, if it could be done at all, would take a major investment in new equipment, the proper software (if it exists), and operators specially trained for such a chore. It's highly unlikely that it could be done at all, and certainly not in the time remaining to us...

EMBEDDED SYSTEMS

Even more serious is the problem with the so-called "embedded systems" or date-sensitive microchips, that function as part of the working electronics in most machines and appliances in every area of modern life. An estimated *25 to 50 BILLION* of these chips are in use worldwide, and if even a tiny fraction of them fail in their date-related functions, they can cause breakdowns in everything from elevators, (which sit at the bottom of their shaft, awaiting a nonexistent safety check), to medical life-support machines, to airplane guidance systems, to industrial equipment that can shut down entire factories. They were never intended to be replaced, as most have no working parts, and many are deeply buried in the interior of their machinery. And *there's no way to know ahead of time which of these tiny microchips will malfunction, and which will not!*

Once they've failed, replacing these microprocessors isn't simple: Unlike correcting a computer program, where a programmer goes into the basic operating system and makes changes with the machine up and running, the machine containing the microchip must be shut down, the chip located, removed, reordered *(and if it's over three years old, it's possibly not being manufactured anymore!)*, shipped and reinstalled, and finally tested. It's a time-consuming problem, and almost impossible in some situations where entire systems have to be shut down (air-traffic control, telephone or electrical grids, for instance). However, in many cases, it's still possible to complete some system-checks before the Y2K, but how can it be done *after* Y2K if many basic supply and delivery systems are malfunctioning or shut down? *Unless business and industry begin testing and replacing these billions of microprocessors now, they will almost certainly be unable to do so later.*

In a Fortune Magazine article in April, 1997, the Chief Information Officer of General Motors, speaking on the manufacturing industry's dependence on imbedded microprocessors said, *"We have a catastrophic situation in all our plants world-wide."*

GOVERNMENT

And what about the government? Aren't they in charge of things? Surely they have the situation under control! *Don't they* ???

Unfortunately, a report on CNN in June, 1998, said that the House Government Reform and Oversight Committee's Subcommittee on Government Management, Information, and Technology, *had given the government an overall grade of "F"* for it's Y2K compliance efforts up to that date. Many departments, including Transportation, State, and Defense won't be compliant until *years* after the turn of the century. Later report cards on the government agencies weren't much better, with only the Social Security Administration considered near compliance.

However, even though they got the only "A" in the Subcommittee's evaluation, it's actually unlikely that the Social Security system will be ready for Y2K either, due to a typical government tendency to "pass the buck": This system, one of the most important government departments, processes payments that support approximately *40 million* people every month. They started their Y2K conversion in 1989, and were only about 1/4 complete as of 1997! Even though they've announced they'd be ready in time, they also announced (early 1998) that they had just found over *30 million* more lines of code that they hadn't realized would need correction! They are currently saying that this is the states' problem, as the codes refer to the interface with state computer systems. So the question arises: who's going to do it, and how can they complete this enormous job in just a couple of years? However, let's hope they do, because *no one wants to contemplate what millions of people will do when their checks don't come, they run out of money, and their families need food and other necessities...*

In addition to the possibility of millions of people without Social Security and other supplemental government checks, who will pay taxes if they think the IRS can't find their records? How will the government run without the current tax structure to pay its expenses? What happens to our economy if the stock markets and banking systems worldwide go down? (The recent deep and frightening drop in the U.S. stock market [early '98] was said to be a reaction to the economic and political events in Asia and Russia, half a world away...) What will happen if we have serious problems right here at home? And in light of the recent terrorist bombings and promises of more incidents, how will we protect our country if the thousands of military computers and embedded chips in military hardware and satellites malfunction?

How will businesses cope without the transportation and communication industries to assist them? (Remember the UPS strike last year?) What about the millions of people dependent on medications and medical life-support systems? What will people do for food if farming equipment and the rail and trucking systems break down; for water if the pumping stations quit; for heat if fuel isn't delivered? Starting to get the picture?

As the comic character Pogo said many years ago:

"We have found the enemy, and he is us!"

NO EASY OUT

There doesn't seem to be any easy out to this. There are a lot of good people out there, working hard to find solutions to this problem, but it's just so enormous, that at this point, it doesn't look like those solutions can possibly come in time. *The implications inherent in a failure to solve the problems in time are simply overwhelming.* Because of this, unfortunately, a lot of people are burying their heads in the sand and refusing to take this issue seriously. And this problem is global in scope: It's been reported that as of May, 1997, only 5% of the businesses in Japan had even begun working on the Millenium Bug, and most of Asia is still reeling from their recent economic troubles. Europe is concentrating on their upcoming conversion to the Eurodollar, and Russia's troubles are so severe that they aren't expected to address the Y2K for some time. So U.S. businesses that are heavily dependent on international transactions are likely to confront serious problems when they try to interface their computer systems with these non-compliant nations. (Note:This book is being written mainly for a U.S. audience, but the basic information is applicable for anyone, worldwide. You'll simply have to locate sources of supply in your own country.)

So how does all this affect you, you say? Well, let's look at a possible scenario:

A LITTLE STORY...

We know that many problems could begin during 1999, and some will almost certainly manifest at year's end. It will be the dead of winter, and cold weather - maybe even snowing or freezing - unless you live in the southern portion of the northern hemisphere or below the equator. Say you went to a small party for New Year's Eve and got home without any problems. You wake up on Jan. 1, 2000, and turn on the bedside lamp...or try to...it's cold in the house, and dark. What gives? You discover that there is no electricity to light or heat the house. Ok, say you have a fireplace, so you build a fire and start to warm up.

You pick up the phone to call a friend about your situation...it doesn't work. Now you're starting to get worried...you can't find out what's happening because you can't use the TV, or the computer. The morning paper hasn't been delivered. You wonder how your elderly parents, who live across town, are doing in this situation. They don't have a fireplace in their all-electric apartment, and probably no extra food, but you have no way to contact them.

Then your kids come in, ready for breakfast. You fix something simple and tell them they'll have to play today without any TV or videos or computer games. They start to grumble. You go outside and find that other neighbors are having the same trouble you are...you begin to get an idea that this might be tied to that "Year 2000 thing" you heard about...naw, surely not. Just an ice storm somewhere... It's cold outside, so you go back in to a house not much warmer. You wonder how long the small stash of logs will last in the fireplace...

You're worried about your parents, so you drive over to their apartment to find them very cold, and confused about not having any utilities. You bring them home to stay with you until this all blows over...now you have a house full of people to care for...

A couple of days go by, it's the end of the weekend, and still no utilities. This is getting serious...The refrigerator is starting to get smelly, and most of the food is gone. The water and sewage systems have gone down, and you're reduced to drinking soda pop for liquids. The kids are driving everyone crazy from being cooped up all weekend. Your parents want to go back to their apartment, but you don't think it's safe. The baby has run out of diapers, and there's no way to wash clothes or handle refuse. Nobody's had a warm bath in a while, you've run out of wood for the fireplace, and everybody's cold and uncomfortable. And you still don't know what's going on because the TV isn't working...

Then a neighbor knocks on the door...they have a medical emergency. Could you help them get a family member to the hospital? You offer to drive, and barely make it to the hospital due to the unplowed snow in the streets and the stalled cars. When you get to the hospital, you are refused admission by the exhausted staff who've been dealing with minimal generator electricity, dwindling supplies, and serious medical emergencies for several days. Things are really getting bad, and you wonder how long this can last.

Leaving the neighbors at their home to deal with their problems, you stop by the gas station to fill up your nearly empty gas tank. It's closed. Then you go by the local supermarket. It's closing too, most of the shelves empty from weekend shoppers stocking up for the "ice storm". No new stock has been delivered, and the manager has no idea when to expect it.

Then, when you get home, your kids look up at you with big, tearful eyes, and say, "We're freezing, and we're out of soda pop and we're thirsty! Yeah, and hungry...when are you going to feed us?", ***and you have no idea what to do...***

And what if this scenario goes on for a week or more...two weeks, a month?

What if it lasts for longer than that? Never mind being able to get to work, dealing with finances, no paycheck, bills... ***How will you feed your family, your pets, locate safe drinking water, treat sewage and waste, heat your home, handle medical problems on your own, and in general, take care of your loved ones, and keep them warm, safe, and secure?***

Now, this is admittedly a serious scenario, but it is entirely possible, given the situation we've discussed above. And things could get even worse, with fires, outbreaks of disease, civil unrest, gangs looting and stealing...These things have all happened before, both in the past and recently, in crisis situations. However, for now, it's enough just to consider the basics of how we'll survive at home for a time, in a world suddenly without the supporting infrastructures that we've come to take for granted.

THE GOOD NEWS

"Wow, that's awful! Is there any good news at all?" you say...

Sure...The good news is that it hasn't happened yet, and we still have most of 1999 to prepare. *Long enough, if we do it right and have a plan.* So, let's get started, and use our remaining months wisely. After all, if nothing this drastic happens, and if we experience just a day or two of inconvenience, we can simply use up any stored supplies, and give thanks that we didn't need them. But getting prepared in a just under a year will take some organization and thought, some time and money. ***So we need to get going on it now.***

> ***"Wisdom ofttimes consists of knowing what to do next."*** **Herbert Hoover**

THE WORKBOOK

That's where the "**BUILDING YOUR ARK**" Workbook comes in...It's your personalized plan for getting through the Year 2000 crisis with a minimum of hassle, worry, and expense. After all, you still have a life to live in the meantime! I've done the research, coordination, and planning for you. Let me walk you through the process with a step-by-step ***ACTION CHECKLIST*** so that you don't have to spend your valuable time figuring out what to do, when to do it, what to purchase, and where to find it. Then you can feel confident that you've done everything possible to prepare for the comfort and safety of yourself and your loved ones.

FOR CAREGIVERS

This book especially is for anyone who is a caregiver, who sees to the feeding, care, safety, and comfort of others. If anyone, whether children, parents, a spouse, partner, friends, neighbors, or pets, is dependent on you for their well-being, then ***you need to put the ideas in this book into action for them as soon as possible.***

SHORTAGES

Remember, the sooner you start making preparations, the easier it will be. In this situation, *time really is of the essence, because shortages of critical supplies can begin as soon as the first of 1999,* when more and more people begin to realize what we're facing. In fact, some order delays have already been reported in the food storage industry. The time to stock up is **now**, when there are no shortages, and no one else has to suffer because of your actions.

WHAT'S IN THE BOOK

In the following chapters, we'll mainly look at the personal aspects of the Year 2000. There are plenty of people working on it from a technical, financial, and political point of view, and we don't intend to deal with those in this book. *Appendix B - Internet Links,* at the end of the book, will give you resources for investigating other aspects of this problem online.

Each chapter is devoted to one major aspect of Y2K preparation, and gives general information on that subject, with suggestions of more specific preparations that you should consider depending upon your location - Urban, Suburban, or Rural. The appropriate products available for each category are listed, along with the current price ranges from all catalogs. An abbreviated catalog code is listed along the left-hand margin beside the reviewed products, so you will know where to order them. Simply go to *Appendix D - Catalogs*, at the back of the book, to find these catalogs and all contact information, along with other references and sources. Included in the text are lists of related books that you may wish to order or purchase locally, to give you in-depth information and instructions on all subjects covered in this workbook.

Most importantly, the Appendix contains the ***ACTION CHECKLIST***, which is your step-by-step master plan for everything you will need. It's set up by category and priority and linked to each chapter, with space for you to personalize the list with your own selected items and plans. This list can be printed out and taken with you when you shop. It's an easy way to get organized and track your progress. The ***ACTION CHECKLIST*** makes everything easier!

HEATING
Chapter 2

Information in this chapter:

You may be wondering why I've placed this chapter first, but remember, the Y2K crisis could become severe in the middle of winter in the northern hemisphere, and unless you live in the extreme southern portions of the U.S. (or further south), it's likely to be very cold outside. This will add to the problems, and must be taken into consideration first, because if your heating system goes down due to a power failure, or you run out of heating fuel, you can freeze to death very quickly. Every winter, in our large cities, many older people freeze in their apartments, simply because they fail to pay the heating bills, or forget to turn on the furnace, and don't realize how quickly hypothermia can set in. As the internal body temperature goes down, so does your ability to think and assess your situation. Freezing is said to be a very easy way to go...you just get drowsy, and everything slows down, and pretty soon, you go to sleep....So it's important to be aware of the symptoms and take adequate precautions. Keeping warm is a priority, and the first assessment you should make is to decide how you will heat your dwelling in the absence of your normal utilities.

KEEPING WARM

If we lose our gas and electrical utilities, don't think that you can get by for the winter with a small fire in the fireplace or a couple of cans of kerosene for a heater. It's going to take a LOT of fuel to keep you warm, unless you partition off a small space to live in and forget about staying very comfortable most of the time. In Japan, where they have lived frugally for centuries with little fuel in a cold climate, they believe in heating the person, not the house. You will want to use some of their methods in order to conserve fuel:

1) Close off all but one small room to live in, possibly the kitchen area. This will be easier to heat and will lower your fuel needs.
2) Better still, move to the basement if you have one, especially if you live in a severe climate. You will need less heat because the earth acts as an insulator and regulates the temperature, allowing for less fuel usage.
3) Hang blankets or other heavy cloths over windows at night to conserve heat.
4) Open drapes during the day to allow sunlight in, if possible.
5) Minimize use of outside doors - lots of heat can be lost with kids running in and out. If the outside door opens into the room you're living in, hang a heavy blanket over it, to stop the loss of heated air when it's opened.
6) Let the house cool down at night, when everyone is sleeping and bundled up warmly, even doing without heat if you can. Never sleep with an open flame burning anywhere in the space!
7) During the day, wear layered, warm, insulating clothes inside the house.
8) Be sure that your dwelling is insulated as completely as possible before the Y2K.

CLOTHING

Even in ordinary times, many people don't dress properly for the weather, especially when going outside in the winter. Did you know that you can lose up to 70% of your body heat if you go out in cold weather without a head covering? During the Y2K, since you probably won't be able to keep the inside of your home very warm, you'll also need to wear more clothing inside the house than you are used to: Stock up on themal underwear, warm caps, socks, and mittens when they go on sale at the end of winter. Layer your clothing to provide insulating airspace. Wool is fairly expensive, and usually requires dry cleaning, but it is the best insulator. Wearing a t-shirt, flannel shirt and a wool sweater will provide more warmth than one heavy and bulky piece of clothing. Be sure to check small children and the elderly often to see that they are warm...they usually don't know to tell you when they are cold.

Since we don't know what will happen to our retail product distribution system, many stores may simply run out of merchandise and be unable to obtain more for a while. So, if you have growing children, stock up on clothes and shoes, in a size or two larger for them, because they can grow a size or more in just a few months. And be sure that everyone in the family has plenty of warm clothes, gloves, hats, some sturdy all- weather boots and a heavy waterproof parka/coat, just in case.

SLEEPING

Again, in Japan, they solved the problem of heating the house at night...they didn't! They simply moved some screens around to make a small space that could be kept warm with body heat; and this was also done in European cultures by hanging drapes around the bed. So you might want to move mattresses into the kitchen or basement, or whatever area is near the heat source, and at night hang blankets from clothesline around the sleeping area. You can also set up a small, one or two-person "pup" tent in the living area to provide a cozy indoor space for sleeping. Use the new "space blankets" made for NASA of super-insulating materials, which can help retain body heat when put under or over your bedclothes. One of the most important purchases you can make is a good sleeping bag for every member of the family. Down bags cost more, but usually have a higher thermal rating. These can be obtained from any sporting goods store, and in many camping/survival catalogs.

Another practice begun in the cold and drafty castles during the Middle Ages is that of everyone sleeping together in one bed. Since the human body maintains a temperature of just under 100 degrees, don't underestimate the value of several warm bodies in the same space! If you're not squeamish, the dog or cat can join you. It shouldn't be too hard to stay warm at night, even in a cold house, if you sleep in thermal underwear, warm bedclothes, a cap and mittens, in a small covered space with other warm bodies, under a nice plump comforter, or snuggled into a down sleeping bag.

THINGS YOU'LL NEED TO SLEEP WARMLY:

(*Note: Catalog Code refers to catalogs listed in Appendix D.*)

CATALOG CODE	ITEM
	1) **AN ENCLOSED SPACE** - stock up on old drapes, sheets, extra blankets, etc., to create an enclosed sleeping space. Garage sales are a great source for these.
CM,MA, SU,SS	a) ***PUP TENT*** - There is a huge variety of these small tents that can be set up indoors and will make a small, warm sleeping space for one or two people. Models range from a "tube tent" made of heavy-duty vinyl for under $10, to more elaborate pop-up camping tents starting at $40.
	2) **OTHER WARM BODIES** - This one's up to you!
CA	3) **THERMAL UNDERWEAR**, tops and bottoms, to wear under your bedclothes. These can be ordered from any good camping catalog, but probably can be purchased locally for less.
	4) **WARM ACCESSORIES** - Wear knitted wool caps to avoid heat loss from the head, and gloves if you tend to put your hands outside the covers.
	5) **BLANKETS AND COVERS**
EE,CM,MA, RM,SA,SC, NP	a) ***WOOL BLANKETS*** - Most catalogs offer a wide variety of blankets, (new and used), usually made for the armed forces - cheaper than those bought in a department store for home use - $10-$40.

b) ***BED COMFORTER*** - If you don't use a sleeping bag, buy a down or Holofil bed comforter for extra insulation - found at any department store.

BA,EE,NP,RM, SA,SC,SS,NP c) ***"SPACE BLANKETS"*** - Superinsulating foil reflects 80-90% of body heat - use under bottom sheet, and on top of comforter or blankets - $2-$15.

d) ***ALL-WEATHER BLANKET*** - Four-layer version of the space blanket developed for NASA - reflects 80% of body heat - could also be used for stadium blanket, auto, camping - $12.

NP e) ***ALL-WEATHER SPACE BLANKET & PONCHO*** - Provides the same protection as d) above, but also has a built-in hood and corner hand inserts so you can grasp the blanket and wrap it around your body. Could be very useful when sitting around a cool room - $14, 6/$13 ea.

CF,CM,EE, f) ***EMERGENCY BAG*** - Foil bag (also called the "Cocoon" or "Space Pocket"), made of same material as space blankets, can be worn or pulled over a sleeping bag, to retain up to 90% of body heat - $7.50-$12.

6) **SLEEPING BAG** - You'll need a good sleeping bag to sleep in, or to spread over your bed like a comforter. There are three general types of bags: rectangular "traditional" bags, (some can be zipped together to make a larger "family-sized" sleeping bag), smaller "cocoon" bags, and fitted "mummy" bags made for more extreme outdoor camping. The type you choose will depend on your sleeping arangements. Some bags have a hood so you can also cover your head in extremely cold situations; however, a soft knitted cap would probably be more comfortable for indoor use. There's a huge variety of these bags available either from camping and survival catalogs or locally from outdoor and sporting goods stores. You'll have to educate yourself on the types of fill and thermal ratings and choose what seems most likely to meet your needs. Generally, down filling is considered superior, but Holofil works nicely for indoor use, and is less expensive. Shop around and talk to the clerks in sporting goods stores - they are usually pretty knowlegable. In general, the lower the thermal rating and the more fill for the cost, the better.

CATALOG CODE **ITEM**

CM a) ***Campmor*** catalog carries a wide selection of sleeping bags, in many styles and thermal ratings - ranging from $40 for a lightweight rectangular model to over $700 for a deluxe expedition bag. They also have child-sized bags for about $50.

MA b) ***Major Army/Navy*** catalog offers a variety of bags, ranging from $20 for a very lightweight rectangular bag, to $350 for a extreme cold weather sleeping system.

SS c) ***Survival Supplies*** carries two military issue bags - an unusual German sleeping bag/parka - $30/used, $50/new, and a Dutch heavy-duty cold weather bag for $40/used, $75/new.

RM d) ***Ready Made Resources*** offers a line of Australian "Wiggy" products, including four sleeping bags - $200-$284.

SU e) ***Survival Center*** catalog carries two bags - a G.I. Intermediate bag, $65/used, and another water-proof bag that converts to a parka, $70/new.

EE f) ***Emergency Essentials*** carries a bag that combines "mummy" warmth with rectangular comfort and cost. Zip two together for a big bed - $69.

NP g) ***Nitro-Pak*** offers polyester, dacron, and Holofil bags including a mummy model - $27-$70.

SPACE HEATING

In earlier times in Japan (again in keeping with their tradition of heating the person and not the space), at dinnertime they placed the dining table in a pit dug in the floor, and put a covered brazier of hot coals under the table. Then they covered the table with a quilted cloth that extended down over the diners' laps, and everyone bundled up and kept their feet warm while they ate! They also had a small cooking brazier on the tabletop, on which they stir-fried the meal, thus adding to the diners' warmth.

HEATING SAFETY

It's obvious that the above scenario has some fire hazards, and I don't recommend it for the average household, but there probably isn't a completely safe heating method to use in an emergency other than a vented propane furnace, or a properly installed woodstove. Fireplaces are notoriously inefficient, and almost any other heater will involve burning some sort of fuel in an unvented area, which can lead to air-quality problems and danger from fuel spills.

You must always keep a fresh air source open in the space where you are using any combustible fuel! Usually just raising a window an inch or so near the heater is sufficient. Yes, there will be some heat loss, but carbon monoxide poisoning is silent and deadly, and not worth the risk. And of course, keep children well away from any heat source.

ALWAYS have an adequate fire extinguisher handy, and install both a carbon monoxide and a smoke detector. Check their batteries often.

As mentioned above, it's going to take much more heating fuel than you probably realize to keep you even marginally warm throughout the winter. This is one area where you can't skimp; you must store enough fuel for the crisis period, and if you can't do so where you live, then consider temporarily moving to where you can.

URBAN

If you live in a city in a multi-family dwelling or dormitory, you may not have much control over your heating system. I remember a severe winter in Chicago in a four-plex apartment where we had steam heat from a basement boiler which served all four apartments. If it had gone out for any reason, we wouldn't have been able to do much about it. So plan to heat your apartment with some kind of non-electric space heater. There are heaters that attach to small propane bottles or 5-gallon bulk tanks. These can be obtained at general merchandise and sporting goods stores and are pretty safe and easy to use. And if your living space is very small, you can probably heat and cook with a propane or solid fuel dual-use heater/cooker. *I cannot recommend staying in an urban setting if you don't have space to store a LOT of fuel.* Plan to use the heater at least 12 hours per day for the duration of the winter. Each heater uses fuel at a different rate, so it's impossible to give a single formula for fuel usage. You will have to figure how much fuel you'll need from the fuel-usage information that comes with each heater. The small propane bottles are fairly safe, but you still should not store them inside a dwelling. If you have no detached space in which to put them, perhaps a friend who does will keep them for you until you need them. If you do plan to store fuel of any kind, you should do some investigation of local fire codes...contact your neighborhood fire station about this, and see if they have any suggestions.

If you live in a climate-controlled high-rise with sealed windows, you will have to learn how to get fresh air into the area, or plan to stay in another location during the crisis. ***Under NO circumstances should you attempt to burn any fuel inside a building without adequate ventilation!***

One helpful thing that you can do to conserve heat is to use insulating clear vinyl film on all windows. This provides more insulation than you might realize, and will cut your fuel usage. You can obtain this film at most hardware stores and from a couple of the catalogs:

IM 1) **VINYL SHRINK FILM** - Increases "R" (insulation) value of a single-pane window by over 90%. Mount with double-stick tape, (included) shrink with hot air from hair dryer - one package covers nine windows - $22.

RG 2) **LOW-E WINDOW FILM** - Reflects summer solar heat, holds inside heat in winter. Heavy-duty, helps make windows shatterproof. Several sizes - $36-$45/15-foot roll.

Also, if you have a decorative fireplace in your apartment, with one of those gas log heaters, don't assume that you also have a chimney suitable for burning wood! Have a professional check this out for you and don't use it if there's any question about its safety.

SUBURBAN

If you own a single family dwelling in a suburban area, you have more options than those in urban situations, and can make any improvements you desire. If you rent, you may have to get the landlord's permission to make some modifications, but it will be worth it. The first thing to do is to make sure that the home is well insulated and sealed for air leaks (*see Urban section above*). If your attic isn't yet insulated, do so right away. If you're a long-term renter, perhaps your landlord will pay for this, or go halves with you. This will make all your heating efforts easier. The landlord may also approve your installing a vented propane heater as a backup for the central heating unit. Fireplaces with gas inserts may not work if the utilities go down, so don't depend on this as a heat source, unless it's hooked up to a propane tank. But many homes have real wood-burning fireplaces, and these can be lifesavers...after all, people lived with no other source of heating for centuries. The only caution is to lay in a sufficient supply of wood to last through the winter, as fireplaces are notoriously inefficient heaters. If you have your own source of wood and a chainsaw, then you have that problem solved. If not, see the section below on wood heat for information on how much wood to store.

The most efficient and useful source of heat is an airtight wood stove, installed on a hearth and vented outside. You can also install an "insert", a small airtight stove made to fit into a fireplace opening and make it much more efficient. Either of these can be a major investment, but the comfort and safety they provide may be well worth it. And since you can cook on top of most woodstoves, it's an ideal solution to both heating and cooking. Plan to spend upwards of $500 for a good airtight woodstove.

If you are in rental property or in a mobile home where fire regulations won't allow you to install a woodstove, you will have to make do with a kerosene or propane heater. You can hook a propane heater up to a five-gallon container, (you'll need a lot of these), or to a large, several-hundred-gallon propane tank, if you have space in your yard for one. (You can also hook your gas cookstove up to these tanks and get double-duty.)

If you feel that the crisis won't last long, and you don't want to make these purchases and improvements, you can also use one of the smaller heaters discussed under the Urban section. *But be careful to store enough fuel to last the winter.*

Read the instructions provided with your stove or heater to determine the rate at which fuel is used, and then decide how much to purchase. Store kerosene and gasoline in metal cans. Both fuels will cause deterioration of plastic containers when it is stored in them for any length of time. Use a fuel saver to prolong the life of the fuel *(see Chapter 14 - Transportation)*. Store the fuel in an out-building such as a garden shed - the further away from your house, the better. ***Don't store any fuel in an attached garage!*** Any fire that starts out there can quickly spread to your house. Contact your local fire station for information on fire codes and safety.

RURAL

If you live in the county, you may already enjoy using a fireplace or woodstove. If not, it would be worth it in terms of safety and comfort to have a good woodstove installed as soon as possible, and lay in a sufficient store of wood. Then your heating and cooking problems are covered.

Or, if you already have a large propane tank in the yard, you could install a wall-mounted propane heater or standing fireplace and connect it to the tank. And you might consider adding another large tank to insure an adequate supply of fuel. Just be sure that the propane tank is full before the fall of '99. These heaters can also be used with the smaller five-gallon propane tanks, but you'll have to store a lot of them. If you normally use electricity for heating, and don't want to switch to propane or wood, consider any of the heating options under Urban or Suburban heating, or consider purchasing a larger free-standing kerosene heater from a hardware or farm supply store *(see section below on kerosene heating).*

Store propane or kerosene fuel in an outbuilding. Don't store any fuel in a barn or other building where animals or flammable materials are kept.

FUELS AND HEATERS

The following list is long, reflecting a welcome variety of heating options. You'll have to decide which method will best meet your needs. When considering this, *don't forget to coordinate your heating and cooking needs,* so that if you are short on space, you don't have to buy and store several different fuels. *Choose whatever method would be safest for your situation, especially if there are children involved.* Alcohol gel and propane are the cleanest burning fuels, with #1 grade kerosene right behind. Other fuels are smelly and combust with higher levels of by-products, (such as carbon monoxide), and are best used outdoors.

Many people are going to ask how large a heater they should purchase, so to find the answer, I consulted two experts, one a good friend of mine who owns a heating and air conditioning business, and the other a consultant at our local gas company. Both gave me the same response - they couldn't answer this question! When I asked them how many BTUs (British Thermal Units - a way of measuring heat) that it would take to heat an "average" room, both were reluctant to answer because there are so many variables - including room size, insulation, ceiling height, and number of windows and doors, etc. - that there is really no reliable way to calculate this. But there are some general guidelines:

Naturally, the smaller the space, the better, especially if you're heating with one of the small liquid or gas heaters listed below. Some safety codes state that you cannot use a heater *over* 10,000 BTUs output in a room used for sleeping, and you should always check your local codes. But it will take a minimum of that much heat to be comfortable in the average (14 x 14 ft.) living room, with several windows and some insulation. If you have a large propane heater or a woodstove, you can probably heat several rooms comfortably. So I'd advise getting the largest and best heater that you can afford, depending on the space you're trying to heat. Most heaters state how many BTUs they produce:

GAS OR LIQUID FUELS/HEATERS

1) **PROPANE SPACE HEATERS** - These can be found in any sporting goods store along with the 16 oz. propane cannisters that they use. They can also be connected to a 5-gallon propane tank, if you have room to store these outside the home. There's a large variety of these heaters available, and most are fairly safe to use with adequate window venting.

CATALOG CODE **ITEM**

CM,NP,SC	a) ***PARABOLIC INFRA-RED HEATER*** - Sits atop a small propane cylinder - 5,000 BTUs - $20-$32.
MA	b) ***HD12 Tank Top Heater*** - Produces 8-12,000 BTUs - fits 5-20 gallon propane tanks - $70.
CM,MA	c) ***Double-headed Heaters*** - Connect to a bulk 5-gallon propane tank - Primus 28,000 BTU heater - $90, Heat Demon 8-24,000 BTU heater - $145.
MA	d) ***Infra-Red Radiant Heaters*** - Operate on 20-100 lb. propane tanks, single, 12,000 BTUs - $119; double, 24,000 BTUs - $165.

2) **PROPANE WALL HEATERS** - These wall-mounted heaters hook up to propane or natural gas tanks. Most vent through an outside wall or a roof, and draw outside air for combustion. If you already have a large propane tank in your yard, these could work well as a substitute for an electric central-heating unit. However, they would be a major investment to install in temporary living quarters.

CATALOG CODE	**ITEM**
BW,CW	a) ***THE COZY WALL FURNACE*** - Heats from 15,000-33,000 BTUs - $400-$600, electric blower - $100 extra.
KW	b) ***MOBILE HOME HEATER*** - 15,000 - 30,000 BTUs - $475-$590. Electric blower - $100 extra.
BW,KW	c) ***WALL-VENTED HEATER*** - sealed combustion/exhaust - 9,000 BTUs - $375-$385.
BW,KW	d) ***ROOF-VENTED HEATER*** - 25,000 - 50,000 BTUs, and has a unit that heats 2 rooms through both sides of a wall - $450-$675.
IM	e) ***VENTLESS FIREPLACES*** **-** Propane models that look like a free-standing fireplace, hook up to large yard tank. Produces up to 40,000 BTUs, 99.9% heat efficiency, safety low-oxygen sensor. Includes logs, piezo-ignition - $600. Smaller model - 6-20,000 BTUs, can be wall-mounted - same features as larger fireplace - $400. Also similar furnace with a wooden mantel - $700.

3) **KEROSENE HEATERS** - These free-standing kerosene heaters heat a large area and can be obtained at local hardware stores for around $100 and up. Note that the average one-room kerosene heater uses 4-6 gallons of kerosene per day, *so to heat just one room for three winter months would require storing 450-600 gallons of fuel!* That would fill eight to eleven 55-gallon barrels. And even more would be used for cooking and lamps. So you can see the necessity for a lot of room for fuel storage!

MA	a) ***PORTABLE KEROSENE HEATER*** - 10,600 BTUs heats up to 400 sq. ft. Runs 12-16 hours on one refill, no installation required. Many safety features - recon-

ditioned - $160.

4) **DUAL HEATER/COOKERS** - If the space you want to heat is small, try one of the dual heater/cooker camping stoves that use either propane bottles or solid fuel cartridges (although these can get expensive for extended usage).

CATALOG CODE	ITEM
CM,SC,SS	a) ***INFRA-RED HEATER/COOKER*** - uses standard propane bottles or bulk tanks. Operates 1 1/2 hours on one 16oz. bottle. Burner varies from 8,000 to 14,000 BTUs, with safety shut-off - $55-$65.
BA,SU	b) ***SNAP-ON STOVE/HEATER*** - Attaches to the top and bottom of a reusable gelled ethanol fuel can - uses minimum oxygen, clean burning - 2,500 BTUs per hour - $8.50, fuel cans - $3.40 each, case of 12 - $40.
CM,NP,SC	c) ***PRIMUS HEATER/COOKER*** - Uses propane canister, can be turned up for cooking or on its side for heating - variable heat - 8,000-10,000 BTUs - $55-$65. Good choice for apartment dwellers.
NP,SC	d) ***SINGLE BURNER*** - Kerosene heater-cooker operates for 16 Hours on its .9 gallon tank - 8,500 BTUs - $90. Good choice if you have room to store kerosene and plan to use it for lighting and heating.

HEATING SUPPLIES

CATALOG CODE	ITEM
	1) **FIRE STARTERS** - Stock a large supply of strike-anywhere matches or butane lighters. (Long fireplace matches are good for lighting heaters.)
CM,SA	a) ***ELECTRONIC IGNITER*** - Electronic spark needs no flints or batteries and gives 100,000 lights, guaranteed - $5-$8. (Good barter item.)

2) **FIRE EXTINGUISHER** - Purchase (and learn to use) a large code-approved A-B-C fire extinguisher from any hardware or department store.

3) **HEAT PROTECTION** - On any flooring except ceramic tile, put a piece of fire resistant material - metal or asbestos - under the heater, (and behind it if it is close to a wall). These can be obtained at any stove dealer or hardware store. ***Keep all flammable materials away from any heaters.***

4) **ALARMS** - Battery-powered smoke and carbon-monoxide alarms, can usu-

ally be found at any hardware store *(see Chapter 9 - Lighting, for information on rechargable batteries to use with these).*

HA a) ***DUAL SMOKE/CARBON MONOXIDE ALARM*** - Combines both functions and uses a 9-volt battery - $65.

FUEL STORAGE

You'll have to determine the rate at which your heater or cookstove uses fuel to know how much to store - most tell you in their instruction booklets. If you don't have a safe storage place, you will have to take a chance and stock up on fuel just before the end of the year, but there is no guarantee that there won't be shortages well before that time. If you decide to use 5-gallon propane tanks, locate a near-by gas station that can supply and refill them for you before the Y2K, and realize that they may not be able to do this for a while after the crisis. So just to be safe, plan to store enough heating fuel to last until late spring in your climate, and more for long-term cooking. *Don't guess at this!* If you use a liquid fuel, you'll need storage cans, which are widely available at general merchandise or hardware stores, or from catalogs. If you're storing a lot of fuel, consider using metal barrels, which you can order from the catalogs or obtain from a local farm or fuel supply store. Only one of the catalogs reviewed in this book (Major) carries metal fuel storage cans or barrels that would be appropriate for kerosene or long term gasoline storage *(fuel cans are also listed in Chapter 14 - Transportation).*

CATALOG CODE **ITEM**

MA 1) **SUPER CAN** - Stainless steel 7-gallon drum perfect for any fuel storage - top handle - $25, flexible screw-on nozzle - $4.

MA 2) **THE EURO GAS CAN** - Heavy-duty 5-gallon steel gas can imported from Germany - reconditioned - $10, flex nozzle - $7.

RM 3) **VAPOR-PROOF FUEL CONTAINER** - Plastic 5-gallon with spout - new - $33, used - $20.

WOOD HEATING

BOOKS

Note: If you're on a budget, check your local second-hand bookstore for the following titles:

CATALOG CODE **BOOKS ON WOOD HEAT**

CL,CG ***"Chimney and Stove Cleaning"*** - A Country Wisdom booklet - $3.

CL ***"Curing Smoky Fireplaces"*** - A Country Wisdom booklet - $3.

LE ***"Guide To Wood Heat"*** - D. Thomas - Covers every aspect to heating with wood from A to Z - $15.

CL ***"Light the Country Fire"*** - Bokrom & Young - How to use wood heat - $10.

CL,SU ***"New Woodburners' Handbook"*** - A guide to safe and efficient wood burning, plus how to select the right woodstove - $13.

CL,CG ***"Save On Firewood"*** - A Country Wisdom booklet - $3.

FIREPLACES

Be sure yours is capable of burning wood. You'll have to remove the gas insert if you have one. Also check the chimney, have it cleaned, and be sure it's working properly. Practice first, if you're not used to building and maintaining a wood fire; it's something of an art! You'll need to stock up on newspaper or other easy-to-light starter material, and small sticks and wood pieces to use for kindling. You can also use the fire-starter paste, but it can get expensive after long usage. See if you can find some "fatwood" - the sap-filled heart of downed trees. Many hardware stores or wood dealers carry this effective and relatively inexpensive fire starter. A small piece will burn fiercely and start most any well-laid fire.

If you're feeling really adventurous, you can learn to cook in the fireplace, although it's probably not a good idea, due to the danger of working in the small space inside most modern fireplaces. The enormous old walk-in fireplaces in European houses were designed to allow room for cooking, with built-in pot or kettle hangers, so cooking in a modern fireplace is not recommended for safety reasons. If you decide to try it anyway, get a sturdy cooking grill on short legs from a camping catalog, and build just a small fire underneath it for cooking. Use heavy cast iron pots to avoid burned food, and long oven mitts to prevent burned hands.

FIREPLACE INSERTS

None of the catalogs that I received include air-tight fireplace "insert" stoves. You will have to obtain these locally. If you want to use your fireplace for heating during the crisis, these smaller versions of the free-standing woodstoves can dramatically increase the efficiency of your fireplace, and can make the difference between just surviving and being comfortable. Prices are usually comparable to a free-standing woodstove, and you must be sure that these inserts are properly installed because they use a stovepipe that must be inserted into and up your fireplace chimney.

AIRTIGHT CAST IRON WOOD STOVES

These can be purchased locally or through several catalogs. There are a large number of good brands; you'll have to study up on them and choose what seems to be the best for you. Most catalogs offer enough information to help you make a selection. Because of shipping costs, purchasing locally would be preferable, if you have a dealer in your area. They also can offer a lot of helpful information on selecting a stove. Depending on the model, plan to pay $500-$2500, plus installation costs. Sometimes you can find a good used stove in the classifieds or at garage sales, but you have to know what you're looking for, as you usually can't return these, and of course, there's no warranty.

Most woodstoves function best with a stovepipe that goes straight up through the ceiling. The only stove that I am aware of that be placed in front of a fireplace and vented out the back and up the chimney is the Ashley (not available through any catalogs in this book - check your local woodstove dealer). If you choose this type of stove, however, be sure that the installers are experienced in this procedure.

Whatever model you choose, you should definitely learn how to use the stove before the Y2K! Be sure the stovepipe draws properly, and that you know how to build and keep a wood fire going, and deal with a chimney fire. One of the best things about a wood stove is that you can also cook on it and keep water hot for washing or bathing! *(See Chapter 7 - Food Preparation.)* There are several grades and many models of these stoves, but all will give good heat. Some have "catalytic combusters" to increase efficiency up to 10% (look for good EPA efficiency ratings), but these produce less attractive flames, and are a bit more technical to operate. Some have non-electric thermostats, and most have see-through doors so you can enjoy the fire. All these stoves radiate heat, but some offer a circulating feature, including optional electric fans (which might not work during Y2K).

There's a lot to consider when making this major purchase, and the Lehman's catalog offers a packet of full-color literature and detailed information on every stove they sell. Call and ask for #L-ST/$5.00, for wood parlor stoves, and #L-ST2/$5.00, for wood cookstoves.

CATALOG CODE	ITEM
LE	1) ***VERMONT CASTINGS*** - The only American-made iron stove, high craftsmanship - five major models, many features - one natural gas model - $1300-$2100.
LE	2) ***JOTUL*** - Cast in Norway - popular in 17 countries - three large models - $1000-$1300, two small box-like models - $500-$900.
LE	3) ***WATERFORD*** - Cast in Ireland - non-catalytic yet meets EPA standards - two parlor models - $1100-$1600, one box stove model - $700.

STEEL AIRTIGHT PARLOR STOVES

These stoves are less expensive, heat as well as, and are almost as airtight as cast iron stoves, due to new firebrick linings and thick metal construction. Unlike many other stoves, they can be installed within 8" of combustibles.

LE	1) ***QUADRA-FIRE*** - Heaviest steel stove - EPA rated as cleanest-burning non-

catalytic model - $1100-$1200.

LE 2) ***EARTH STOVES*** - Both catalytic and non-catalytic models - $1000-$1200.

LE ***STONE WOODSTOVES***

The Hearthstone models are made of beautifully colored and textured soapstone that cannot warp or crack like steel, and radiates heat three times longer - Three wood models - $1300-$1900, gas model - $1200-$1500.

OTHER WOOD STOVES

There are a number of less expensive wood stoves, which burn hotter and faster with less pollution, so they don't have to meet EPA standards, (which can add as much as $300 to the cost). But they usually use more wood and aren't as efficient heaters. These might be a good choice if you have a supply of wood on your land and can cut your own. If you must purchase wood, get more than you would for an airtight stove. Some of these stoves are approved by the Underwriters Laboratory (UL).

CG,LE 1) ***POTBELLY STOVE*** - The traditional round, tall "caboose stove" - burns both wood and coal - $300-$600.

CG,LE 2) ***BOXWOOD STOVE*** - Small, oblong cast iron stove with cooktop - $129-$450.

LE 3) ***LINCOLN PARLOR STOVE*** - looks like more expensive parlor stoves - $350.

CG,LE 4) ***FRANKLIN FIREPLACE*** - Can be used like a fireplace with doors open, not very efficient - $325-$660.

LE 5) ***STEEL STOVE*** - Called "cheapest stove made in N. Am." - boxwood style - $200.

LE,SU 6) ***PORTABLE FOLDING STOVE*** - Set up at last minute - $140-$150.

7) ***FOUR DOG "PORTABLE" STOVES*** - Patterned on the Jotul, made of lightweight 3/32" steel with airtight gasketed door and heat-retaining smoke baffle. You can line sides and bottom with fireproof brick and add a stainless steel hot water font that heats about five gallons. Three sizes - The largest Four Dog model weighs 55 lbs. and costs $175. Call 612-517-6527 for more information and prices. Perfect if you don't want to spend a fortune or set up a permanent woodstove. (Be aware that legal regulations prevent the manufacturer from stating that the stove can be used indoors, but people have done so quite successfully, using the usual cautions for any wood stove.

STOVE KITS

CG,LE,SC These allow you to take a 55-gallon metal barrel and turn it into a low-budget, airtight heater. You can use one barrel or stack another on top, and will need some skill and tools to put them together. The kits do not include the barrels, so you'll have to obtain those locally, and also the stove pipe and other installation equipment. The barrels can be obtained from many local sources, sometimes for free - check the Yellow Pages. *Be sure any barrel you use is clean of any chemical that it might once have contained!* Kits cost $40-$80.

A SAFETY TIP: Whenever you install any woodburning stove, it's crucial to be sure that the surrounding walls and floor are covered by a non-flammable material, such as metal, ceramic tile, or asbestos. Keep any flammable materials such as drapes and furniture well away from the stove at all times.

FIREWOOD

You'll need a log carrier and a year's supply of dry hardwood, stacked under cover, preferably close to the house. Firewood is usually sold in "ricks", which is a stack of logs approximately 2'x4'x8', or in "cords", which are stacks approximately 4'x4'x8'. Since usage varies so widely due to the variety of wood, stoves, and climates, you will just have to ask around your area to determine the amount of wood to purchase. For example: when we heated with wood on a small airtight stove, we used about a cord per winter season in our relatively mild climate (it snows a couple of times each winter, with an occasional ice storm). So if your climate is severe, plan to stock up on several cords, at least.

Purchase or cut your wood "green" during late winter/early spring of '99, before the sap rises, and allow it to dry all summer and fall under some kind of light cover - plastic will do. Undried "green" wood is cheaper, but there's nothing worse than trying to get a fire going with damp or poorly-cured wood! Prices now vary widely due to location (between $50-$100 per cord), and there's no way to estimate what it will cost by the winter of '99. So don't wait until the fall of 1999 to purchase wood...there may not be any available, or the price may have sky-rocketed, and it won't have time to cure and dry before you have to use it.

OTHER WOOD HEATING EQUIPMENT

NO 1) **CHAINSAWS** - You can probably get a chainsaw locally, but the Northern catalog carries five gas-powered models ranging from $100-$240. Get the best model you can afford.

IM 2) **CHIMNEY FIRE RETARDANTS** - These are powdered chemical retardants that can usually be purchased from a stove supplier or any hardware store. Store near the stove. Also, use chimney cresote cleaners to prevent chimney fires.

3) **FIRE STARTERS** - You might want to stock something to help you get that

fire started:

CATALOG CODE	ITEM
MA	a) ***FIRELIGHTERS*** - Combines the convenience of a match with tinder, and burns up to six minutes. Great for starting fireplaces, woodstoves, and lighting charcoal - 20 per box/$3, 4 boxes/$10.
MA,NP,SS	b) ***FIRE RIBBON OR FIRE PASTE*** - Fuel-in-a-tube burns on anything - odorless and tasteless. One tube lights dozens of campfires, fireplaces, woodstoves - $3.75-$4.
NP	c) ***FIRE STARTER STICKS*** - All-weather fire starters, odorless, non-toxic, burns completely - 12 sticks/$2.
SS	d) ***HEXAMINE FIRE-STARTER TABLETS*** - Can be used in a campstove or to start wood fires. Six tabs per tube for $.95.
SC	e) ***WET FIRE TINDER*** - Burns at 1300 degrees, non-toxic, odorless, smokeless - will burn even floating on water - $7/12 cubes.
NP,SU	f) ***LIQUID FIRE STARTER*** - Gelled alcohol, no toxic fumes, no petroleum - 16oz. squeeze bottle - $3.75-$4.29, case - 24/$86. This would work with charcoal stoves and grills, also.
	g) ***FATWOOD*** - the resin-soaked heart of downed trees, it's sometimes called "heartwood". Many home and garden stores carry bundles of this in the winter months. It burns intensely and a small piece will easily start a fire. Most heartwood also smells wonderful when it burns.

CG,IM,LE 4) **ACCESSORIES** - You'll need the usual fireplace accessories: ash bucket, shovel, poker, fire-retardant rug to place in front of the stove; all of which can be purchased in the non-electric catalogs or at any hardware store, and sometimes at flea markets.

HA,IM 5) **SMOKE & CARBON MONOXIDE DETECTORS** - Don't forget to install good alarms and check the batteries often (*see #8 under GAS OR LIQUID FUELS section above, and in Chapter 13 - Safety*).

SC a) ***CARBON MONOXIDE DETECTOR*** - Wall-mounted patch turns dark with carbon monoxide leaks - put beside any stove or heater - $6.

There is so much variety in heating options that it shouldn't be too hard to locate something that works for your particular situation. Just use care when setting it up, be sure you know how it works, and try it out before you have to use it for daily heating. *And be sure to coordinate your heating fuel with that used for lighting and cooking.* It can save time, money, hassle and storage space.

WATER
Chapter 3

Information in this chapter:

WATER STATISTICS

Today, in our society, we take clean water for granted. But in most undeveloped parts of the world, obtaining sanitary water is a major problem, resulting in many serious diseases and a high death rate. Here's some interesting facts about water:

* The EPA (Environmental Protection Agency) recently reported that ***95% of the world's fresh water is now contaminated.***
* According to the World Health Organization, contaminated water is the largest health problem in the world ***- 50,000 people die each day worldwide, due to waterborne diseases.***
* The CDC (Center for Disease Control) estimates that one million people in the U.S. get sick from microbiologically contaminated water each year, and a thousand die as a result.
* ***Waterborne gastrointestinal infections account for 80% of all diseases in the world.***
* 25% of all hospital beds worldwide are occupied by people who are ill due to waterborne diseases.

Even in our modern culture, ***the delivery of sanitary drinking water is not something that we can be assured of in the future.*** In Aug., 1997, CNN reported that scientists fear that the world is running out of supplies of clean fresh water. And since most public water systems are run by computers and embedded microchips, in a crisis such as the Y2K it is possible that the delivery of potable water to your home could be interrupted, not only by a failure in the electric pumping systems, but by any number of unexpected factors.

A SCARY STORY...

In the *Sun-Herald* newspaper in Australia, 4/26/98, it was reported that a Y2K compliance-simulation test for microprocessors at Coff's Harbor water storage facility revealed that the system would have dangerously malfunctioned: The entire chemical holdings - normally used in carefully regulated amounts to purify the water - would have been dumped into the water in one batch. Experts say that *this would have had the potential to kill the town's entire population of 60,000 people!*

So even if water continues to be delivered to our homes, we have to be alert to the danger of contamination from many unsuspected sources. In my rural area, hardly a week or two goes by without an area water system announcing a "boil-water order" because of some contamination in their lines. So our best bet during the Y2K crisis is not to drink from any municipal or other water supply, at least until communication services are back in place and it's officially announced that the water has been tested and is uncontaminated.

WATER, WATER, EVERYWHERE...

"Dig the well before you're thirsty." Chinese Proverb

We can live for 30 days or more without food, but since our bodies are composed of almost 70% water, *we can live without it only three to four days.* (By the time we get thirsty, we are already 3-4% dehydrated and have lost almost 15% of our muscle strength!). If our normal water supplies are cut off, we can't just go out and fill a jug at any pond or stream as our ancestors did, because our bodies are no longer adapted to the pathogens now present in all untreated water. As mentioned above, ***there are virtually no safe natural water sources left anywhere, even in the most primitive areas.*** Sadly enough, no camper or hiker anywhere in the world can now drink from seemingly pristine mountain streams and springs due to the presence of such pathogens as Giardia.

Therefore, obtaining a source of clean water for both internal and external use during the Y2K crisis is vital, and ***you will have to store or purify all your water supplies.*** *Unless you have a deep well that you know produces pure water, you must treat any water that you drink, or in which you bathe, or wash dishes.* If the water is very polluted, also treat it for washing clothes, especially for infants. ***Never make an exception to this!*** (*Refer to Chapter 8 - Sanitation and Cleaning, for more information on bathing, washing, and using "greywater".*)

Be sure to have at least two sources of water and two methods of purifying water, in order to have a backup system if either one fails. *Do not take any chances with this!* You don't want to have to deal with a dangerous and debilitating illness during the crisis period.

HOW MUCH WATER TO STORE

For storage, ***you must provide a minimum of one gallon of water per adult per day for drinking and cooking, and another gallon for washing and bathing.*** Children, nursing mothers, and those who are very active or ill may need more (a man engaged in heavy labor in hot weather can consume 2-5 gallons per day). If this sounds like a lot of water, realize that during normal times, the average person uses approximately 110 gallons per day for all their activities (including flushing toilets, and watering lawns). According to a report on cities aired recently on cable TV, New Yorkers use *170 gallons a day!* Military troops in the field use about

15 gallons per day, so we're not talking about storing much water at all - two gallons a day are a real minimum. Store more if you can. Fortunately, in cold weather, when the Y2K could be most severe for the northern hemisphere, our water needs are lower than in warm weather, when perspiration increases water loss.

To figure how much water to store: Multiply the number of persons in your group by two, and then multiply that figure by the number of days you are preparing for, and you will know the minimum number of gallons to store.

Learn the location of the incoming water valve, so you can shut off the water if you suspect contamination from water or sewage lines, and stop it from entering your home. Also, shut off the valve and drain the pipes (saving the water, of course!) if the weather is very cold and the pipes could freeze.

URBAN

If you live in an urban area in an apartment, condo or high-rise, you probably won't have much storage space. You might want to set aside a closet for water storage, but be aware that water is very heavy (8 lbs. per gallon), and don't put too much weight on the floor in one place, especially in older buildings! And remember, the smaller one or two-liter and one-gallon containers can be stashed here and there around the house. In addition to investing in a good water filter, your best storage options would be to:

1) Purchase distilled water in convenient 1-5 gallon containers .
2) Fill your own sterilized containers with filtered or purified water.
3) Fill 1 or 2-liter pop bottles with filtered water (and freeze, if desired).
4) Use water from the hot water heater and toilet tank.
5) Filter water from your waterbed, if you have one, or if not, think about getting one. Be sure it has no chemicals in it.
6) Purchase small containers of boxed or bagged water if storage space is very limited.
7) Fill the bathtub and any other large containers you have space for, if you suspect any problems with the water supply.
8) *Purchase the best filter/purifier you can afford, and use it on any water that you haven't personally purified and stored.*

If you're in a building with gutters, ask the manager about setting up a cistern system using barrels under the gutters. Get with other residents to locate storage spaces. Use the parking garage, if possible. Locate any nearby water sources such as swimming pools or ponds in parks, etc. However, don't depend on outside sources, as inclement weather could force you to remain inside; and because of its weight, carrying water over any distance can be extremely difficult. If you plan to use a vehicle to carry water, be aware that fuel for the vehicle is likely to be scarce and hard to obtain.

SURBURBAN

If you live in a single family dwelling, with a yard, no matter how small, you can set up a pool, or a gutter/barrel cistern(s), or barrel storage in your garage, or a combination of all, to add to your in-house storage. Use all of the sources listed under the Urban section, also, and don't forget a good filter/purifier. If you have a hot tub or an in-ground swimming pool, be sure to clean and refill it just before the winter, and purchase a cover. Remember, *don't add pool chemicals*!

RURAL

You are probably used to providing your own water, or at least part of it, so you have more options than the city or suburban dweller. If you are on a rural water system, don't depend on it. *The best source would be a deep well* with a metal hand pump installed. Plan to put in your own well, or set up a cistern or barrel storage system. If you have a pond, lake, or river nearby, you can use this source, if you have a way to carry the water to the house, or you can invest in a solar pump. And you can also use any of the ideas listed under Urban and Suburban. Remember, *you must have a good filter/purifier in order to use any water source except a tested well.*

OBTAINING POTABLE (DRINKABLE) WATER

BOILING

Even though it uses valuable fuel, boiling is still the safest method of purifying water because it kills most harmful viruses and microoganisms. (But realize that only filtering will remove many harmful chemicals.) To sterilize water: bring the water to a rolling boil for at least 10 minutes, and allow for some evaporation. If the water is cloudy, you can boil and then strain the water through a cloth. Let the water cool before drinking. To improve the taste of boiled or stored water, add oxygen by pouring it back and forth between two containers. However,if you don't want to use precious fuel, and lose water to evaporation, there are other methods that are safe:

FILTER/PURIFIERS

The one absolutely necessary item to stock besides food and a heat and cooking source, is a really good water filter/purifier. They are faster and more convenient than boiling or chemical purifiers. You can get simple drip filters in department stores, but these are not made for our purposes. I'm talking about a wilderness survival filter/purifier that can take really polluted water and turn it into something drinkable. If you have one, you can be assured that (within reason), no matter the source of your water, you can probably make it safe to drink. Adding chemical purifiers to the water can increase your security. It's tempting to save the money and just try to store enough water in containers, but you can't afford to chance running out of drinking water. One of these filter/purifiers allows you to utilize water sources that you couldn't use otherwise, and could literally save your life. A good filter/purifier should remove all types of microorganisms and chemical contaminants. Some typical contaminants are :

* ***BACTERIA*** - These are present everywhere, and they are invisible, their size varying down to a microscopic .2 microns. Not all are agents of disease, but some can cause typhoid, dysentery, cholera, and e.Coli infections.

* ***VIRUSES*** - These are the smallest pathogens, some as small as .0004 microns. Many can pass through the finest filter, but fortunately, tend to adhere to particles in the water which can be removed. Any filter you choose should be able to remove particles down to a minimum of .2 microns.

* ***PROTOZOA*** - These are one-celled animals, much larger than viruses or bacteria, and survive in the form of cysts or spores. Giardia and cryptosporidium cause intestinal diseases, and others cause malaria and sleeping sickness.

Chemical contaminants can include a huge variety of substances, such as pesticides and farming runoff, and factory waste that has made its way into the water supply.

TYPES OF FILTERS

It's important to understand that ***there are two major types of filters***:

1) **MICRO-FILTERS** - These eliminate most protozoa and bacteria, usually down to .2 microns in size. Generally speaking, a microfilter works well on water from relatively clean natural sources - ponds, lakes, streams, wilderness rivers, rainwater, etc. Some of these filters can process up to 10,000 gallons and more before a cartridge change, so you should use them for most external water needs, such as bathing, washing, etc. However, *if you plan to drink or cook with the water*, you must *add a chemical purifier or use a filter/purifier if you suspect any viral and/or chemical contamination (from unknown upstream sources in most rivers, or leaking sewage, for instance).*

2) **FILTER/PURIFIERS** - These remove not only protozoa and bacteria, but **also inactivate or kill viruses**. Filter/purifiers use a combination of micro-filtration and iodine to kill viruses down to .004 microns in size, and other microorganisms usually less than .2 microns in size. *Filter/purifiers must be used if you suspect that your water comes from any sources containing viruses, including standing water, untested wells and other sources mentioned above, especially if you have to use it for drinking or cooking.* Purifiers process much less water than micro-filters before a cartridge change - usually around 100 gallons or so.

Some filters also have a carbon matrix to sweeten the water and remove unpleasant tastes. This could be important with children and the elderly, to encourage them to drink enough water.

CHOOSING A FILTER

When choosing a filter, don't just look at price alone - look at the intended use and the cost per gallon of the filtered water. The more expensive filters usually have more features, are easier to use, are better constructed and filter more water per gallon before you have to change the cartridge. You might plan to use a combination of a ceramic filter for economy and general filtration needs, and just in case, have on hand a second, less expensive filter/purifier to use for water that you suspect is contaminated with heavy chemicals or viruses. Or you could add one of the chemical water purifiers listed below to the ceramic-filtered water. But don't take any chances if you have to use water from an unknown source! *It's better to overdo your filtration and treatment than to miss something potentially deadly in your water.*

The micro-filters and filter/purifiers listed below are regarded as the best available for treating unpotable water. They've been used worldwide by outdoor expeditions and have a good track record. ***Be sure that any model filter you buy can remove the types of microorganisms listed above.*** These filters can be found at better sporting-goods stores, and be aware that the prices vary widely. Try to get the best price for the number of gallons that can be filtered before cartridge replacement. When you purchase the filter system, get enough extra cartridges to process more water than you think you'll need. (Helpful hint to extend your filter's cartridge life: Tie a coffee filter over the water inlet of your filter to keep it clean longer.) The listings below (where it is available), give the estimated cost per gallon (ECPG) to produce potable water.

(Note: Catalog Code refers to catalogs listed in Appendix D.)

CATALOG CODE	ITEM
NP	1) **AquaRain WATER FILTER** - A gravity-operated table model, which can process up to 21 gallons a day. Stainless steel housing with four ceramic carbon-core filter elements. Removes most common bacteria and protozoa. Processes a minimum of 2500 gallons before the carbon element wears out, but unit will still produce thousands of gallons of safe water (ceramic elements can be cleaned over 100 times before replacement) - Contact Tray Morrison at **800-350-2757** for more information, current prices, and to order, or use the Nitro-Pak catalog - $249-$275, extra filter elements (uses four at once) $35 each.
	2) **KATADYN FILTERS** - ***All of these are micro-filters (not purifiers),*** that work only with fresh, not salt water, and would be adequate if your water is not contaminated by viruses, or if you also add a chemical purifier. Considered the best and most economical by many long-term worldwide users, including the International Red Cross, WHO, NATO, Navy SEALS, U.S. Forest Service, etc. The filter element is impregnated with silver to prevent algae or bacteria growth. Works even with turbid or silt-laden water. Filter element can be cleaned up to 300 times before replacement.
CM	a) ***REGULAR*** - Mechanical ceramic filter to .2 microns. Output - a quart per minute - $250. Replacement filter - $165.
BA,CM,LE, NP,RM,SU	b) ***MINI CERAMIC*** - Removes 100% of pathogens, down to .1 mi-cron. Cartridge filters up to 2,000 gallons - $100-$150. Replacement filter - $60. Interchangable ceramic and carbon elements - estimated cost per gallon -

(ECPG - $.07.)

LE,NP, RM,SU c) ***MINI CARBON*** - Activated carbon element reduces chemicals and odors. Filters up to 150 gallons. Interchangable ceramic and carbon elements - $99-$139. Replacement cartridge - 2/$30-$59.

BA,LE,NP, RM,SU d) ***POCKET*** - Uses ceramic filter - to .2 microns, cartridge filter life is 13,000 gallons - $249-$299. Replacement filter - $140-$165. (ECPG - $.02.)

BA,CF,EE,LE, NP,RM,SU e) ***COMBI*** - Only portable filter that combines ceramic and carbon elements - removes 100% of harmful microorganisms and chemicals. Ceramic filters up to 13,000 gallons, carbon granulate filters up to 60 gallons - $165-$185. Replacement media - ceramic - $75, carbon granules - $20. (ECPG - $.01+.)

NP,RM f) ***SIPHON*** - No pumping, works on gravity pressure - removes all bacteria and parasites to .2 microns - $96-$99, replacement filter - $75.

BA,LE,MA, NP,RM,SU g) ***TABLE-TOP*** - Pour-and-drip filter system, holds 2.5 gallons, produces up to 12 gallons per day - filters up to 26,000 gallons - $235-$275. Replacement filter - $75-$140. (ECPG less than $.01.)

CF,MA,NP, RM,SU h) ***EXPEDITION*** - Group-sized filter with same technology as the pocket model and a piston hand-pump - produces a gallon a minute. Filters up to 10,000 gallons - $725-$875, replacement filter - $90. (ECPG - $.03.)

NP i) ***CHLORINEX SYSTEM*** - If you think your municipal water system will function, you can install this whole-house system the kitchen sink - provides two-stage ceramic and carbon filtration - $375. Replacement carbon filter - $55, replacement ceramic filter - $75. (I'd still get another source of water, however.)

3) **PUR FILTER/PURIFIERS** - These are ***purifiers*** that use a patented two-stage system combining a filter to eliminate protozoa, and resin beads containing an iodine compound to kill the remaining viral organisms. Iodine is bonded to the resin beads preventing it from affecting taste and color of the water. Activated charcoal granules remove chemicals and improve taste. *Note: these purifiers treat considerably less water per cartridge than filters.*

CM,MA,NP, RM,SC,SU a) ***HIKER*** - *NOT classified as a purifier.* Has most advanced anti-clog filter and pre-filter to remove most microorganisms, plus inner carbon stage that removes bad tastes and chemicals. Filters up to one quart per minute. Treats 200 gallons - $55-$60, replacement cartridge - $25-$30.

CM,EE,MA, NP,RM,SC b) ***VOYAGER*** - Compact, lightweight, guaranteed not to clog for 1 year - removes all microorganisms. Filters one quart per minute. Treats 100 gallons - $68-$75, replacement cartridge - $35-$40.

CM,MA,RM, NP,SC,SU c) ***SCOUT*** - Lightweight purifier, filters up to one quart per minute, removes most organisms. Treats 100 gallons - $80-$90, replacement cartridge - $40-$45.

CM,MA,RM, NP,SC,SU d) ***EXPLORER*** - Purifier has only self-cleaning filter with built-in brush - removes all microorganisms -Treats 100 gallons. Double-action pump produces 1.5 quarts per minute - $125-$130, replacement cartridge - $40-$50.

MA e) ***CARBON CARTRIDGE*** - For Scout or Explorer models - filters chemicals, improves taste - $20.

MA,CM,SU f) ***PIONEER*** - Features a .05 micron pre-filter, treats 20 gallons. Removes most organisms, produces 1 liter per minute - $30-$35, replacement cartridge - 2/$8.

SC,SU g) ***PUR PORTABLE*** - Tabletop version removes most organisms. Treats 100 gallons - $50, replacement cartridge - $30.

RM,SC,SU h) ***SURVIVOR-06 SALT WATER PURIFIER*** - For shipboard use, purifies salt water using reverse osmosis. Produces 1 pint every 1/2 hour - $555. The Survivor-35 model produces up to 1.2 gallons/hour - $1,500. Sea-tested in actual survival situations.

CM,SS 4) **FIRST NEED FILTERS** - One model filters to .4 microns, another to .1 micron. Removes most organisms. Self-cleaning pre-filter, treats 100 gallons - $53-$75. Replacement filter - $30-$33.

CM 5) **MSR** - Two ceramic filter models:

a) ***MINIWORKS*** - Removes most microorganisms, chemicals, odors, with Marathon Ceramic 205 element. Produces 1 liter in 90 seconds - $60, replacement cartridge - $30.

b) ***WATERWORKS II*** - Filters to .2 microns, and removes most chemicals. Lever handle for easy use - $125, replacement element - $30, membrane - $35.

6) **SWEETWATER** - Micro-filters *(NOT purifiers - but the Guardian Plus has a purifier attachment)*. Numerous safety features such as "end of life" filter indicator, and pressure relief system. Filters to .2 microns.

CM,NP a) ***WALKABOUT*** - Small lightweight, handles muddy water. Produces .9 liter per minute, eliminates 99.9999% of all microorganisms - $35, Treats up to 100 gallons - replacement filter - $13-$15.

CM,NP b) ***GUARDIAN*** - Called easiest to pump with lever handle. Eliminates 99.9999% of all microorganisms - $50-

$60. Treats up to 200 gallons - replacement filter - $20-$25.

CM,NP c) ***GUARDIAN+PLUS*** - Modular purifier system with Viral-Guard, a snap-on iodinated resin cartridge that kills viruses. Produces .7 liter per minute, treats 200 gallons - $70-$80, replacement cartridge - $20-$25.

CM,NP d) ***PREFILTER SILT STOPPER*** - prevents intake of algae, silt, and cysts and extends life of filter - $10. Replacement filters - $12.

SS 7) **PRESS-2-PURE** - Portable bottles/canteen remove harmful microorganisms, dissolved solids, metals, chemicals, sediment, radiological radon 222 - FDA and EPA approved. Treats over 200 gallons - 18-32 oz./$25-$27.

NP 8) **PENTAPURE SPORT WATER FILTER/PURIFIER** - Non-pumping, developed for NASA astronauts on the space shuttle - EPA registered. Each bottle filters up to 26 gallons, about 200 refills. Produces 1.2 quarts per minute. Might be good for one person with ample water storage, as a backup - $33, replacement filter set - $25, replacement cyst pre-filter - $9.

SU 9) **WATER WASHER** - Suggested to be used with filters that do not use carbon to sweeten the water taste. Said to reduce chemicals, pesticides, herbicides, - can process thousands of gallons - $60

SC 10) **SURVIVAL STRAW** - Not a filter but a system that destroys bacteria and viruses and removes fungus, chlorine, heavy metals, pesticides, and carcinogens, plus eliminates bad taste and odor. Immerse directly into water supply and drink. Meets FDA and EPA standards. Tested to purify over 5,000 gallons - $30.

RM 11) **PORTABLE UV WATER PURIFIER** - Produces potable water using an 8 "C"-cell battery pack. (also has AC and 12-volt converter). Produces about 8 gallons on one set of batteries. Water drips through activated carbon filter, and past a quartz-shielded high-intensity ultraviolet light in bottom chamber to kill microorganisms, - $138 (could be used with a solar battery recharger.)

As you can see, there are many models to chose from, and it can get a bit confusing ...you will have to read about them in the catalogs and decide for yourself which one meets your needs. When you purchase a filter, if it uses a replacement cartridge, invest in several extras at that time. ***Don't stint on this piece of equipment! You can't afford to drink unsafe water.***

SOLAR WATER DISTILLERS

For those who like to do-it-yourself, and know the benefits of distilled water, you can take almost any water source and purify it by distillation. Water is heated to boiling and the steam is then condensed and collected, leaving any contaminants behind. Volatile chemicals are also boiled off.

RM 1) **SUNWATER SOLAR DISTILLER** - Portable - no power required. Eliminates salts, minerals, bacterial and radioactive minerals, reduces chlorine, pesticides, THMs and chemical fertilizers. In rare cases of extreme pollution, may require carbon filtration also.

For 1 person - 2 liters/day - $350.
For 2 people - 5 liters/day - $570.
For 3-4 people - 8 liters/day - $790.

RM ***"Solar Still Manual"*** - W. R. Breslin - Complete plans and instructions for building your own 3-gallon-a-day solar still - illustrated - $13.

CHEMICAL PURIFIERS

There are several substances used to treat water with a purifier/preservative, and each of them has its benefits and drawbacks. *All except the oxygen type should be avoided by pregnant women.*

1) **CHLORINE BLEACH** - Bleach may be used to treat already potable water and prevent growth of organisms during long term storage, but *don't rely on it for purifying already-contaminated water, (such as pond water), as* ***it has little effect on hard-shelled protozoans such as giardia and cryptosporidium***. However, when you fill containers from your home water supply for long term storage, it's a good idea to add some bleach (or liquid oxygen, below), to be sure the water stays potable. Use plain liquid bleach with 5.25% sodium hypochlorite and *no soap or other additives such as fragrance.* Here's how much bleach to add:

Amount of Water	**Clear Water**	**Cloudy Water**
1 Quart	**2 drops**	**4-8 drops**
1 Gallon	**4 drops**	**8-16 drops**
5 Gallons	**1/2 tsp.**	**1 tsp.**
50 Gallons	**1 Tbs.**	**2 Tbs.**

After treating the water, let it stand for 30 minutes if it's warm, and 1 hour if cold. Be sure not to add too much bleach to the water, as that can be as dangerous as not adding enough - *chlorine is a deadly poison.* Expect a slight bleachy smell. Before using, pour back and forth between containers to diperse the smell and oxygenate the water. Also, if you can wait before using it, cover the water loosely and let it stand for 24 hours, as the chlorine taste and smell will evaporate.

2) **WATER PURIFICATION TABLETS/LIQUIDS** - These can be found in many outdoor and survival catalogs and contain iodine, which is an effective water purifier. They usually have a three-year shelf life, so be sure they are fresh when you buy them, although I've never found any that

had an expiration date on the label. Your best bet is to use a supplier that has a rapid inventory turnover.

WARNING: ***Anyone who is pregnant or who may become pregnant must not drink water treated with iodine!*** Miscarriage or fetal deformation could result. *Anyone with thyroid probems or allergic reactions to eating shrimp, should also avoid using iodine. If in doubt, ask your physician.* Otherwise, extended consumption of iodine-treated water can cause the skin to become yellowish, but is not harmful... (however, considering the above cautions, I tend to favor other methods).
If you treat laundry water with iodine, it can stain the clothes. Iodine imparts a strong taste to the treated water, and some iodine kits come with a second treatment that removes this. If you are using regular iodine, put the water in a flavored drink mix to hide the taste, or put it through a carbon filter. If you don't have one, get clean, food-grade charcoal from your pharmacy and pour the water through it to remove some of the iodine taste. (Don't use barbecue charcoal or bricquets as they are impregnated with chemicals.)

After you treat water with iodine, wait 30 minutes, or one hour if the water is cold.

CATALOG CODE	ITEM
CM,MA,EE,NP, SC,SS,SU	a) ***POTABLE AQUA*** - (Also military iodine tabs) makes questionable drinking water bacteriologically safe. Bottle of 50 tabs (treats up to 50 quarts) - $4-$7.
CM,NP,SC	b) ***POTABLE AQUA PLUS*** - two-bottle system: first tablet purifies water, second removes iodine taste and color. Bottles of 50 - $4.50-$11.
NP,SC	c) ***POLAR PURE*** - concentrated iodine crystals, not affected by age, air or temperature. One bottle treats up to 2000 quarts of water for less than one cent per quart - $12-$13. Said to be the best iodine purifier.
MA	d) ***TRAVELER'S FRIEND*** - Contains a highly potent extract of grapefruit peel, pitch, and seed, diluted with deionized water. Certified non-toxic, effective against more than 50 pathogens, including Giardia, e Coli, and Salmonella. No iodine, no off taste - one bottle treats 10.5 gallons untreated water, 16 gallons of filtered water -$12/3 bottles.

BA,CF,RM, SC,VR 3) **LIQUID OXYGEN TREATMENT** - This process, called "Aerobic 07" or"ION", destroys harmful microorganisms by the release of oxygen ions into the water, since most internal pathogens are "anerobic", and can't live in the presence of oxygen. With unlimited shelf life if stored under refrigeration, one bottle treats over 200 gallons of water. Use 8-10 drops per 10oz. glass of water. Allows tap water to be stored over five years without rotation, and unlike iodine, is clear, tasteless, and *completely non-toxic.* It can also be used to cleanse produce and food preparation surfaces. A good multi-use sanitizing product, and about the same cost as chlorine disinfectants. Concentrated, one ounce treats 55-gallons for storage. Small 1oz. - $13, large 2.33oz. (contains about 1400 drops) - $18-$20. For more info. go to: **http://waltonfeed.com/ion3.html.**

NP 4) ***OXY-STABILE*** - Stronger version of oxygen purifier - allows water storage up to five years. Kills harmful microbes, bacteria, parasites and viruses, Odorless and tasteless. Two ounce bottle treats 110 gallons - can be used as a disinfectant - $19, 6/$18 each.

MA,RM 5) ***KATADYN MICRO-PUR*** - Keeps *pre-filtered* water fresh and drinkable for up to 6 months. Safe, non-toxic, and tasteless, contains a simple *silver compound that prevents bacterial growth without the need for chlorine, iodine or other chemicals.* Shelf life - 5 years from date of manufacture - Treats 250 gallons/$12-$13, 2,500 gallons/$25, 12,500 gallons/$75. *(See the Colloidal Silver information in Chapter10 - First Aid and Health.)*

WATER SOURCES AND CONTAINERS

Below are some helpful books on water sources and usage. If you're on a budget, check with your local second-hand bookstore for the following titles:

CATALOG CODE	BOOKS ON WATER
MA	***"The Drinking Water Book*** - Ingram - What's in your tap water, evaluates filters and bottled water, and more - $16.
BA,CG, CL,MA	***"The Home Water Supply"*** - Stu Campbell - How to find, filter, store and conserve water - everything you need to know - $19-$24.
RM	***"Rainwater Collection (for the Mechanically Challenged)"*** - All aspects of water management, from collecting to storage and pumping - illustrated - $18.
RM	***"Rainwater Harvesting"*** - A manual for developing countries, but excellent information for anyone collecting runoff and rainwater - $23.

The following are some suggestions for obtaining water other than at the faucet. ***DO NOT USE any container that has held any kind of inedible chemical or substance!*** This is very important, as no matter how well a container is cleaned, most will retain some residue that will leach into the water and contaminate it, sometimes with fatal results.

1) **DISTILLED WATER** - Purchase distilled water in one or five-gallon containers at the grocery store. You can also take your own containers and fill

them at stores that have this service. For long-term storage, (over several months), add purifier to these just to be safe. Do not use empty plastic milk jugs, no matter how tempting! These can't be completely cleaned of the milk, and it can leach out into the water, sometimes carrying pathogens. The 5-gallon distilled or spring-water bottles that some companies deliver water in are ideal for storage, but they can be expensive to purchase. Glass one can cost over $20 each, but you can occasionally locate them at flea markets and garage sales for less.

2) **FILTERED OR TAP WATER** - If you have a kitchen sink or whole-house water filter, just prior to the end of 1999, simply gather a supply of containers and fill them. You can also use plain tap water. It's said that this water can be stored short-term without any purification, but I'd add a chemical purifier just to be safe, especially if you plan to store the water for several months or more.

3) **SODA POP BOTTLES** - Save the big two-liter plastic soda pop bottles, wash thoroughly, and fill with water. If you freeze them, they will help keep the food in your refrigerator or freezer cold for some time afterwards if the power goes off. Don't fill the ones to freeze over 3/4 full, as ice expands. Purify these if storing long-term.

4) **HOT WATER HEATER** - Don't forget that you can drink and use the water from the hot water heater and the storage tank (not the bowl) of the toilet, although I'd filter and/or purify the "toilet water" for drinking or cooking, just to be safe! And *don't use it if you have put any kind of chemical bowl cleaner in the tank.* To drain the hot water tank, be sure that the electricity or gas is off and turn off the water intake valve, then open a hot water faucet and fill containers. Later, be sure the tank is filled again before the gas or electricity is turned on.

5) **WATER BED** - A water bed holds a lot of water, some up to 400 gallons, but *be sure that they don't also contain toxic chemicals. If you have one without internal baffles,* drain it just before you think you'll need it, wash it out, and refill with clean water, adding 2 oz. of bleach per 120 gallons. You can use this water for washing or cleaning, and filter it for drinking. Of course, then you'll have to find another place to sleep!

6) **PACKAGED WATER** - Some survival and camping outfitters offer sterile water in foil packets or boxes. These are somewhat expensive, but might be a solution for those with very limited storage, and are good to use in first aid situations. Also great for travel with kids!

CATALOG CODE	ITEM
CF,EE,MA,SA, SC,SS,SU	a) ***AQUA BLOX*** - Foil-lined sterile "juice boxes" filled with 8.5oz. of pure drinking water. Minimum shelf life - 5 years. 3/$1.95-$2.50, case of 27/$15-$20.

CF — b) ***AQUA BLOX LITERZ*** - Same as 8 oz. above, in liter size - $3.

BA,CF,EE, MA,NP,RM, SC,SA,SS — c) ***POUCHES*** - Approximately 4.2oz. of purified sterile water in airtight metalized "retort" pouches - can store for 5+years and withstand temperature extremes - $.25-$.60 each, less by the case.

7) **BOXED WATER** - These are specially-made rigid cardboard boxes with liners, that you fill with water for storage.

CF,EE — a) ***BASIC 25 GALLON BOXED WATER KIT*** - 5 five-gallon mylar bags in durable cardboard boxes with handles - can be stacked three-high - 5 boxes/$25.

NP — b) ***H2O BAG 'N BOX KIT*** - Includes a triple-layered foil-liner bag with built-in spigot and hand cut-outs - 6 boxes/$43.

8) **BATHTUB/CONTAINERS** - Fill the bathtub(s) just before you think you'll need the water, use it for bathing, and filter it for drinking. Also, most general merchandise or hardware stores carry large plastic tubs with lids that sell for under $15 that would make great water storage containers.

9) **2-7 GALLON SPIGOT-CONTAINERS** - Many catalogs and stores with camping sections also carry 2-7 gallon water containers with pouring spigots that you can fill and purify for storage. You can also use the round plastic 5-6 gallon food storage buckets, but you have to dip water from them, as pouring is messy.

CATALOG CODE	ITEM
MA,NP,SC, SS,SU	a) ***COLLAPSIBLE CARRIERS*** - Folds flat when not in use. Easy-pour spigot, heavy-duty food grade polyethyl--ene. 1.5 to 5 gallons, prices range from $6-$11.
BA,MA,RM, PP,SA,SC	b) ***RIGID PLASTIC CONTAINERS*** - Heavy-duty plastic water jugs with spigots - 2 to 7 gallons, $6-$17.
MA	c) ***HEAVY DUTY SWISS WATER BAG*** - 5-gallon black rubberized bag with spigot, useful for carrying and/or solar heating bathing or washing water - used, excellent condition - $7.

10) **STORAGE BARRELS/DRUMS** - You can sometimes obtain used, food-grade 55-gallon barrels from food service companies. C*lean them thoroughly before storing water in them.* Realize that, although it may not be hazardous, the taste of whatever was stored in them previously can still leach out into your drinking water. It's preferable to purchase new water barrels in several large sizes (15, 30, and 55 gallons), fill them well before the time needed, and add purifiers. They can be stored in garages and out-buildings, and must be covered with a tight lid. Remember, wa-

ter is very heavy, and you can't move these barrels after filling, so be sure to have some small buckets or containers available so you can decant water from the barrels and take it into the house.

CATALOG CODE	ITEM
CF,MA PP,SU	a) ***POLYETHYLENE BARRELS*** - 15 to 55 gallons with lids - $26-$83. MA catalog has used 55-gal.(food grade)- $40, and SU - $16.50.
MA,SC	b) ***POLYETHYLENE BARRELS*** - With lids, some with folding handles - 15-55 gallons - $30-$73. (Some catalogs offer discounts for quantity purchase.)
CM,RM	c) ***POLYETHYLENE BARRELS*** - 5-55 gallons - prices range from $12-$50.
CG,LE	d) ***WOODEN BARRELS*** - These two catalogs offer a wide variety of old-fashioned oak and basswood kegs which range in size from 5-40 gallons. Some are lined with paraffin and some are charred inside. Some have a bilge bore with bung (a hole in the side with a stopper). They are considerably more expensive than the plastic barrels - $75-$200.
CF,MA,PP,NP, RM,SC,SS,SU	e) ***BARREL SIPHON/PUMP*** - Insert siphon into barrel and pump to start water flowing and use water to the bottom of the barrel. Best for filling containers - fits 15-55 gallon barrels - $12-$18.
NP	f) ***BASIC HAND PUMP -*** Simple, vented plastic hand-pump adusts to fit 15-55 gallon barrels - best for dispensing-water directly from containers - $15.
NP,SC,SU	g) ***SPIGOTS*** - Allows easy dispensing of water when using smaller barrels - $3-$5.50.
CF,MA,NP, PP,SU	h) ***BUNG WRENCH*** - Use to open the bung or plug on a water barrel - $9-$14.

11) **SWIMMING POOL/HOT TUB** - Purchase a children's play pool, a larger above-ground swimming pool, or use a hot tub or in-ground pool. Fill it after summer usage, keep it covered, and *free of chemicals.* You can later filter and purify the water for use. *DO NOT use pool chlorine for purifying drinking water - it's not for human consumption!* A cover is important to keep debris and pollutants out of the water.

12) **RAIN BARREL/CISTERN** - If you have gutters on your house, consider setting up a cistern storage system. It's pretty simple: Purchase a ready-made cistern or use a water barrel or any clean 55-gallon drum, and place one under each downspout of your gutters to catch rainwater. There are kits that allow you to attach a diverter to the downspout so the water from the gutters flows into the barrel. After they are full, be sure these containers are closed with a tight-fitting lid. You can also set up a hose system from the gutters or cistern to flow into a large over-

flow pool (such as those in #11 above) to collect even more water. Systems similar to these were widely used in earlier times and provided most of the household water needs. As long as it rains periodically, a cistern can supply you with plenty of usable water.

CATALOG CODE	ITEM
HA	a) ***RAINSAVER CISTERN*** - Assembles in minutes to hold 60 gallons. Top and bottom spigot attach to a hose. Special fittings allow several cisterns to be connected for more capacity. Debris screen, liner, reinforced base, overflow valve, and cover. Made from recycled plastic - $129.
LE	b) ***DOWNSPOUT RAIN CATCHER*** - Installs easily to any metal or plastic downspout. Rust-resistant, galvanized steel - $11.50.

NO 13) **PICKUP WATER HAULER** - Durable resin tank fits pickup bed between and over wheels, vented lid - 150-465 gallons - $140-$280.

RM 14) **COLLAPSIBLE WATER TANKS** - If you are hauling water from a pond or river via truck, use one of these - 10" opening makes filling easy - heavy-duty plastic Kolaps-A-Tank carriers - 73-1340 gallons - $250-$800.

15) **WELL PUMPS AND RURAL SOURCES** - If you live in a rural area and have access to a stream, pond, lake, river, cistern, or your own well system, you're all set. However, you will need to install a hand pump for the well or cistern, and have it working before the end of '99. These can be obtained from local farm supply stores or several catalogs:

CATALOG CODE	ITEM
	HAND OPERATED WELL PUMPS
CG,LE,NO,RM	a) ***INDOOR WELL PUMPS*** - Sometimes called "pitcher pumps" - attach to a countertop and pump water to the sink - $85-$250.
CG,LE,RM	b) ***OUTDOOR WELL PUMPS*** - Attach to a deep well - will need extra fittings - $135-$541. Pump adapter - $50.
LE	c) ***WELL BUCKET*** - Galvanized steel cylinder fits almost any drilled well, allows you to draw up over two gallons of water manually if pump is out - $33.
	SOLAR WATER PUMPS
RM	a) ***FLOWLIGHT SLOW PUMPS*** - Takes water from spring, cistern, pond or stream and pushes it as high as 400 feet. Depending on the model, will supply between 50 and 3,000 gallons per day. (Not a water filter.)

Forged brass housing - 1/4 HP/$475, 1/2 HP/$675.

16) **FROZEN WATER** - If you live in a very cold climate, don't forget snow and ice! Just be sure to use untouched snow from clean drifts. Bring this snow or ice inside to melt and use it as from any other unfiltered source.

Water is one of the easiest and most inexpensive of all supplies to locate and store, if you do it ahead of time! If you wait until it's too late, you may find that it becomes one of the most valuable items that you need. Don't neglect this vital aspect of your preparedness plan just because there seems to be lots of water around now. *You'll miss it when it's gone...*

FOOD STORAGE
Chapter 4

Information in this chapter:

Next to air and water, food is the most important substance that we regularly need to maintain life. It's the first thing we seek after we're born, and we continue to be concerned with it at least three times each day for the rest of our lives. And yet, as important as it is, most of us give little thought about how our food is produced and brought from the farm to our tables. Unless we're farmers or backyard gardeners, we just go to the grocery store and pick up whatever we need. It's always there, and since most of us have never really gone hungry for any period of time, we normally don't pay that much attention to the subject. And yet, if we don't, we could easily go hungry...

OUR VULNERABLE FOOD SYSTEM

"Farming Is Everybody's Bread And Butter" - Bumper sticker.

Hunger isn't a stranger to millions of people in third-world countries, and many of them die from malnourishment or the diseases that it causes each year. Although there is said to be enough food available worldwide to feed everyone, the problem seems to be in the distribution systems within each country, and is often connected to the whims of the current poltical or military regime. And, as we have recently seen with the terrible suffering from Hurricane Mitch in Honduras and Nicaragua, weather disasters can prevent vital supplies from being properly distributed in times of emergency. So, lacking the security of our modern, efficient food production and distribution systems, eating regularly is an uncertain luxury for many people around the world. And what would happen here in our rich and overweight country if that same production and distribution system that we so casually rely on were to falter or fail? How would we feed ourselves and our families? How many of us have the land or the know-how to grow all our own food? **Obtaining enough food during the Y2K crisis could become a serious problem**

for a number of reasons:

1) Due to modern, mechanized, large-scale farming practices that dump large amounts of chemcals on the land, we are rapidly destroying the organic life and fertility of our vital topsoil. This makes us increasingly dependent on the production and distribution of these same chemicals to continue producing crops.
2) Our practice of mono-cropping with only a few varieties of hybrid seed leaves our food supply vulnerable to a one-season destruction from various pests and/or diseases.
3) Due to pressure and mergers from the huge hybrid seed conglomerates, the small farmer and backyard gardener is in danger of being denied the use of open-pollinated seed that insures the continuity of our genetic diversity and long-term food production. *This is a serious danger,* as it affects our basic ability to grow any food crops at all *(see Chapter 6 - Food Production, under Gardening).*
4) Our highly mechanized food farms operate with large machinery dependent on the oil and gas industry to deliver its fuel supplies.
5) Packing, canning and freezing plants, that process the raw produce, are dependent on computers and embedded systems in order to function.
6) Our food grain reserves are at an all-time low, with only a few months' supply available at any time. (The U.S. Dept. of Agriculture projected last year that the nation's grain supply would reach a 22-year low, and the El Nino-induced drought from the summer of '98 will further affect crop levels.)
7) The production of livestock is dependent on the computer-regulated distribution and delivery of feed and fertilizer.
8) The loss of thousands of small farms nationwide to the huge farming conglomrates, has reduced the ability of any area to locally supply its own produce, making most cities dependent on long-distance food shipments.
9) The reliance of our food systems on the rail and trucking industries for delivery of their products, makes them very vulnerable to any breakdown in this computer-operated network.
10) Most grocers stock no more than a half a week's supply of food at any time, relying on frequent shipments from their regional warehouses, who in turn, depend on shipments via rail and truck from their suppliers, and so on...
11) More and more people rely on frozen or pre-packaged foods from the grocery store, or eat out on a daily or weekly basis; therefore, fewer and fewer people, especially those in urban areas, are able to produce any of their own food supplies, or even know how to do so.

These are some of the many weak links in this chain of food production, all the way from the fields, to the packing plant, to your local grocery store, to your dinner table. It isn't much of a stretch to see where breakdowns could occur at many places along the way. And if they do, *how long do you think it would be before your grocer's shelves are emptied and you are out of food?* If there is any disruption in our computers and utilities during the Y2K, it's almost certain that, due to it's enormity and complexity, our food system will be one of the first to break down.

STOCKING UP

Where will this leave you and your family? Do you currently have at least a six month's supply of food stored in case of emergency? The Morman Church is so certain that almost anyone can expect to need these supplies at any time that they require their members to store a year's supply of food. And they've been proven right on many occasions. Stored food can get you through many crises - loss of employment and income, weather disasters, illness, and so on. And now that we are facing very uncertain times ahead, it also would seem prudent for us to set aside a good store of food. *The time to take care of this is now, as shortages are certain to become prevalent as the Y2K draws near and more and more people begin to stock up.*

FOOD PRESERVATION

Before modern food processing and refrigeration, native peoples and our own ancestors had learned many clever ways to keep the harvest. They had to - their very lives depended on it. They learned to keep meat on the hoof until needed, and then slaughtered and smoked it. They used root cellars for storing many winter vegetables, and buckets set in cool streams or wells for keeping perishable dairy products. Cheesemaking, pickling, salting, wine-making, and air drying all developed from the need to preserve many kinds of foods. And more recently, canning has developed as a reliable method of preservation. It took an enormous amount of effort and time for people to develop these techniques, often by trial and error over many generations. And in times of plague, drought, and social unrest, many were unable to supply all their food needs, and did in fact, starve. So today, most of us don't really appreciate what it takes to provide the nutritious and ample diet that we currently enjoy. We have simply forgotten how to provide a store of food for ourselves *(see following chapters on Food Preservation and Production).*

FOOD STORAGE REQUIREMENTS

When you store foods, you must meet several requirements in order to keep the foods edible as long as possible. If you can remember the initials **CDD**, you will know the key ingredients to food storage: ***Keeping your food COOL, DARK, AND DRY can insure that it will not spoil from the following enemies of stored foods:***

1) **TIME** - Since you know the year that the Y2K crisis is likely to begin, time is not as crucial a factor as if you were storing long-term for an unexpected natural disaster. However, *plan to have your food storage completed at least by July, 1999,* as many problems are expected to begin by then, or before *(see timetable in the Preface).*

   Most foods that you buy at the grocery store can be safely stored - if properly packaged or repacked - for a year or more on your kitchen shelves without a major loss of nutrients. The expiration date on many foods, excluding perishables such as dairy, is just a suggested guideline, and food doesn't instantly go bad on that date. (This will allow you to obtain many of your foods locally for a reasonable cost.) However, even though foods don't lose calories when stored, the quality of vitamins, proteins, fats and some other constituents diminish over time. So if you begin stocking up early in 1999, you might want to continue to rotate the food purchased from the grocery store, (if supplies permit), to be assured of a fresh stock at the beginning of the Millennium.

2) **HEAT** - If at all possible, foods should be stored in a cool place as heat will quickly render many foods inedible, even dry foods such as grains and beans. Never store any foods in an attic or other very warm location, such as a small, closed storage room or metal building. In general, the lower the storage temperature (above freezing), the longer the food will last. Some people have been known to bury their sealed plastic food buckets in the ground, which maintains a uniform cool temperature (in the low 50s). Of course, many foods, including meats and some dairy foods and powders can be frozen, but then you'll have to eat them up right away if the power goes off. However, if you have frozen a lot of water in soda pop bottles in your freezer, *(see Chapter 3 - Water),* then it may keep the food for a while after the electricity goes off, until it melts. And freezing beans and grains for at least 24 hours will kill any insects that may be hiding in them. But in general, don't depend on your freezer for any long-term storage during the Y2K crisis. Fortunately, the crisis will begin during the winter, so if it's below 40 degrees consistently outside, you could move your now non-electric refrigerator or freezer onto a back porch or into the garage, (not an easy job!), or store some foods in a cool chest or other container in the same space. Any container placed outside your home is subject to theft and/or marauding animals, so be certain that it can be locked or otherwise secured.

If you live in a suburban or rural area and have a discarded refrigerator or freezer, or can locate one, consider making it into a "mini-root cellar" for year 'round food storage: Have a large hole dug in the ground and line the hole with heavy plastic to retard rusting. Remove the motor and shelves and sit the refrig erator or freezer in the hole on its side. Fill the hole around the appliance with some of the removed dirt and pack it down. The door will then serve as the lid, as on a chest freezer, and you can stack hay over it for further insulation. This should keep many foods quite well, as the temperature underground is fairly stable and cool all year - around 52 degrees. *(Be careful to keep children away from this cooler...they love to get into such places, and can suffocate if the lid closes on them).*

There are also some small propane-powered refrigerators for those who have access to a large propane storage tank, and although expensive, they might be very useful if you live in a warm climate, have to keep medications or baby formula cold, or just want to enjoy the luxury of it:

(Note: Catalog Code refers to catalogs listed in Appendix D.)

CATALOG CODE	ITEM
LE	a) ***SERVEL PROPANE AND KEROSENE REFRIGERATORS*** - A tiny flame heats an ammonia mixture (permanently sealed inside a cooling unit) which then cools via evaporation and condensation.

Proven effective since the 1920's, the freezers maintain zero degrees! Noiseless, constant cooling, no venting needed - built in Sweden. In addition to the following small models, Servel also manufactures standard-sized propane refrigerators and freezers used worldwide.

* ***Portable Refrigerator*** with handles - (looks like average-sized ice chest, holds 1.17 cubic feet), runs on electricity or propane cylinder, thermostat, makes ice cubes, plastic cabinet - $419.

* ***Portable Deep Freeze*** - Steel cabinet, 1.5 cubic feet, runs on 12-volt or 115 volt electricity or propane cylinder, pre-set thermostat, steel carrying handles, stackable storage baskets - $619.

* ***Built-In Mini Refrigerators*** - Made for recreational vehicles and vacation cabins, can also use free-standing. Models from 1.9 to 8 cubic feet - two models have separate freezer door - $515-$1375.

RM b) ***EXPLORER REFRIGERATORS/FREEZERS*** - Portable units, similar to those described above, and also non-portable, free-standing 5 and 7 cubic-foot gas deep freezers. They also manufacture standard-sized refrigerators. Most models run on AC/DC or propane and look like ice chests:

Model FP20 - .6 cubic ft. - uses 8oz.LP gas per day - 360.
Model FP40 - 1.25 c.f. - uses 7oz. LP gas per day - $419.
Model FP50 - 1.5 c.f. - uses 8oz. LP gas per day - $489.
Model FP70 - 2 1/8 c.f. - uses 8oz. LP gas per day - $580.
Moel FP100 - 3 1/8 c.f. - uses 12oz. LP gas per day - $780.

3) **MOISTURE** - Water promotes the growth of bacteria and molds, and in general, will rapidly spoil foods in long term storage. Moisture levels in any cereals, grains, beans, or dehydrated foods should be under 10% if they're to be kept for any length of time. Unfortunately, it's not always easy to determine the degree of moisture in home-dried foods. If you purchase food prepackaged, be careful to check on this with the company you use, as many don't monitor either the moisture or the oxygen levels in their products...another reason to use a company with experience and a good reputation.

If you dry foods yourself before the Y2K, purchase a good book on dehydrating, follow directions carefully, and use a dryer with an adjustable heat setting so you can control the degree of dryness. If you're drying with solar heat, just be sure that the foods are hard and brittle, not leathery and soft. Most powdered foods must be stored in very dry conditions in a metal container that doesn't "breathe" and allow the intrusion of moisture. In general, the cooler and dryer the foods, the better.

Moisture can also corrode metal storage cans, allowing them to leak oxygen. So never store your foods on the ground or on a concrete floor, but on some kind of pallet or shelves, and keep them away from any outside or concrete walls so that air can circulate around them.

4) **OXYGEN** - Oxygen is implicated in the formation of peroxygen or free-radicals when it combines with foods, most notably fats. This is the process by which foods become rancid, and this is the reason for vacuum packing many foods (including grains) that have even small amounts of fat in them. Also, insects and most harmful microorganisms can't live in an oxygen-free environment.

   Oxygen is removed in packaging through two methods: the addition of the heavier gases nitrogen or carbon dioxide, (which is usually a professional operation), and reduction through a chemical reaction with the use of oxygen-absorber packets. You can purchase these for packaging your own foods *(See Chapter 5 - Food Preservation).*

   If you purchase your storage food, be sure that it is packed with less than 2% oxygen in the headspace of the containers. It's said that only two companies achieve this level - Mountain House and Vacu-Dry Co. *(Note: Many firms distribute the Mountain House brand. The Vacu-Dry company distributes their products under the name "Perma Pak". See Appendix D for contact information.)*

5) **ANIMAL/INSECT PESTS** - A hungry rat can chew through just about anything except a metal can, which is why most long-term food storage plans use them. It's rare, but they've even been known to get into the hard plastic 6-gallon buckets. So if you're putting up your own food, and especially if you're storing it where you can't check it every day or so, be sure that it is safe in rodent-proof packaging. One or two rats or mice can devastate your entire storage program in a day or so. And don't think you can't have them - they're everywhere. You may have to set some traps. Also be careful to keep your storage space free of insects; use pest strips and roach houses to trap them. A certain number of insects and insect parts are allowed by government inspection agencies to be present in grains and other bulk foodstuff sold for human consumption, (just think of it as added protein!). So you may want to put your bulk foods in the freezer overnight to kill any bugs, before you pack them yourself, or add Diatomaceous Earth (DE), a natural insecticide powder that's harmless to humans. You can obtain DE at natural food warehouses and some organic gardening outlets, or see the listing below.

6) **LIGHT** - Light can break down many nutrients also, and direct sunlight can heat the storage containers up like ovens, so it is considered a good practice to store all foods in a dark place.

7) **ROUGH HANDLING** - You might not think of this, but if you handle the freeze-dried food packages roughly, the contents can easily crumble, and you'll end up with powdered food!

Some foods, because of their chemical makeup, seem to take to storage better than others, but if you are careful to keep your foods COOL, DARK, and DRY, they should be ready for you to eat when you need them.

SHELF LIFE OF SOME STORAGE FOODS

How long can you expect your foods to last? There are many variables in this question, as you've seen above, and it all depends on the conditions under which the food is stored. The military and the USDA have developed some guidelines, but they are only valid under certain conditions. Some prepackaged foods kept under ideal conditions have been found to be still tasty after twenty years! Since we aren't going to be storing our food supply that long, this isn't a crucial question. But it's helpful to know which foods are the most likely to need your careful attention to keep them at their freshest. Most foods will last longer than the experts say, but no one has really researched this question. Here are some conservative estimates for food stored unopened, in proper containers and under optimum conditions:

INDEFINITE - Honey, sugar, salt, instant coffee, tea, and cocoa, unflavored gelatin, bouillon products, wheat, white rice, dried corn, soft drinks. (Grains of wheat from Egyptian archaeological sites have been found to be still viable after several thousand years.)

TEN YEARS - Most grains, dried beans and peas, vacuum-packed coffee.

FIVE TO TEN YEARS - Pasta (dry), Crisco and other shortening, instant milk, egg powder, baking powder, cornstarch, cheese powder.

FIVE TO EIGHT YEARS - Dehydrated fruits and vegetables.

UP TO FIVE YEARS - Bouillon, flours, powdered margerine, processed liquid vegetable oils.

TWO TO THREE YEARS - Brown rice, textured vegetable proteins, most dried herbs and spices, dried soup mixes, beverage powders.

UP TO 18 MONTHS - Canned meats, vegetables, peanut butter.

ONE YEAR - Jelly, hard candy, canned nuts, ready-to-eat cereals and uncooked instant cereals, canned fruits, juices, and vegetables, canned condensed soups, natural liquid vegetable oils, lard.

SIX MONTHS - Most foods in store packaging, boxes, etc., dried fruits, crackers in metal containers, potatoes, canned citrus juice.

So you can see that if you can obtain most of your storage foods in the year before the Y2K crisis, they will probably last long enough for your needs.

GENERAL RULES FOR STORING FOOD

1) As much as possible, select and store foods that you regularly eat, or if you're purchasing a prepackaged food storage program, be sure that it's food your family will eat. You can purchase "variety packs" from some suppliers that allow you to try out their various foods before you purchase them. In fact, this might be a way to determine whether you decide to choose a prepacked plan or do it yourself.

2) Be sure to store some "fun foods", even if you do purchase a prepacked plan. These can be almost anything that can be stored that you consider a treat. You don't want to eat them all the time, but these foods can help you psychologically more than you realize when you're under stress.

3) If you suspect that your water supplies will be limited, be careful to store low-sodium foods, as salty snacks and canned foods can make you really thirsty. If you don't drink enough water, it's easy to become dangerously dehydrated. Also, the liquid in many canned vegetables and fruits can be part of your daily allowance, if it is a plain-water pack and not salty or sugared.

4) Store more food and other supplies than you think you'll need, because you could always be faced with having to help others, and no one wants to turn away anyone whose children are hungry.

5) Keep your food storage plans to yourself, unless you plan to feed the neighborhood! It's one thing to be able to assist others in need, and another to ask for trouble.

6) Plan to include some "live" fresh foods in your meals every day, either sprouts or garden or windowbox lettuce and greens. They're easy to grow, and provide essential vitamins and enzymes for good health. Give some to your pets, too. (This will be discussed further in Chapter 6 - Food Production.) But remember, *the way to continue to eat well after the Y2K crisis is to be able to produce some of your own food,* if possible. Don't neglect this aspect of food storage if you have access to the smallest plot of land or even pots on the porch. "Storing" food out in the garden is a viable and healthy option! So open-pollinated seeds are also an important part of any food storage plan.

PREPARING YOUR FOOD STORAGE PROGRAM

Before you begin to work on your chosen food plan, please refer to the Appendix A - Food, for helpful information on caloric requirements, general nutrition, how much food to store, and computer software that helps you calculate how much food you'll need to buy. There are basically four ways that you can set up your food storage program:

* **PURCHASE A PREPACKAGED FOOD PLAN**
* **CREATE YOUR OWN FOOD PROGRAM**
* **USE A COMBO STORAGE PLAN**
* **DO A LOCAL PURCHASE FOOD PLAN**

First, let's look at the advantages and disadvantages of each plan, so you can get a feeling for what would be most appropriate for you:

1) **PURCHASING A PREPACKED PLAN**

a) ***Advantages*** - If you lack the time, have no interest in dealing with food, and can afford it, this is the way to go. These food storage companies have developed the art of packaging a wide variety of foods for long-term storage that will suit almost any diet. Actually, the cost-per-meal is very low, possibly lower than you already pay for your everyday meals, unless you decide to use only the expensive freeze-dried foods.

b) ***Disadvantages*** - These prepacked food plans can cost thousands of dollars, and can be almost beyond the reach of many people to purchase all at once. And you'll be letting someone else decide what you will eat. The packers are already experiencing some delays in filling orders - up to eight months as of Nov., 1998 - and this will only increase as time passes. Unless you order your food plan before the end of 1998, it's very possible that you could never get it. Also, because we know the exact date that the Y2K problems will begin, we don't really need food packaged for very long-term storage, (although it's always a good idea to have some set aside in case of natural disasters).

2) **CREATING YOUR OWN STORAGE PLAN**

a) ***Advantages*** - This method is for the do-it-yourselfer who likes to do more with food than just eat it! Essentially, you will provide, prepare and home-pack almost all of the foods in your plan. If you enjoy planning menus, cooking and nutrition, then this could be a rewarding and fascinating way to go. It's also the least expensive method.

b) ***Disadvantages*** - This method will take time, study, and organization. You'll have to learn about nutrition, what foods to store, how to store them, and where to obtain them. Then you'll have to locate storage containers, purchase certain preparation appliances, grow or purchase the foods, prepare and put them up, and tend to all the details involved in this type of project. Unless you'e a full-time homemaker with no small children, or a Martha Stewart clone, this plan is probably not practical.

3) **COMBINATION PLAN**

a) ***Advantages*** - In this plan, you would purchase most of your bulk grains and beans (and some other foods) from a wholesale food warehouse, and pack them yourself. If you wish, you'd also can or dry some fresh vegetables in season which you have grown or purchased locally. Then you'd order some specialty items, that you don't have time or skill to prepare properly, from the prepackaged food companies, and round it all out with items from the local grocery store. This method will save you both time and money, and is a good compromise, especially if you begin by ordering the pre-packaged storage items you'll need right away. Small orders are more likely to be shipped promptly than large ones.

b) ***Disadvantages*** - You will still have to spend the time to make your plans, and do some of the storage, but packaging grains and beans is simple (*see Chapter 5 - Food Preservation)*. And you can purchase any fruit or vegetables canned that you don't want to can or dry yourself. Who knows, you might even discover that fooling around with your food is fun!

4) **LOCAL PURCHASE FOOD PLAN**

a) ***Advantages*** - If you don't have time, energy, or skills to set up your own food program, but you find the all-at-once cost of purchasing the prepacked food plans to be prohibitive, you can still stock up from the grocery store and local food warehouse. This plan has the advantage of being simple to do - you just double-purchase many of your regular foods each time you shop, and the cost is absorbed in your weekly food expenses.

b) ***Disadvantages*** - You'll have to be careful to provide good nutrition with this plan, and not stock a lot of snack foods. This plan requires some skill in knowing what foods to purchase economically, as canned beans, for instance, are much more expensive than dried. You'll still have to repack dry foods in tins or buckets. Also, there will be some foods, such as dairy, that you can't provide for long-term storage with this plan. You'll need a lot of space to store the bulky, heavy canned goods, and a cool environment in which to keep them for any length of time.

PURCHASE A PREPACKED FOOD PLAN

If you decide to let someone else put up all your food and just purchase it and stash it away, there are quite a few companies that can do this for you. Some have been doing this for many years, and some are fairly new on the storage-food scene. Since you will use this food within a couple of years, the quality of packaging is not quite as critical as it would be if you were purchasing it for long-term storage. However, poor quality can affect taste and nutrition, too, so still try to purchase from a reliable firm.

Since some of these food plans can take up quite a bit of space, be sure to locate a cool, dry place to store them before they arrive. Be sure that that your food plan is nutritionally balanced, includes sprouting seeds, and that you know how many calories each prepack unit offers per person per day. Some are barely above starvation needs *(see Appendix A - Food, to figure caloric needs for your family)*. If there are certain foods in the pre-packaged plans that you know your family won't eat, see if the company will substitute. This is important to insure full use of your food for the money you spend. Also check to see if they offer a money-back guarantee if you're not satisfied with the quality or service. You may have to call and talk to several companies before deciding which to use. Information on most of the companies and their products is found in the various catalogs *(and in Appendix B -Internet Links).*

And after you've obtained this store of food, you can stock your pantry with extra items that you know your family will enjoy, and use these foods along with your pre-packed ones. Be sure to get a variety of seasonings and canned goods.

1) **WHAT'S AVAILABLE** - Prepacked food comes in several forms, and many complete storage plans contain a variety of them. Most are some variation of dehydrated food, as this method retains nutrition and taste longer than with any other long-term method, such as canning. Traditional high-heat canning methods reduce the nutritional content of food 60-80%, whereas dehydration, done with low heat and circulating air, causes less than 10% nutrient loss.

Because of the huge variety in dietary preferences and of the foods available in these packs, it is impossible to list everything here. You will have to obtain the catalogs, contact the suppliers yourself, and decide what is appropriate for you and your family. I'll try to sort out some of the more confusing terms and methods used, as each catalog has its own ways of displaying and listing the storage plans and it's not always very clear what they're offering. Comparison is difficult due to the individuality of each supplier's programs. Some food plans contain only one type of storage food, and many contain a mixture. So there are a few basic things that you should know before you attempt to sort it all out.

Also, be sure to buy a couple of cookbooks especially for storage foods *(see Chapter 7 - Food Preparation)* as there are some special techniques to successful cooking with them. I'll list what catalogs carry what type of foods and give you a little information about them to get you started: Bon Appetit!

CATALOG CODE	ITEMS
BA,CL,NP, RM,SC, SS,SU	a) ***STANDARD DEHYDRATED ("AIR-DRIED") FOODS*** - Commercial dehydration processes remove almost all of the moisture from foods, and most companies then pack them either in heavy-duty, double-enameled cans or in six-gallon plastic buckets. **Cans** are packed by inserting the contents, and before they are sealed, injecting an inert gas to retard any further oxygenation or vitamin loss, and to preserve flavor and taste.

The most common can sizes are the #10 (1 gallon) and the #2 1/2 (1 quart). Some companies also include plastic snap-on tops to reseal the cans after they have been opened.

The **six-gallon plastic buckets** are packed by filling them directly with the food and adding oxygen absorbers, or by first sealing the food in metalized non-porus bags after replacing the oxygen with nitrogen, as are the cans discussed above. You can buy a new "Gamma" twist-off bucket lid to more easily reseal these containers *(see Chapter 5 - Food Preservation).*

What's available: Most grains, beans, vegetables, and fruits can be dried, and most anything can be vacuum or nitrogen-packed in cans or buckets. You'll find everything from granola to baking soda, meatless entrees to cheese powder, herbs to vitamins. About the only thing that you can't store successfully by this method is meat products which are usually freeze-dried *(see Freeze Dried below).* However, some food programs offer meat in wet-pack (MRE-retort) pouches. Both of these processes cost quite a bit more than air-dried foods.

Advantages: Most properly packaged, low-oxygen foods will remain edible for up to ten years if stored under optimum conditions, and field experiments have shown that this is a conservative estimate. The cost is less than freeze-dried foods, and it's a lot less work than putting up your own foods. Dehydrating reduces the bulk of the food by about 80%, allowing you to store more food in less space than regular canned and other store-bought goods. Each pound of dehydrated fruits or vegetables is equivalent to 8-12 pounds of fresh or frozen produce! *(More about home dehydration in Chapter 5 - Food Preservation.)*

Disadvantages: The cans and buckets can be heavy to lift, and once they're opened, the food will begin to deteriorate and must be used or resealed in a low-oxygen environment. *(See Chapter 5 - Food Preservation for information about using oxygen absorber packets - OAPs.)* Some people don't like the taste of dehydrated foods as well as freeze-dried food. This process does not cook the food, so it requires reconstitution in water and heating or cooking, which can be a problem in low fuel and water situations. Also, this method is a bit more expensive than drying and vacuum-packing foods yourself, depending on where you purchase the foods.

BA,CL,CM, b) ***FREEZE-DRIED*** foods have almost all the moisture removed

NP,SC, SS,SU

by a "space-age technology": The fresh or cooked food is first flash-frozen at -50 degrees F. and then, at low heat, the ice is drawn off as a vapor. The food is usually then packed in special foil packages, but it can also be packed in the same cans and buckets as standard dehydrated foods.

What's Available: There are many entrees, fruits, vegetables, eggs, orange juice, tofu, meats, desserts, soups, snacks, and more!

Advantages: Freeze-dried foods retain most of the color, flavor, texture and taste of fresh foods, and are preferred by many to standard dehydrated and canned foods. They can also be freeze-dried cooked and as entrees, and are ready to eat with just the addition of a small amount of water and heat. They are lightweight and easy to transport and store. This is one of the few effective long-term methods for storing meats.

Disadvantages: Freeze-dried foods retain most of their shape and take up more room in storage than dehydrated foods, even though they are reduced in weight by 80-90%. They are also considerably more expensive, and selections are more limited than with standard dehydrated foods.

EE,MA,NP, RM,SC, SU,SS

c) ***MEALS READY-TO-EAT (MREs)*** - Many catalogs carry these ready-to-eat meals, (also called retort-pack), first developed for the military. Many jokes have been told about these foods, but most people who use the newer versions find them quite palatable. Everything you need is included in a heavy sealed plastic bag, including utensils. There is a good choice of meat-centered entrees, precooked and packed in a pouch, and each comes with side dish, dessert, crackers, cracker spread, beverage powder, gum and towelette (you can also get cases of entrees or desserts only). They are usually sold by the case of 12 entrees. Prices vary widely, so shop around.

Advantages: These are very handy to have in case of unexpected emergencies, as there is no refrigeration, no cooking, no water and no preparation needed! However, if desired, the entree pack can be heated in water or on any warm surface, or in the special heater-packs described below. Even when you have another store of food, sometimes it's good to have something to fall back on when you're ill, or too busy or tired to prepare a meal. They're lightweight and store for 5-7 years at room temperature.

Disadvantages: MREs available to the private sector are military surplus, and supplies depend on which items the government is currently producing. Most suppliers have little control over their stock, so you should check with them before ordering. Sometimes old stocks are sold off at reduced prices, so try to locate dated cases to be sure you're getting fresh supplies.

EE,NP,SC,SS * ***INSTANT MRE HEATER*** - A unique flameless heater for the MRE entrees. Add water to activate - heats to over 200 degrees in minutes. Can also be used as a hand warmer. One time use - $.79-$1.50, reusable packs - small, heats one pouch - $20, large, heats 3-4 pouches - $25.

d) ***OTHER EMERGENCY FOODS*** - There are some very interesting products devised to assist in real emergency situations, and we can use some of them for the Y2K crisis to fill out our nutritional program *(also see suggested nutritionals in Appendix A - Food)*.

BA,MA,NP, RM,SA,SC * ***SURVIVAL FOOD TABS*** (also Life Tabs) - Developed for the U.S. Army Special Forces, these are ultra-high-calorie food tablets that provide all essential vitamins and minerals, protein, fat, dextrose and lactose (sugars). Said to provide more calories and nutrition ounce-for-ounce than any other food. 100% digestible, - taste like a malt ball. Can be used to prevent starvation in extreme emergency situations, or added to supplement storage food diets for those engaged in strenuous activity - 12 tabs equal a day's nutrition. But *do not use to replace regular meals if they are available.* Estimated shelf life, 10 years - 120-180 tabs - $20-$25.

* ***EMERGENCY FOOD BARS*** - Provide supplemental food and energy in emergencies. Great to carry in the car, and to use when unable to prepare food - 5-year shelf life.

NP,RM,SC * ***MAINSTAY*** - Taste like lemon cookies - 2400 or 3600 calorie vacuum-packed pouches. Pouch provides 3 days food for one person - 2400 calories - $5, 3600 calories - $7

BA,EE,NP,SS * ***DATREX*** - All-natural ingredients, no preservatives, U.S. Coast Guard approved. Tastes like crunchy coconut cookie - 3600 calories - $4.50-$8.

CM * ***SPORTS BARS*** - Provide complete nutrition - CM carries Clif and Power Bars - best tasting in a survey were the Balance Bars, which along with many others, can be found at grocery and natural health stores - average cost - $1.50-$1.75 ea.

Given the above information on how food is prepackaged, and after studying the Nutrition Section in the Food Appendix and the catalogs, you should be able to make an informed decision on which food program to choose. Talk to the people at several of the storage companies...they have experience and can give you advice. Many will work with you to help you obtain a food program tailored to your needs.

BOOKS

CATALOG CODE	BOOKS ON STORAGE FOOD
	"Creating The Complete Food Storage Program" by Skipper Clark - $15 plus $4 S&H to Skipper Clark, 96 Canyon Highland Dr., Ororville, CA 95966. This is a complete overview of most methods of storing and packaging foods. If you're going to do any of your own food packaging, you *MUST* have this book!
SA	***"A Pantry Like Grandma's"*** - Overview and explanation of storing dehydrated, low-moisture foods - $3.
SA	***"Food Banking Guide"*** - Everything you need to know to set up, store and enjoy your family food reserve - $10.
CF,RM	***"Making the Best of Basics*** - James T. Stevens - A standard text covering all aspects of preparedness, including detailed food storage plans - $20.

CREATE YOUR OWN FOOD PROGRAM

If you know a bit about nutrition, enjoy meal planning and food preparation, and have access to good fresh foods, you might consider creating most of your food storage program yourself. It will certainly save money, but it will also take some time, effort, and planning on your part - especially planning! But whatever cost and effort you expend to prepare a food storage program from scratch, think of it as insurance that you're paying for up front: *whenever* you need it, you'll be glad you spent the time and did the work!

1) SUGGESTIONS FOR CREATING YOUR OWN FOOD PROGRAM

a) Prepacked food plans come already nutritionally balanced, so when preparing your own program, you should read the nutrition section in the Food Appendix to refresh your knowledge of this vital information.

b) Buy a good book on creating your own food program, and study it (see above). I highly recommend "Creating the Complete Food Storage Program" by Skipper Clark *(see booklist above)*. There's more than enough information in this book to get you started.

c) Decide on the period of time for which you want to store food. I would suggest no less than six months, and preferably a year, as you can always eat up the extra if the crisis ends sooner. It would be good not to have to purchase food during any recovery period, when there are bound to be shortages and long lines in the grocery stores, money could be scarce, and prices sure to be very high.

d) Watch your family's food intake for at least two weeks, and inventory everything you eat. Divide this inventory into three categories *(See Appendix A - Food)*:

* ***Carbohydrates*** - Most grains, fruits, sweets, and vegetables, including beans, are mainly carbohydrates.
* ***Protein*** - Meats, seafood, soy foods, eggs, dairy, and lesser amounts in grains and beans.
* ***Fats*** - Fats are solid or liquid cooking oils, margarine, and are in dairy, eggs, and most meats.

When you plan your menus, try to see that you get a ratio of about 40% carbohydrates, 30% proteins, and 30% fats. The fat ratio may seem high, but not if it's coming from unsaturated fats such as good olive oil. This is the ratio suggested by Barry Sears in his book "*Enter the Zone*" which explains why we can eat a low-fat, high carbohydrate diet and still gain weight and have blood sugar problems. You need "good" fat to stay slim! (It's all chemistry, and is a fascinating look at how our body uses food.)

e) Multiply your daily dietary needs by the number of days you are planning for your program, for example: If you're planning to store food for six months, then you'll need about 180 breakfasts, lunches and dinners (and snacks) for each member of your family. *(See the Appendix A - Food, on calculating the amounts to store for adults and children.)*

f) Decide how you will eat during the crisis and try to make the menus nutritionally balanced, appealing, and simple. Cooking on a different stove, possibly without any oven or other familiar appliances, will be a change, and can limit your possiblities. This is no time to try to be a gourmet cook! Study a couple of Dutch oven and storage-food cookbooks to give you an idea for one-pot dishes and other simple recipes *(see Chapter 7 - Food Preparation)*. Decide on your menus first, in order to know what foods to stock. You'll also have to take into account the special dietary needs for any infants, ill, or elderly who live with you *(see Chapter 11 - For Parents)*. Make a list of at least a month's menus and then multiply them for as many months as you need. You can vary each menu a bit as you repeat it.

g) Using your menus, make a list of all the food that you estimate your family will need for this period of time. Don't faint! It can look like an awful lot of food, and it is...we don't realize how much we normally consume over a long period of time. Don't forget to include things like snacks, condiments, and seasonings. You can look at the food plans in the catalogs to get an idea of how a food storage program breaks down, and plan your own around this. *(Also, see the Appendix A - Food, for the amounts of food suggested to store per person.)*

h) One of the first things to do is to begin collecting your equipment. If you're going to put up much of your own food, you'll need the proper equipment in order to do the job right. *(We'll cover this in Chapter 5 - Food Preservation.)*

i) Investigate ordering your bulk items, grains, beans, etc., from a wholesale food warehouse. These are your most inexpensive sources for many of the foods you will pack yourself. *(See the list of warehouses in Appendix A - Food.)*

j) Make a month-by-month shopping list and begin purchasing your foods. Use the ***ACTION CHECKLIST*** to keep track of your needed food purchases, and use the "buddy system" to begin stocking up on those items that you can purchase from the grocery store each week.

Plan to purchase any fresh foods over the spring and summer of '99 for drying or canning. You can buy storage canned goods or prepacked foods in fall or winter. You'll have to plan your schedule to accomodate the time it requires to process food at home.

The closer to the Y2K that it is when you begin this program, the faster you'll have to work, or else rely mostly on purchased foods. I figure it will take at least six months for someone with a reasonable amount of time to devote to it to put up all the food needed for an average family. So don't start this plan unless you have time to finish it.

k) If you get caught short on time or money, put up what you can, and know that anything you can do will help. ***If I had to store just a few items, here's what I'd get:***

BASIC FOOD STORAGE SUPPLIES:

* A wide variety of bulk *whole* grains and beans, including popcorn and whole-grain pastas - these are very inexpensive and provide high-quality nutrition.
* Canned fish and meats, if you eat these.

* Shortening, and a good olive oil for cooking or salads.
* Canned vegetables & fruits in waterpak, and fruit juices .
* Tinned crackers, cookies, condiments, seasonings (including a butter-flavored seasoning).
* Sprouting seeds - and several jars to sprout in.
* Honey or other sweeteners, jellies and jams.
* Nut butters and canned nuts.
* Teas, coffee, and drink mixes.
* Dried fruits, soups, sauces, seasoning mixes, and salad dressings.
* Nutrition bars, multi-vitamin and mineral tablets, with extra Vitamin C., other nutritionals - (*see Appendix A - Food).*
* MREs - a case of entrees for those days you can't or don't want to cook.

You can live a long time on the many variations of beans and grain carbohydrates (and meat proteins), seasoned with mixes or your own herbs and spices. Don't worry about baking yeasted breads, which are the mainstay of many storage plans; chances are you won't have a good oven, and there are many delicious and nutritious unleavened breads that are easy to prepare in a skillet or Dutch oven. You can grind the grains for tortillas, pita bread or biscuits. Add the meat or fish occasionally for protein and fat, and sprout seeds for enzymes and vitamins. You'll get extra fats in the oil and nuts, and the sweeteners can add flavor and carbohydrate energy when needed. For times when you just can't prepare food, you can substitute an MRE or a nutrition bar for a light meal. Be sure to include many of the nutritious food supplements mentioned in *Appendix A - Food.* This is not an ideal diet, but it will sustain you for a long time for very little money and preparation.

COMBO STORAGE PLAN

If you feel that doing it all yourself would tax your time or knowlege, you can elect to use a combination method for your food storage plan. Since most canned and well-packaged foods will last several years when kept properly, if you plan carefully, you can easily create a storage program of groceries from the local supermarket supplemented with basic grains and beans from a wholesale natural foods warehouse. Then you can purchase any needed extras that you can't put up yourself, such as freeze-dried dairy, fruits and meats, from the food storage outlets. This can result in considerable savings.

Your best bet when shopping for foods is always to shop locally and not pay shipping costs. Try to locate a returned freight warehouse where they sell overruns and dented canned goods. You can sometimes realize over 50% savings on many of your usual grocery items. It's even worth it to periodically drive a distance to stock up for your program, if there's no warehouse nearby. The only caution is to be certain that no packages have been opened, and the canned goods, even though dented, are not bulging on the ends. This signals that the food is spoiled, and if eaten, could cause serious and often fatal botulism poisoning.

Decide which prepackaged foods you want to use, and order these early. Then you can order your bulk grains and beans very inexpensively from a wholesale food warehouse and pack them yourself. This is the program that I am using for my family.

1) Read the section "Create Your Own Food Plan" above, to get an idea of the first steps to take in your Combo plan.

2) Then decide what items you will dry or can, and purchase the storage and preparation equipment you need. You can do this part of the plan during the summer months, when fresh foods are available.

3) First, order from prepack food storage companies anything that can't be safely put up at home: canned dairy products such as cheese and butter powder, whole egg powder, stew blends (for convenience), and any vegetables you don't can or dry yourself, freeze-dried fruits and meats, and MREs for non-cooking days.

4) Obtain your bulk purchases from a wholesale natural food warehouse *(see Appendix A - Food).* These carry most food items in bulk, and usually their prices are better than a natural food or grocery store. But you will have to check each item, as there's no hard and fast rule. Bulk grains and beans are almost always cheaper, often organic, and come in large sizes (25-50 lb. bags). You can also get bulk TVP, dried herbs, dried soups, seasonings, sprouting seeds, vegetable oils, pasta, bottled fruit juices, canned vegetables and fruits by the case, personal products - shampoos, soap, cleaning products - detergent, and many, many more items. Buying in bulk from these warehouses can save you a lot of money and is worth the small amount of extra effort. Call and ask them to send you their catalog.

   When you get the catalog, mark the items you want and take it (or a list) with you when you go to the grocery and natural foods store. Compare prices by checking the amount offered for the cost per unit of weight or volume. You'll need a hand calculator for this. Choose the items that you can get for less from the warehouse, make up your order and call it in.

   When you receive your order, you can then repack the bulk items into the 6-gallon poly buckets, using a dessicant, oxygen absorbers, and/or vacuum-packing *(see Chapter 5 - Food Preservation).*

5) When you have purchased what you need from the prepackers and the wholesale warehouse, you can complete your plan at the local grocery store or retail food warehouse. Here you can find most condiments, crackers, canned foods, seasoning mixes, soft drinks, and snack foods, to round out your food storage plan.

If you shop carefully, you should be able to save a great deal using this plan. Even if you decide not to put up any of the food yourself except some of the bulk grains and beans (which are very simple to do), you'll find this method is a good program for the money and time expended.

LOCAL PURCHASE FOOD PLAN

If you're a very busy working person or don't have time to spend on an extensive and complicated food program, (or the money to order one of the prepackaged storage plans), you'll have to rely on local shopping. You can provide most of the needed foods this way, but you may have to order dairy foods from the prepack companies, as they are not storable otherwise without refrigeration. Here's a suggested plan:

1) First, read the nutritional information in *Appendix A - Food,* and the section on Creating Your Own Food Plan, to get an idea of what and how much you will have to purchase, and how long certain foods can be stored.

2) Realize that there will be some foods that you will have to pay more for if you buy them at the grocery store in small packages, but you are essentially paying for the convenience of not having to repackage them yourself from bulk.

3) You will have to locate a large space to store these foods as they are much bulkier than the prepackaged plans. You'll also have to provide a cool and dry environment, as many of these foods aren't packed to last very long if exposed to heat and moisture. An ideal place would be a basement with a de-humidifier. Then, if you move down there for the crisis period, your food will be readily available.

4) Once you have your basic storage food list, begin "buddy" shopping by simply picking up a certain amount of the items on your food list each week when you do your regular shopping. Divide the items on your storage food list into weekly groups according to the number of weeks left until the Y2K, (or better, until about two months before). Mix these groups up, as you don't want to be stocked up on only one type of food at any one time. These extra purchases will increase your overall food bill, but it's easier on your budget than purchasing it all at once in the prepacked plans.

5) Repack any foods in flimsy packaging. Obtain empty metal tins such as those used for cookies, fruit cakes, etc., from flea markets, or grocery or general merchandise stores. Be sure the lids fit tightly. You can also get the six-gallon plastic buckets from local food processors, such as bakery shops, and store the food packages in these. Put foods in plastic bags and seal in the tins or buckets with dessicant or oxygen absorbers *(See Chapter 5 - Food Preservation).* Use and replace (rotate) any canned goods until about two months before the end of 1999, if stocks are readily available, to insure fresh supplies.

PACKING EQUIPMENT FOR STORAGE FOODS

When you purchase most bulk items, you will have to repack them in order to store them, even for a short time. This is best accomplished by removing all oxygen from the food and sealing it in an airtight container. The easiest and most economcial method is to use the six-gallon poly buckets, just as commercial packers do. *For more information on this and other methods of storing foods, see Chapter 5 - Food Preservation.*

FOOD PRESERVATION
Chapter 5

Information in this chapter:

If you decide to do some of the work in your food storage program, you'll need to know about the various techniques of preserving foods. There are several methods that adapt well to the home kitchen, and allow you to take advantage of fresh produce in season. Here are the different preservation methods and some advantages and disadvantages of each:

DRYING FOOD

Technically, this method differs from the commercial dehydration process in that foods dried commercially usually contain between 2-4% moisture, whereas it's usually only possible to dry foods at home to 10-20% moisture. Drying food is pretty simple:

1) Select only unblemished and very fresh produce; almost any fruit or vegetable can be dried. Slice or cut into suitable pieces, small enough to dry quickly.
2) Place on a plastic screen or wooden (not metal) tray with some kind of holes in it to permit air circulation.
3) Put the tray(s) into an electric dryer (if you have one), an oven with a pilot light or on low heat, or place in the sun.
4) Foods dried outside in the sun must be covered with cheesecloth or a screen to keep it clean and insect-free, and brought inside each night.
5) Dry food until it is leathery, but not brittle, (unless you will be packing it for long-term storage). You'll have to watch the food, especially if drying in an oven or in very hot weather outside, to prevent it from over-drying.
6) If possible, vacuum pack the food in a heavy plastic bag and store all dried foods in a tightly closed container.

Each food has its own drying requirements, and it's best to study the subject a bit to learn all the details of working with this method. Dried foods store well when vacuum-packed *(see section below on Packaging Storage Foods).*

1) ***Advantages*** - For storage, drying reduces the bulk of the food, thus allowing more food to be stored in a smaller space. Also, dried food loses only about 3-5% of its nutritional value, and will last much longer without refrigeration than fresh food. Many fruits and vegetables are suitable for drying, and taste reasonably good when reconstituted in water. Dried fruits make tasty snacks eaten just as is. Drying food is simple, and requires no expensive equipment; you can make either electric or solar dryers yourself from simple instructions. There are a number of good books available on the subject (*see booklst below*), which give you all the necessary details.

2) ***Disadvantages*** - Drying does not sterlize food; there are still microorganisms present which become latent in the dried state; hence scrupulous cleanliness must be observed when preparing foods for drying. Drying depends on having a steady source of low heat, either an electric dryer, a gas oven, or several continuous days of sunlight. Care must be taken to dry the foods to a low enough moisture content, or it will still spoil in storage, and it's hard to know when it's ready. Home-dried foods don't store as long as commercially dehydrated and canned, unless also vacuum-packed. Some electric dryers work better than others, so shop carefully for this appliance, and choose the best model you can afford.

3) Since you'll probably be preparing most of your dried foods before the Y2K period, you might want to use a convenient electric dryer; but if you want to continue processing foods by this method after the crisis period, consider also building or buying a solar or air dryer.

CATALOG CODE **BOOKS ABOUT DRYING FOOD**

(Note: Catalog Code refers to catalogs listed in Appendix D. Also, if you're on a budget, check your local second-hand bookstore for these titles and others listed below.)

NP,SC,SU ***"The ABCs of Home Food Dehydration"*** - Barbara Densley - Explains the complete drying process with many helpful hints - 112 pgs. - $9-$12.

RM,SU ***"Dry It, You'll Like It!"*** - Gen MacManiman - How to dry foods, plus plans for building your own dehydrator - $7.

NP,SU ***"Home Food Dehydrating"*** - Jay & Shirley Bills - Economical, do-it-yourself methods of drying foods - $11-$12.

CF,CL, RM,SU ***"How To Dry Foods"*** - Deanna DeLong - A comprehensive manual covering many drying techniques, including making your own dehydrator - $15.

PP ***"How To Dry Foods Easily"*** **VIDEO** - Deanna DeLong - Step-by-step instructions on how to dry and pack food, and info. on equipment - $19.

CL,RM,SU ***"Making and Using Dried Foods"*** - Phyllis Hobson - Step-by-step instructions for drying and storing over 100 foods, plus recipes for preparing them - $13.

CANNING FOOD

People have been preserving food by this method for at least a century, and it has proven its effectiveness. Almost any food can be canned, but acid foods, such as fruits and some vegetables (tomatoes) are the safest, because the acid in them inhibits the growth of spoilage microorganisms. Although simple, canning requires some knowledge of the processes required, and stringent safety practices. So ***don't attempt to can anything without first studying the techniques, and following directions carefully***.

1) ***Advantages*** - Canning is a proven method that will allow you to store tasty, edible foods for at least a year. The process is simple, and requires no special skills. Canning jars and lids are relatively inexpensive and easy to obtain at any general merchandise store. Canning is a simple way to process and preserve many jams, jellies, tomato sauces, soups, and other cooked foods.

2) ***Disadvantages*** - Canning significantly reduces the vitamin and enzyme content of most foods due to the high heat required in the process. Although simple, this process demands that certain stringent sanitary and processing requirements be met in order to produce a safe product. *There is always the danger of very serious food poisoning from improperly processed food.* Almost all foods except those high in acid must be heated under pressure, so this requires the purhase of a pressure cooker especially made for canning. Canning jars take up much more storage space than dried foods, and are subject to breakage. Although canning jars and rings are a one-time purchase, for long-term canning, you must stock up on the jar lids, which can only be used once.

Briefly, here's a simple outline of the process:

1) Select fresh, blemish-free foods and wash thoroughly. Cut into suitable pieces for packing in jars, or prepare according to your recipe, if putting up already cooked foods such as soups, or catsup.

2) Pack foods tightly into sterlized canning jars, either raw or cooked. If raw, pack using a cold or a hot-pack, depending on whether the food is covered by cold or boiling water or syrup. Cold-pack works for acid foods, but hot-packing is required for most vegetables and meats. Cooked foods should be packed while boiling hot.

3) Clean jar-rims and seal with sterilized two-piece lids.

4) Process jars either in a "water bath" or a pressure cooker for a pre-determined time which varies for each food. If the lids don't seal tightly, you must repeat this process.

NOTE: You can also preserve food in metal cans, like the ones found in grocery stores, but this requires the purchase of special cans and sealing equipment. Be sure to get cans coated with a food-safe coating such as "C" enamel. Most people pass on this process, because it does take some expensive equipment, but information is listed below for those who wish to try it.

Several of the books about food preparation listed below will give you complete instructions in canning methods. Follow instructions carefully, in order to insure a safe and long-lasting product.

OTHER PRESERVATION METHODS

Salting, brine pickling and smoke curing have long been used to preserve certain foods, but they usually require some skill and preparation, although if you have a garden, you may wish to try making some pickles and sauerkraut. If you live on a farm, you are probably already familiar with butchering and smoking meats, which is a subject too involved to go into here. *Full instructions for these processes can be found in any of the food preparation books listed below.*

Over the centuries, the Japanese discovered many fascinating methods of food preservation which we can also use: There's an interesting process of making pickles by inserting cut pieces of of certain vegetables, such as broccoli, carrots, cauliflower, etc., into a crock of miso, the salty paste made from soybeans *(see Appendix A - Food)*. Left for several days, these "pickles" are a delicious condiment to eat with grain dishes, and provide elements which are helpful in digesting grains and beans. The miso can be reused many times. There are other easy methods of fast pickling using bran and salt that are much more digestible than the traditional vinegar pickles.

If these methods sound interesting to you, you may wish to investigate the healthy dietary practices of the Macrobiotic system. (Macro = greater, Biotic = Life). *(Information and recipes can be found in several of the books carried in the Natural Lifestyle catalog. See Appendix D - Supply Catalogs.)*

CATALOG CODE	BOOKS ABOUT FOOD PRESERVATION
LE	***"The Ball Blue Book"*** - The basic guide to canning, freezing, drying, pickling, etc. with dozens of recipes - $6.
RM	***"The Busy Person's Guide to Preserving Food"*** - Janet Chadwick - Step-by-step, illustrated instructions for preserving foods and recipes for using them - 216 pgs. - $13-15.
CL,LE,SU	***"Canning and Preserving Without Sugar"*** - Norma M. MacRae, R.D. - Helpful procedures for people on sugar-free diets, and good for anyone! - $13.

CL ***"Keeping the Harvest"*** - Chioffi & Mead - Latest techniques, equipment, and USDA guidelines for home preserving - 216 pgs. - $13.

CL,SU ***"Putting Food By"*** - Hertzberg, Vaughn, & Green - Large book with great ideas for preserving and storing food - $13-$14.

MA,RM,SU ***"Stocking Up"*** - Carol Hupping - THE classic on all types of food preservation, with useful recipes - $18-$30.

FOOD PROCESSING EQUIPMENT

As with most things, the proper tools will make the job of food processing easy and effective. Below is a list of some of the specific utensils that you will need if you dry or can foods. Know that there are many other useful food preparation utensils available that can make the job easier and add to your food supply, such as strainers, juicers, cider presses, butter churns, etc., which can be found in the catalogs or at any general merchandise store. However, we will just focus on the basic equipment needed to create a food storage program:

1) **FOOD DRYING EQUIPMENT** - When drying foods, it's tempting to use reg ular window screens to lay the foods on, but be certain that the screening is nonmetallic to prevent the food from picking up unknown substances. Many books on food drying include plans for building simple drying screens, electric dehydrators, and also solar "ovens". These use air heated by the sun to circulate up through a box containing the foods to be dried. There are several manufactured air-drying appliances, and also some "dehydrators" with stacking trays, a heat element, and sometimes a fan to circulate air and speed the drying process. You may want to try several methods to see which works best for you.

CATALOG CODE **ITEM**

CG,LE,MA, NP,RM,SC a) ***THE PANTRIE*** - A hanging mesh air dryer with five shelves that can also be used as a sprouter, or to grow wheatgrass. Comes with complete instructions, sprouter tray, and one-year warranty - $39-$60.

RM b) ***SUB/OVEN*** - Air or solar dryer, crafted of solid oak - use in oven or sun. Instruction and recipe book included - 4 trays (4 sq. ft.) - $49.

LE,NP,RM c) ***THE EXCALIBUR*** - (electric dehydrator) Rear-mounted heating unit and fan - fully automatic with adjustable thermostat. Claims to be 2-5 times faster than competition - no tray rotation - easy-clean mesh trays, low electric useage - recipe book included - (small size - $110), 5 trays (8 sq.ft.) of drying space - $140-$157, 9 trays (14 sq. ft.) of drying space - $170-$199.

MA d) ***FOOD DEHYDRATOR*** - (electric) Round, clear plastic,

	5-tray food dryer with heater and circulator fan - two fine drying screens and instrucion booklet - $50, two extra drying trays - $11.
CG,CM,PP	e) ***AM. HARVEST/SNACK MASTER PRO*** - Opaque, round, plastic 4-tray (expandable to 12) electric dryer - adjustable thermostat, patented fan system - instruction book - no tray rotation - $80-$133, extra trays - 2/$20.

2) **CANNING EQUIPMENT** - Canning supplies are widely available, usually in your local grocery store, along with many small utensils that make the job easier, such as corn cutters, food mills, jar and lid lifters, etc. However, the professional-sized pressure cookers required for safe vegetable and meat canning may have to be ordered. Most home-canners use glass jars and lids, but some invest in a machine which seals metal cans before they are processed.

CATALOG CODE	ITEM
CG,LE	a) ***ST. IVES CAN SEALER*** - Only "true" canning method, seals metal cans, sizes #1,2,2.5,3, and all standard fish cans - setup takes about 15 minutes. Simply prepare food, pack in can, seal (takes 30 seconds), and for long term storage, heat to 170 degrees in an oven - $125-$144.
CG	b) ***#2 CANS*** - With all-purpose enamel finish - sold by carton of 168 - $250.
NP	c) ***#10 CAN SEALER*** - For putting up your own storage foods - professional-quality manual and electric models. Manual model cans up to 60 cans per hour, electric model, up to 200. Perfect for groups - one year warranty - Electric canner - $1200, manual canner - $500.
RM	d) ***PROFESSIONAL #10 CANNER*** - Similar to a) above - $770.
NP	e) ***#10 CANS*** - box of 6 - $15, case of 54 - $115, pallet of 424 - $448. Boxes for storing 6 cans in -25 boxes - $70. *(Almost anything can be sealed in these cans for safe-keeping, not just foods.)*
CG,CF, LE,MA	f) ***PRESSURE COOKER/CANNERS*** - Seals jars at 250 degrees to kill harmful microorganisms. Only USDA-approved way to preserve meat, fish, poultry, and all low-acid vegetables. No gaskets to crack - cast aluminum, sides are 1/4 inch thick. Vent steam pipe and pressure regulator, safety valve - owner's manual. Can also use to pressure-cook any food. One year warranty - US made - extra parts available, 10.5 qts. (7 pt./4qt. jars) - $100-$150, 15.5 qts. (10 pt./7qt. jars) - $119-$162, 21.5 qts. (18 pt./7qt./4 1/2 gal.) - $135-$175.

NOTE: *Lehman's also has instructions on how to use these pressure canners for sterilizing medical equipment. Ask for free literature, #L-MS.*

LE g) ***NON-PRESSURE CANNER*** - For simple "water canning bath" of acid fruits - high capacity, square, stainless steel vessel for processing large amounts of food. Made by Amish - holds up to 15 quarts or 48 pints - $119, jar rack to fit bottom of pan - $10.

CG,NP, PP,RM h) ***HOT STEAM CANNER*** - A two-piece pot that uses steam from only 3 pints of water to process food, and saves time, fuel, and water. *Suitable for canning acid foods only.* Capacity - 7 qts. - steam dome inverts to become a 15 quart kettle, base and rack become a roaster - $25-$45.

LE i) ***STAINLESS STOCKPOT/CANNERS*** - Heavy-duty round stockpots can be used for many cooking chores, including canning. Bottom is bonded aluminum for good heat transfer. Seven sizes from 7.5 qt.(processes 4 pt./2 qt.) - $82, to 60 qt. (processes 30 pt./16 qt./4 1/2 gal. - $250.

PRESERVING EGGS

I have read about traditional methods of preserving fresh eggs, but have never tried any. Some people have immersed them in brine (salt and water), and others buried them in containers sunk deep underground, both with varying results. The idea has been to seal the pores of the shell so that oxygen can't get inside the egg and spoil the contents. Now, one catalog company offers a method they say was developed during the Depression, that will store fresh eggs for a year and more without referigeration! A friend has used it and says it works. Use the freshest eggs you can get.

CATALOG CODE **ITEM**

SU * **KE PEG** - This is a gel that you smear over the eggs, sealing the surface pores and preventing spoilage of the contents - store in a cool place said to prepare up to 40 dozen eggs - $20.

FOOD PACKAGING

The process of preserving foods in jars or cans provides them with their own storage package, but dried foods, bulk grains and beans, and powdered foods also need to be properly packed for long-term storage. Do-it-yourself packing saves money and allows you to store your choice of foods. There are several methods:

1) **LOW-OXYGEN PACKING** - This method involves several techniques of replacing the oxygen in a can or poly bucket:

a) The container can be flushed with a heavier gas, usually nitrogen or carbon dioxide, thus driving the oxygen out.
b) The oxygen can be removed by a vacuum process, which draws all the air out of the container.
c) Packaged oxygen absorbers can be packed in the container.

Flushing a container with nitrogen requires the use of special equipment, as does vacuum packing of cans, and are best done professionally. Several food storage books, including **"Creating The Complete Food Storage Program"** by Skipper Clark, give details of the nitrogen procedure, and of the method listed below *(see books listed in Chapter 4 - Food Storage). If you decide to pack foods at home, you will need to study the correct procedures and obtain the proper equipment in order to insure a well-packed product.*

Almost any grain or bean/legume can be successfully packed for short-term storage (several years) at home. Here is a brief out line of this simple process, but *get more details from a food storage book, and follow directions when using the OAPs:*

a) Place the dry food to be packed into a five or six-gallon storage bucket (with lid) and dust with Diatomaceous Earth (DE) to discourage bugs. This is a white powder derived from ocean plankton that is harmless to humans, but dehydrates and kills insects. Get food-grade DE, (not that used for swimming pools) from any natural food warehouse, store, or catalogs. (See h) under products listed below.)
b) Add several O*xygen Absorber Packets*, (OAPs), which are also harmless to the food, or a palm-sized piece of dry ice, either of which will reduce the oxygen content in the bucket.
c) If using OAPs, seal the bucket immediately. If using CO2, set the bucket with lid on loosely and watch until the ice has disappeared, then seal the bucket with plastic caulking and label it.
d) If you'll be storing the foods for a longer time, you can also line the bucket with a mylar bag before filling, and heat-seal it for further protection.

Many catalogs have these packaging materials:

CATALOG CODE	ITEM
CL,MA,NP, NP,SC,SU	a) ***PLASTIC/POLY BUCKETS*** - These are the familiar white, five or six-gallon plastic pails used in the food industry. They are ideal for storing many dry foods, but be aware that they are also very heavy when filled. Many restaurants or bakery shops throw them

away and will let you have them free or for a small charge. Or, you can order these from most catalogs listed in this book - 3.5 gallon - $5, five gallon - $6-$12, six-gallon - $7-$8.

CL,MA,NP, PP,SC b) ***GAMMA SEAL LIDS*** - Most plastic six-gallon buckets come with a snap-on lid which is hard to reseal. This ingenious item solves that irritating problem. Snap a rim on the bucket and simply screw the lid on to that! Seals most 3.5 to 7 gallon buckets. Comes in several colors - virtually unbreakable - $7-$10 ea., 6/$37.50-$50, 10/$75-$80.

CL,NP, MA,SC c) ***MYLAR BUCKET LINERS*** - Triple-layer bags that act as a vapor, light, and oxygen barrier, and are ideal for packing foods in the buckets. You will need some way to heat-seal the bags - some people use an iron set on Low, (practice first!) and others purchase a hand-held heat-sealer often offered on TV - liners $1.75-$5 ea., 6/$15, 10/$1.65ea.

NP d) ***HEAT SEALER*** - A commercial grade heat sealer for use with the mylar bags - useful if you're prepacking a large amount of food - $200.

MA e) ***BAG SEALER*** - Small, handheld - uses 2 "AA" batteries for heat to seal bags airtight - A/C adapter - $25.

Note: *Foods prepacked in buckets with mylar liners, oxygen absorbers, and flushed with nitrogen, are sometimes called Super Pails.*

CL f) ***PLASTIC FOOD-GRADE LINERS*** - These use a tie to seal, and are a bit less expensive, but can also leak oxygen - okay for short-term storage if tied very tightly - $2 ea., 6/$10.

CL,MA,SC g) ***OXYGEN ABSORBER PACKS* (OAPs)** - Suggested use is one for every 2.5 gallons of container. You must also have a way to vacuum reseal the unused packs (you can use the small hand-held vacuum pump listed below under Vacuum Packing, or your vacuum cleaner, and a heat sealer). Most suppliers suggest using them all at once, so you will have to be ready to pack a lot of your food when you open the package - 50/$25, 150/$30.

NP,SC h) ***MOISTURE ABSORBING DESICCANT PACKETS*** - Filled with silica gel that removes any residual moisture. Can be used to store almost anything, from dried foods, to valuable paper documents, and can be reused indefinitely. Vacuum seal in a mylar bag for excellent preservation - $.39 ea., 10-50/$.32, 50+/$.27, large - up to 10 gallon buckets - $4, 12+/$3.50ea.

MA i) ***PERMA-GUARD DIATOMACEOUS EARTH*** (Fossil-shell flour) - Food grade, specifically refined for mixing into grains for storage. Destroys insects by dehydration - easy, safe, harmless to humans, contains trace minerals, no taste, does not dissipate - 1 lb./$5, 5 lbs./$15, 10 lbs./$25.

CL j) ***BUCKET OPENER/GAS WRENCH*** - If you decide not to use the Gamma Seal Lids, this handy little instrument will make removing and replacing bucket lids a bit easier. Can also be used to turn off gas valves - be sure to get one made of metal for durability - $7-9, with water barrel cap (bung) wrench - $12.50-$13.

2) **VACUUM PACKING** - Most dried foods will benefit by also being stored in a vacuum. This simply involves removing all oxygen or air from a food package and sealing it. This is easily done at home, if you are packing food in plastic or mylar bags, and there are several methods you can use:

a) ***SODA STRAW*** - This process does not create a perfect vacuum by any means, but it will remove a lot of the oxygen in any small dried-food package. Simply take a soda straw and insert it into any zip-lock plastic bag or mylar storage bag, and suck the air out, moving the contents around to be sure you get it all. You will see the bag conform to the shape of the contents as the air is removed. This is the simplest and easiest method, and will work for well-dried foods that won't be stored for long periods.

CL,PP,RM b) ***PUMP-N-SEAL*** - Vacuum seal your food containers with this little hand-operated pump. - with instructional video - $17-$20, replacement tabs - $10.

c) ***VACUUM CLEANER*** - If you attach a piece of an old nylon hose over the intake hose of your vacuum cleaner, you can use this to remove air from the larger mylar storage bags before sealing them. This also won't give a perfect seal, but will suffice for most grains and beans, especially if you've inserted an oxygen absorber to remove any remaining air. (See below for the mylar bags.)

RG,RM,SC d) ***ELECTRIC VACUUM PACKER*** - This is a small electric appliance that removes the air and seals a plastic bag in one operation. It uses a cut-and-seal bag system, and has many automatic features. Originally created to vacuum pack foods for freezing, the frozen foods can be boiled and microwaved in the bags, which can then be reused. But it can also be used to seal dried foods for storage, and has an adapter for use with jars. Comes with bags and instruction video, in two models - Food Saver Professional II - $329, and a smaller version, Food Compact II - $180-$225. Also, RG carries the Magic Vac brand - kit with bags and manual - $300.

e) ***VAC-LOC BAGS*** - USDA approved, multi-layer bags for use with the vacuum-packer above, available in two styles - pre-cut - 8"x11" packs of 50/$27, or rolls 8" or 11" wide in one or two-roll packs, 20' long - $14-$45.

If you are packaging foods for a long storage period, you will have to take more precautions than if you plan to use them within a year or so, but always take care to seal the food as well as possible in order to keep out moisture, oxygen and pests. Remember, CDD!

FOOD PRODUCTION
Chapter 6

Information in this chapter.

Providing your own food is one of the oldest and most rewarding occupations for anyone. This is evidenced by the millions of people who engage in backyard gardening, even in this day of convenient grocery stores, whose abundant shelves make obtaining food easier than at any other time in history. And yet, there is something magical about bringing in that perfect, ripe, delicious tomato, or a basket full of freshly picked greens, that tempts many to develop the patience and skills needed for any gardening endeavor. Somehow, nothing else tastes as good or satisfies as well as something that we've grown ourselves.

Many of us now have lives that don't allow us space for a garden, or we're too busy with families or jobs to work in one. But if our food supplies are interrupted during and after the Y2K, even for a short time, it will be necessary for most of us at least to produce some fresh greens for vitamins and enzymes. *Nothing can take their place in a stored food program.*

And fortunately, nothing could be easier than sprouting a few seeds or growing some greens on a windowsill! Nothing lifts the spirits like the sight of something green and growing in the midst of a mid-winter crisis. So this chapter will explore some very basic and simple ideas about keeping some fresh food on your table, year 'round.

SPROUTING

"Eatin' greens is a special treat; it makes long ears, and great big feet. (But it sure is awful stuff to eat!)" Thumper in Walt Disney's "Bambi"

In spite of the little rabbit's distaste for greens, we all need them every day to maintain good health. And nothing could be simpler than sprouting. We don't know who first discovered the process as a food source, but it's been around for many years. Almost any seed, including beans and grains, can be soaked overnight and encouraged to sprout. This process creates some amazing changes in that little seed:

* Many of the proteins in the seed are converted to available amino acids.
* Starches are converted to simple sugars, requiring little digestion and providing quick energy.

* Vitamin content increases dramatically with sprouting - soybeans *increase their Vitamin C content 700%!*
* Uncooked sprouts contain enzymes necessary for many of our body's most important functions.
* Both humans and animals benefit from the addition of sprouts in the diet; sprouts provide a low-fat, high fiber, immune-enhancing addition to any storage-food plan.

So you can see that sprouts are certainly a valuable food, and worth the little trouble it takes to keep a tray or jar of seeds growing at all times. Most any seed can be used for sprouting, but there are several that are well suited - try alfalfa (most commonly used), any grain, soy beans, mung beans, lentils, fenugreek, cabbage, radish, and broccoli seeds (delicious, and filled with anti-cancer substances!). Many food storage plans also include mixed packs of sprouting seeds, but you can obtain them from any natural food store very inexpensively. *Never use any seed treated with pesticides and intended for planting* (for safety, they're usually dyed a bright color). They can make you very ill.

Sprouting is like composting: there's been an awful lot written about it over the years, but it's basically a simple operation:

1) Wash and soak the selected seeds or grains overnight in pure water. Drain and save the water for use in cooking.
2) Put sprouts in a container, such as a quart jar, with a screen over the mouth (lid kits can be purchased, or use a piece of nylon hose or netting held on by a rubber band).
3) If you're doing a lot of sprouts, purchase one of the sprouting units listed below. Or just use a lot of jars.
4) Keep the sprouts moist but not wet, and rinse at least twice a day, allowing them to drain in-between rinsings.
5) Most sprouts prefer to start in a dark, cool environment, 70-80 degrees, then in light once they've started to grow. If you're using a clear glass jar, wrap it in a towel until the sprouts are almost ready to harvest. The darkness encourages them to grow, seeking the light.
6) Don't crowd them...they need room to grow. A tablespoon of small seeds will fill a quart jar. One ounce of seed will produce about one cup of mature seeds. You'll soon learn how much to sprout for your daily needs.
7) Different sprouts require different growing periods - most are ready to eat within 2-5 days. Buy a good sprouting book that will give all the details for each type of seed *(see booklist below)*. You'll soon get used to the time it takes for each type of sprout to mature.
8) Just before eating, expose the sprouts to the light for several hours to increase the chlorophyll content. Don't set them in the sun for a long time, or they'll dry up and die very quickly.
9) Rinse a final time in a bowl to remove any seed husks and eat. Don't discard the rinse water, especially in low-water situations; strain it and use for cooking or making mineral tea *(see Appendix A - Food)*.

Sprouts will keep about a week in the refrigerator. If you lack refrigeration, you'll have to sprout smaller amounts and eat them all in a day or two. This means you'll need to set up several jars or larger units to keep a supply growing at all times.

(Note: Catalog Code refers to catalogs listed in Appendix D. If you're on a budget, check out local second-hand bookstores for the titles below.)

CATALOG CODE	BOOKS ON SPROUTING
NP	***"Rita's Sprouting Book"*** - Rita Bingham - Learn the ins and outs of sprouting, with 70 recipes - $6.
SA	***"The Savvy Survivor's Sprouting Guide"*** - Add megavitamin power to your diet - how to grow 22 varieties of sprouts - $8.
SU	***"Sprout It!"*** - Steve Meyerowitz - From seed to salad in one week - how to grow more than 30 fresh greens in the kitchen - $11.
SU	***"The Sprouting Book"*** - Ann Wigmore - Combination guide to sprouting and excellent recipe book - by an expert - $8.
SU	***"Sprouting for All Seasons"*** - How and what to sprout, including delicious recipes - $12.

SPROUTING SUPPLIES

CATALOG CODE	ITEM
CL,NP, RM	1) **SPROUTING SEED PACKS AND MIXES** - If you live where you can't obtain the seeds locally, you can order them packed for long-term storage from several of the prepackage companies. Prices average about $120-$260 per 46 lb. poly bucket, depending on seed varieties. NP recomends storing 35-50 lbs. per person for a year. Smaller packs also available Seeds packed in triple-layered foil bags - prices range from $3-$7 for 1.5 pounds, to deluxe mixes of ten different seeds at $10 for 5 pounds.
SU	2) **POLY BUCKETS SEED PACKS** - Poly buckets packed with 7 lb.of alfalfa seed - $22.50, and mung beans - $29.
	3) **SPROUTERS & SPROUTING KITS** - There are several kinds of sprouters available, some complete with their own seeds:
LE,MA	a) ***KITCHEN SPROUTER*** - Two trays, 8 1/2" square, with lids, seeds and and instructions, to get you started - $13-$14.
BA	b) ***READY RESERVE SPROUTING KIT*** - Six #2-1/2 cans of sprouting seeds with four varieties - alfalfa, peas, lentils and wheat, plus a stackable, two-tray sprouter kit, drain tray, cover, instruciton booklet - $34.
RM	c) ***SPROUTING SEED SPECIAL*** - A large kit including seven

1.5 lb. bags of assorted sprouting seeds and a triple-decker sprouter - $41.

NP d) ***SPROUTMASTER KITS*** - Two trays (no size given) - divider allows multiple variety sprouting - with Quick Guide To Sprouting - single kit - $15, triple kit - $37.

SA e) ***SURVIVAL SPROUTING KIT*** - A long-term storage sprouting kit with six #2 1/2 cans packed with 20 varieties of seeds for sprouting or gardening - includes sprouting trays with lids and a Sprouting Guide - $75.

SC f) ***BIOSTA THREE-TIER SPROUTER*** - Round, clear plastic stackable sprouters with three levels and a drain basin - $28.

CG,LE,MA, g) ***THE PANTRIE*** - A hanging mesh food dryer with five shelves - can also be used as a sprouter, or to grow wheatgrass (*see below*) - with complete instructions, sprouter tray, and one-year warranty - $39-$60.

WHEATGRASS

If you soak and sprout grains of wheat (or rye, or barley) for a day, then plant them in a shallow pan filled with about an inch of clean soil, they'll grow into lovely green grass that you can cut off and eat or juice (*see equipment listed below*). *This is potent nutrition - wheatgrass contains all 8 essential amino acids, and supplies good amounts of most vitamins and minerals.*

I keep a small pot of wheatgrass growing all winter for my cats, and they love it! No matter what Thumper says, you can't eat better food than a green salad made of sprouts and wheatgrass!

Many people like to extract and drink the nutritious juice from wheatgrass, which is said to have potent health properties. Go slow with this, it's "strong medicine"! A small shot glass is more than enough for the average adult; start with half a glass.

(For more information on other green foods, see Appendix A - Food.)

CATALOG CODE **BOOKS ON WHEATGRASS**

SU ***"The Healing Power of Chlorophyll"*** - Bernard Jensen - Survival and health based on the bio-chemical properties of chlorophyll - $7.

CF ***"The Wheatgrass Book"*** - Ann Wigmore - A classic about the health properties of growing and eating wheatgrass - $9.

SU ***"Wheatgrass, Nature's Finest Medicine"*** - Steve Meyerowitz - Used for many ailments and nutritional remedies - $6.

If you decide to try juicing wheatgrass, you'll need a special juicer:

CATALOG CODE	ITEM
CG,CL,LE, MA,PP	1) **HEALTH FOUNTAIN WHEATGRASS JUICER** - Also a fruit press - clamps on to any suitable surface - cast stainless steel - 7 lbs. - $50-$60, 10 lbs. - $90, 23 lbs. - $172.

GARDENING

There's no room in this book to go into the enormous subject of gardening, but I'd strongly advise it for anyone who likes to eat fresh, good food! If you have no experience in growing things, purchase a good gardening book or two - there are literally thousands in print - and learn a bit about feeding yourself (*see booklist below*). Pay special attention to the books that discuss growing food year around in small spaces. There are also a huge number of gardening sites on the Internet, with just about any information you could desire *(see Appendix B - Internet Links)*. Gardening is a fascinating hobby, and easier than you might think, so give it a try.

NOTE: I am not including the process of hydroponic gardening because, although it does grow food fast in a small space, it requires electricity to run water pumps, a special growing medium, chemical nutrients, and lots of water, none of which may be available during the Y2K period.

URBAN

No matter where you live, you can always grow a small amount of fresh greens to enjoy and to promote good health. If you're an apartment or dormitory dweller, with no land to use, you can still have an any-season "garden":

1) Get a book on container gardening, *(see booklist below, and Internet gardening sites)* and follow their advice in choosing seed varieties, planting those that have little space requirements and are suitable for the time of year in which they'll be growing.

2) In winter, fill a bread pan or similar deep pan or box with a soil mixture from a garden shop (be sure to tell them what you are doing so they can give you the correct mixture). Then set this pan or "windowbox" in a sunny window and plant your greens. Keep them watered but not wet, and they'll provide you with cut-and-come-again greens all winter.

3) In summer, when you can set something outside in the sun, if possible, take a large plant pot, or a plastic laundry basket or other similar container, (line it with a plastic bag split open to fit the basket), and fill it with a good soil mixture. Plant the same way as your windowbox, and water well - soil dries out quickly in small containers during warmer weather.

4) Any container-grown plants will need frequent feeding, so get a good organic fertilizer when you purchase the soil. And keep a keen eye out for pests... in a small garden, they can do a lot of damage overnight.

SUBURBAN

If you have any yard space at all, it can probably be turned into a productive garden. I remember during WW II, my grandfather and many neighbors had small "victory garden" plots in their backyards and vacant lots. We ate a lot of good food that way - food that our over-taxed farming system couldn't produce for us during wartime. Most of these backyard farmers had no experience, but learned from one or two neighbors who did, and all were able to produce some food for their families. We can do the same, if after the Y2K there are food shortages, which is very likely, given the fragile interconnectedness of our present food systems *(see Chapter 4 - Food Storage).*

Get a good general gardening book, and check out the numerous sites on the Internet on this subject, and begin now to put in a small backyard garden. Deep beds are the most efficient and simplest no-till method for the inexperienced. You don't need a lot of expensive machinery to use this method, just some way to outline the space and keep it contained, and some decent soil. Gather leaves all fall, add your kitchen scraps, and start a compost pile to add to the soil next spring. John Jeavon's methods in his classic book, *"How To Grow More Vegetables..." (see below),* have been used successfully by amateur and expert alike. Just follow his instructions, and you'll soon have a garden!

RURAL

If you live in a rural area on any amount of land, and you aren't already gardening, now's the time to get started. There are many things to consider, and building a large garden takes some planning and preparation. It takes time to create a truly productive garden plot, but you can begin now, and reap a good harvest, even the first year. The easiest, no-plow method is to build deep beds, which can be as simple as outlining the bed with concrete blocks, rocks, or other material, and filling it with good soil. The complexities of composting, all-season cropping, and so on, are subjects best studied in one of the general gardening books in the booklist below. The books about four-season gardening will show you how to produce some food almost all year around. And if you have the space, build a greenhouse to complete the setup. There is also a wealth of good gardening information on the Internet *(see Appendix B - Internet Links).*

Below are just a few of the very many excellent gardening books available. These have been chosen for their specific aid to gardening beginners working under difficult conditions:

CATALOG CODE	BOOKS ABOUT GARDENING
SU	***"Big Book of Gardening Skills"*** - A complete reference, with charts, tables, and over 450 illustrations - $19.
CL,SU	***"Container Gardening"*** - a Country Wisdom booklet for those with limited space - $3.
CL,LE RM,SU	***"Cold Climate Gardening"*** - Lewis Hill - Covers all aspects of producing food in a harsh climate, and of extending harvests - illustrated, 320 pgs. - $13-$15.

CL,SU ***"Drought Gardening"*** - A Country Wisdom booklet for those in low-water areas - good ideas for anyone - $3.

"How to Grow More Vegetables (Than You Ever Thought Possible...)" - John Jeavons - The classic best-seller about how to set up and use a deep bed garden system - get from bookstore - $15.

"Let's Get Growing" - Crow Miller - An old-timers' secrets on how to grow your food - get from bookstore - $24.

RM,SU ***"New Organic Growers Four Season Harvest"*** - Eliot Coleman - An experienced gardener tells how to eat from your garden all year long - recommended - $18.

SU ***"Self-Sufficiency Gardening"*** - Financial, physical, and emotional security from your own backyard - $14.

CF,CL ***"Solar Gardening"*** - L & G Poisson - How to harvest year 'round from the garden, using solar appliances - recommended - $25.

CL ***"Successful Small Gardens"*** - Louise Riotte - How to grow vegetables anywhere you live - $12.

CF,SU ***"Survival Gardening"*** - John Freeman - Enough nutrition to live on from 1,000 square feet! - $9.

CL ***"Warm Climate Gardening"*** - Barbara Pleasant - Comprehensive guide to gardening in humid or dry regions - 202 pgs. - $13.

SEEDS

I hadn't intended to put any specific information here on seeds, but I've run across several things that have changed my mind:

Not many people take the time to think about the basis of our entire food supply - our seeds - *but without them we would be unable to produce any food, and would quickly starve.* Recently, a friend emailed me the address of an article dealing with our loss of open-pollinated seeds, and hence, the genetic diversity that allows us to continue to feed ourselves. I think that this article is so important that ***I encourage you to read it and give a copy to everyone you know.*** This problem strikes at the very base of our entire life on earth, and we can't let this loss occur. Even if you don't garden, you do eat!

If you want to read the article, go to **www.arkinstitute.com/98/up0606.htm.**

Once you read this article, you will understand the vital importance of keeping the tradition of gardening with open-pollinated seeds alive and well. If you wish to garden in this way, please visit another website which can provide you with a good supply of these seeds -

www.arkinstitute.com/seeds.htm.

If you want to learn more about saving and sharing this vital seed inheritance with others, please contact an organization that is doing an amazing job of preserving these old seed varieties for all generations to come:

Seed Savers Exchange, 3076 N. Winn Rd., Decorah, IA 52101
319-382-5990 phone, 319-382-5872 fax

Call them for information and a brochure. They do not currently have a website or email. To get an idea of what they do, go to **www.csf. colorado.edu/perma/diversity/whealy.html** for a talk given by Kent Whealy, founder of Seed Savers Exchange. If you order their FREE seed catalog, they include all information on how to join the SSE, and receive their other catalogs and books.

Also, go to: **www.ianr.unl.edu/pubs/NebFacts/nf92-80.htm** for a list of seed comanies, and look under "Specialty Seed Companies" for those that carry open-pollinated "heirloom" seeds.

In addition to Seed Savers Exchange, another excellent source for open pollinated seeds is:

ABUNDANT LIFE SEED FOUNDATION - P.O. Box 772, Port Townsend, WA 98368. Call: 360-385-7192 order phone, or 360-385-7455 fax. Their $2 catalog features a large variety of heirloom and open-pollinated seeds at good prices. You may order as a customer, or join the foundation to support their work.

CATALOG CODE	BOOKS ON SEEDS AND SEED SAVING
SU	***"New Seed Starters Handbook"*** - Nancy Bubel - How to save seed and start your own garden plants - $16.
LC,LE,MA, RM,SU	***"Saving Seeds"*** - Marc Rogers - Practical, how-to advice on raising, harvesting, and saving seed - illustrated - $10-$13.
CF,MA, RM,SU	***"Seed to Seed"*** - A complete seed-saving guide for 160 vegetable crops, with detailed information - $20-$21.
CL,SU	***"Starting Seed Indoors"*** - A Country Wisdom booklet - $3.

Many catalogs and food storage plans also carry open-pollinated garden seeds. *Even if you don't plan to garden, these seeds could become very valuable barter items:*

CATALOG CODE	ITEM
BA,RM	1) **READY RESERVE PREMIUM** - This is an assortment of 17 varieties nitrogen-packed in a #2 1/2 can. One can will plant a garden

plot 65' x 124' - $17.

MA,PP,SC 2) **FAMILY GARDEN EMERGENCY SEEDS** - 25 packs of open-pollinated garden seeds (except the corn), sealed in individual foil packets. Will plant a basketball-court sized garden - should remain viable for at least five years - #10 can - $23-$25.

SU 3) **SURVIVAL GARDEN SEEDS** - 15-20 (as available) open-pollinated vegetable varieties in a #10 can - $32.

4) **BACK TO EDEN SURVIVAL SEED KIT** - This small, family-owned company produces vacuum-packed, open-pollinated seed kits, specifically assembled for your local growing zone. They supply four zone areas: Zones 1-3, 4-6, 7-8 and 9-11, so you can obtain the seed especially suitable for your growing conditions. Seeds are vacuum-packed to protect them from insects, moisture, and other spoilers. Packs include approximately 55-60 varieties of the most popular garden food seeds. The seeds are guaranteed to be true-to-name and viable when shipped. Cost is $97 plus $11.50 S&H - *a very good price.* You can reach them via the Internet at: **www.tlchub.com/seeds/index.shtml** or call The Greenhouse between 9 a.m. and 4:30 p.m. MT to order: Phone 970-527-3375 or fax 970-527-6221.

This should get you started in this fascinating field. You and your family will benefit from your gardening efforts, and who knows, you may end up having a new hobby! And there's nothing like the security of knowing that you can provide some of your own food in hard times.

FOOD PREPARATION AND COOKSTOVES
Chapter 7

Information in this chapter:

***NOTE**: I'm placing the information about cookstoves ahead of the section on cooking because the type of cooking and utensils you use will depend somewhat on the kind of stove you choose.*

EMERGENCY COOKING

Hopefully, there will be no loss of utilities during the Y2K crisis, but if so, there is no place where this loss will be felt more keenly than in the kitchen. Without electricity or cooking gas, most modern kitchens aren't set up to function well at all. Cooking during a crisis can become a major headache if you insist on continuing your usual kitchen habits. In the food preparation section, I'll discuss some of the changes that could prove useful to the cook, and in this section, we'll look at the different ways that you can cook food if all the utilities are down. It's pretty simple: you just need a safe heat source and something to sit a pot on. *When using any open flame, the same safety precautions used for heating must be observed, and **always provide adequate ventilation.***

It doesn't take a very big flame to cook over, even a candle will do. But for three meals a day, unless you have a woodstove, you'll want to get a good campstove that can be used safely indoors *(see Cooking Fuels and Stoves below)*. Perhaps the safest way is to place a sheet of metal over your present stovetop and set a campstove on that (the sheet metal provides a stable base for the stove). Then you can cook as usual in the kitchen, where it's most convenient. If you have to cook in another room, be sure to include some kind of fire-proof material to set the stove on (metal, ceramic tiles, bricks), and *be very careful not to allow any combustibles near the cooking area.* We'll discuss the best types of cooking utensils to use on these various stoves in a following section.

URBAN

If you live in a high-rise, apartment, or dormitory, where ventilation is poor or not always under your control, and where fire hazards are high, choose a solid-fuel or alcohol stove that burns cleanly, and do as little cooking as possible. In this case, you could store MREs and canned foods *(see Chapter 4 - Food Storage)*. If you find you cannot open any windows at all, ***do not attempt to use any flame for heating or cooking,*** and try to get to a safer place before the crisis begins. Otherwise, any small stove listed below would work fine, placed on top of your kitchen stove or on a non-flammable surface, with a nearby window raised about an inch. If you have a usable balcony (be sure it is constructed to hold weight!), you can also set up a charcoal grill or a campstove out there and use that when weather permits.

SUBURBAN

Chances are you have some sort of outdoor cooking device already, either charcoal or LP gas, which you could use if the weather isn't too cold. You might also set up a temporary cooking area in the garage (move the cars out), or on a screened or glassed-in porch. These could be safely used for most cooking, with proper ventilation. For cooking in milder climates, if you have a supply of wood, you can simply make a campfire in a circle of stones in the backyard. Although these methods can be used during milder weather, you still will need to provide some sort of indoor cookstove when the weather turns nasty. (Who wants to stagger out into a cold garage first thing in the morning and spend fifteen minutes getting a charcoal fire going, just to get your first cup of coffee or tea!)

If you have a fireplace, you can use that, but you'll have to practice cooking over a small wood fire on a grill. If you've installed a woodstove, you can cook on top of it, but you still might want to provide a campstove as a backup in case the weather warms up and you don't want to build a fire in the woodstove. As mentioned above, put a piece of sheet metal over the unused burners on your kitchen stove to provide a stable surface, and set a campstove on that.

RURAL

As usual, you seem to have the most options. If you already have a large propane tank hooked up to your gas cookstove, then all you have to do is make sure that the tank is full before the crisis begins, and continue cooking as usual. You might consider ordering another tank if you're planning on using propane for heating, also. It still might be prudent to get a small campstove such as the Sierra Stove, listed below, that burns a variety of fuels. If your home is all-electric, then you'll definitely have to provide another cookstove. If you have a woodstove for heating, you can cook on that, use your fireplace, or cook outside on a grill or campfire if weather permits. If you have room, and the extra money, you might want to opt for a wood-burning kitchen cookstove, especially if you have a woodlot and access to all the firewood you need. And you can also set up a temporary kitchen in an attached garage or on a porch as described above under the Surburban heading.

COOKING FUELS

It's helpful to understand the wide variety of different fuels used in the standard camping stoves. Most use one of the following:

1) Propane in 16 oz. bottles, bulk 5-gallon (LP), or 250 to 1000-gallon yard tanks.
2) Liquid camping/lantern fuel (sometimes called white gas or Coleman fuel) usually in one-gallon cans.
3) Butane gas in cartridges.
4) Kerosene, usually stored in five-gallon cans.
5) Unleaded gasoline.
6) Solid "sterno" type fuel cannisters (gelled ethanol) and solid fuel bars or tablets.
7) Charcoal.
8) Wood fuel - kindling, wood scraps, twigs, etc.
9) Denatured alcohol.
10) The sun.

Propane, butane, kerosene and lantern fuel burn cleaner than unleaded gas, *which should not be used indoors at all.* However, unleaded gas runs about 1/4 the cost of lantern fuel, and 1/20 the cost of propane. Alcohol and the solid fuels burn cleanest, but are probably the most expensive, and charcoal and scrap wood the cheapest. So your choice of fuel for cooking will depend on where you will be cooking - indoors or outdoors, or both - how much you want to spend, and coordination with your heating and lighting fuels. In the listings below, BTUs refer to the amount of heat produced *(see Chapter 2 Heating).* Here's what's available from any sporting goods store or camping and surival catalog, listed by the type of fuel used:

COOKSTOVES (Listed According to Fuel Use)

PROPANE FUEL

(Catalog Code refers to catalogs listed in Appendix D.)

CATALOG CODE **ITEM**

1) **ONE BURNER CAMP STOVES** - Bottled propane is probably one of the safest indoor fuels to use, as it won't spill. There's a variety of small, one-burner camp stoves that that attach to or sit atop a propane bottle:

MA a) ***CAMP CHEF*** - Both table-top and four-legged models - $60-$96. Another single-burner with short legs - $86. All three produce 30,000 BTUs.

SA,SS b) ***COLEMAN*** - 6,400 BTUs - $16-$20,

CM,NO c) ***"KING KOOKER"*** - Heavy-duty on tripod legs - 170,000 BTUs - $50-$75.

CM,NP,SC d) ***PRIMUS*** - Converts from a heater to a cookstove - 9,000-14,000 BTUs - $55.

CM,SS e) ***TRAIL SCOUT*** - 8,000 BTUs - $20.

NO f) ***HI-PRESSURE*** - 140,000 BTUs, on legs - $180.

MA,NO,NP 2) **DUAL-BURNER STOVES** - Outdoor two-burner on legs 30,000 BTUs per burner - Camp Chef/$185-$199, King Kooker/$80.

MA 3) **COLEMAN CAMP STOVES** - Two to three burners with lid, used like a regular stove 8,500 BUTs per burner - 2 burners/$40-$60, three burners/ $130.

4) **HOTPLATE STOVES** - Bare-bones, cast iron, one to three-burner "hotplate" stoves. These are usually seen at camp cook-outs and fish-fries. They produce a lot of heat for their size.

NO a) ***HEAVY DUTY*** - Single burner/$40-$75, double burner/ $115, triple burner/$155.

MA b) ***PORTABLE CAST IRON STOVES*** - lightweight - each burner produces 15,000 BTUs - single/$40, double/ $70, triple/$100, heavyweight - each burner produces 35,000 BTUs - single/$70, double/$150.

LE,NO c) ***PROPANE GAS COOKERS*** - 14,000 BTUs per burner - Single burner/$20-$52, double burner/$40-$79, triple burner/$60-$99.

RG,RM 5) **PORTABLE KITCHEN** - Energy-efficient single or dual burners single burner - $100, double burner - $180, with broiler - $320.

6) **PROPANE GRILL** - If weather permits and you already have an outdoor (LP) propane gas grill, stock up on bulk LP fuel tanks or hook it up to a large yard-tank.

LIQUID CAMPING FUELS (COLEMAN/WHITE GAS)

CATALOG CODE **ITEM**

MA 1) **CAMPING STOVES** - Usually Coleman - with attached liquid fuel tank - one, two or three-burner models. Some also use unleaded gasoline, which should only be used outdoors. Standard camping stoves with lids - 7,500 BTU one-burner $60, 16,000 BTU two-burner/$90, 17,000 BTU three-burner/$150.

CM 2) **PEAK** - "The Feather 400", 7,500 BTUs one-burner - $40.

BUTANE GAS

CATALOG CODE	ITEM
EE,NL	1) **BURTON PORTABLE STOVE/MR. MAX** - One-burner, operates like your regular kitchen stove - $60. Butane fuel cannisters - 12/$50-$60.
SA	2) **MOUNTAIN LITE STOVE** - One burner, sits atop a butane bottle, has fold-out supports for larger pans, stainless construction - $27. Fuel cartridge - $4.
SC	3) **PORTA-CHEF** - One burner, auto ignition and safety shutoff - $50, refill cartridges - 3/$15.
NP	4) **THE SCORPION III** - Stainless steel one-burner, legs fold. Adjustable flame - $35, 6oz. fuel cannisters - $4.

KEROSENE

CATALOG CODE	ITEM
MA,NP,SC	1) **SINGLE BURNER** - Heater-cooker, .9 gallon fuel tank, (could combine with kerosene lighting) - $90-$99.

GASOLINE

CATALOG CODE	ITEM
MA	1) **COLEMAN GASOLINE CAMP STOVE** - Model 435F499, two burners - $90. (*Outdoor use only.)*

MULTI-FUEL STOVES

These are all one-burner camp stoves that use several different fuels.

CATALOG CODE	ITEM
CM,MA	1) **COLEMAN** - Ultralight dual-fuel #440-700 uses white gas or unleaded gasoline - $50-$60.
CM,SU	2) **MSR MODEL XGK SHAKER** - Burns just about anything, including leaded gasoline, very small backpacking-type stove - $90-$95.
CM,SC	3) **PEAK** - Model 442 uses same fuels as MSR above - $50-$70.
CM	4) **PEAK** - Apex II uses camp fuel (white gas), kerosene or unleaded gas, -$55.

CM,SU 5) **PEAK** - Uses white gas or kerosene - 60-$70.

CM 6) **THE TURBO BLEUET** 270 - Uses Gaz 270 or 470 propane/butane cartridges (not included) - $30.

GEL AND SOLID FUEL STOVES

Some small, one-burner portable hiking/camping stoves use solid "Sterno" type alcohol-gel fuel cannisters, or hexamine tabs and triozane bars. They are good for short term usage, burn cleanly, and are safer than liquid fuels, especially around children, but are probably too expensive to be used for any extended period of time. They are a good choice if you live where you simply can't store any other kind of fuel, such as a high-rise or dormitory. At least you could heat up canned food and boil water for mixes and hot drinks.

CATALOG CODE	ITEM
NP	1) **ALCO-BRITE** - Uses alcohol gel, gives off only CO2 and water vapor - $15, can of fuel - 16oz./$4.29. Probably safest to use in small apartments, dorm rooms, etc.
EE	2) **THE HOTSHOT** - Stove in a box uses two cans of fuel - $7.50, fuel cannisters - $3.50 each.
CM,SC, SA,SS	3) **KWIK-COOK** - Folds-up, burns Sterno, Mega-Heat, other canned heat, or solid fuels - Trioxane, hexamine, etc. - $8.
BA,SU	4) **"SNAP-ON" STOVE/HEATER** - Attaches to reusable gelled ethanol fuel can, also used for space heating, clean burning - $8.50-$10.50; fuel cans - $3.25-$3.40 ea, 12/$38-$40.
NP	5) **ESBIT POCKET STOVE** - Original German Military "Tommy" stove - stainless steel, can hold a gallon pot - $7, fuel tabs - 12/$5.
NP,SC, SS,SU	6) **THE WING** - Folding steel camping stove uses solid fuel tabs - $3-$8. Extra fuel tabs - 8/$3.

GELLED ALCOHOL AND SOLID FUELS

CATALOG CODE	ITEM
SA,SS	1) **HEAT GEL & MEGA HEAT** - Alcohol gel in a can that won't spill or evaporate - long shelf life - $3.29-$3.65. (see stoves #1-2 above).
SA	2) **STERNO** - Canned heat used in many small camping stoves - two 5/8oz. cans - $2.19 (see stove #3 above).
NP,SS	3) **SOLID FUEL** - Solid trioxane bars and hexamine tabs can be used with

most small folding camp stoves such as Esbit and Wing - stores indefinitely - great as fire starters - 3 bars/$.99-$1.25, 6 tabs/$1.75.

CHARCOAL

Charcoal cooking is familiar to many from weekend cookouts. But *a charcoal fire should never be started indoors* - bring it inside only when the coals have burned down to the gray-white (cooking) stage. Even with good ventilation, this is not advised; it's best to use it in the garage or on a porch. Use the paste fire-starter (*listed in Chapter 2 - Heat ing*), to start the charcoal instead of more flammable starter fluids.

CATALOG CODE **ITEM**

RM 1) **THE VOLCANO STOVE** - a double-walled, cool-bottomed charcoal cooker with an ingenious draft system that can bake, boil, fry, stir fry, roast, using only a few charcoal bricquets. Sits safely on counter or table and cooks two meals a day for two months on one 25 lb. bag of charcoal! Small model - $70, large - $100. A line of accessories expands cooking options - in a set with the stove - $199.

RM 2) **CHARCOAL GRILL** - Any outdoor charcoal grill can be used if the weather allows. These are widely available at any outdoor or hardware store. Sportsman grill - $80. (*Also see the Pyromid stove below.*)

MIXED FUELS

These stoves use a variety of different types of fuels.

CATALOG CODE **ITEM**

CM,RM,SC 1) **THE SIERRA STOVE** - Uses anything that will burn: twigs, bark, scrap wood, pine cones, charcoal, etc. Battery-powered blower keeps fire hot, lasts for 8-10 hours. (Use with solar battery recharger.) Includes a grill for mini-barbecuing - $40-$50 (combine with battery-powered lighting).

BA,CF, EE,SU 2) **THE PYROMID OUTDOOR COOKING SYSTEM** - Uses charcoal, wood chips or Sterno, and thermal feedback to generate very high temperatures. Sets up in 15 seconds, stores flat. With accessories, becomes a grill, stove, oven, roaster or a smoker. Has its own cookbook.

8" stove (1-2 people) - $35;
12" stove (2-6 people) - $80;
15" stove (4-8 people) - $130;
18" stove (6-12 people) - $180.

ALCOHOL FUEL

CATALOG CODE **ITEM**

CM 1) **THE TRANGIA #28** - One-burner campstove uses denatured alcohol - $25.

SU 2) **ALCOHOL STOVE** - $22.50.

SOLAR COOKING

Using a solar-powered "oven" to cook foods is a unique and little-used method, but it's simple and efficient. If you run out of other fuels, you can always rely on the sun to provide heat for cooking! If you live where you get lots of sun even in winter, this might be a good choice. On cloudy days, you'd just have to use other fuel or eat something cold. Even though the initial purchase price is high, remember, you won't have to buy any fuel. If you are handy, you can build one of these yourself for very little cost. Several solar cookbooks contain construction plans *(see cookbook section below)*. Build or purchase one early and practice cooking with it.

Basically, most solar "ovens" focus the sun's rays through a glass cover into an insulated box with reflective surfaces, in which the food is placed; the focused heat cooks the food. Solar cooking takes somewhat longer for food to reach hot temperatures than flame cooking, but once the proper heat is reached, regular cooking times apply. You must keep an eye on the oven and turn it with the sun as it moves along its path. Casseroles and one-dish meals are ideal for solar cookers; any recipe designed for a slow-cooker will work well.

CATALOG CODE **ITEM**

LE,CF,RS 1) **THE SUN OVEN** - Rugged fiberglass case with interior shelf and self-leveling mechanism. Bakes, roasts, stews, - reaches temperatures of 360 to 400 degrees - can be used to purify water and sterilize medical supplies - $159-$229.

KW,RS 2) **SOLAR CHEF** - Uses 16 mirrored segments for high power and conventional cooking time at up to 500 degrees - 2 sizes - $320-$385.

RM 3) **FOLDING BACKPACKER SOLAR OVEN** - Made from 97% paper products, weighs only 1 lb, 12oz. Reaches 375 degrees, and cooks almost anything - $44.

KW 4) **COMPACT SOLAR COOKER** - Lightweight unit folds flat - recipes included - $16.

5) **INSTRUCTION BOOKS**

KW ***"HOW TO BUILD PETE'S SOLAR SLOW COOKER"*** - Step-by-step instructions for building a wooden oven using parts from the hardware store - $3.

KW ***"SOLAR STOVETOP COOKER PLANS"*** - Make your own cooker out of cardboard - pattern, instructions, recipes - $12.

WOODSTOVE COOKING

If you're fortunate enough to have a parlor woodstove with a flat top surface, you can cook quite well on that *(see Chapter 2 - Heating)*. This works fine as long as the weather is cold and you are using the woodstove for heating. However, in warmer weather you'll have to provide another source of cooking heat. Any pots and pans will do, but heavy cookware such as cast iron works best for woodstove cookery. There are a number of books out about woodstove cooking, but it is pretty simple: Once you have a good fire going, you can boil water and cook as usual on the top surface, but you can't control the heat very well. So it's best to prepare simple food that doesn't require exact temperatures. In the old days, Grandma kept a large kettle of stew going on the woodstove at all times, and everyone just ladled some into a bowl whenever they wished. You can also heat and boil water and fry in a skillet on top of a wood-stove, and even make biscuits in a Dutch oven. It just takes practice, so you should install your stove as soon as possible, and get used to cooking on it before you have to.

CATALOG CODE **ITEM**

CG,LE 1) **WOOD-BURNING COOKSTOVE** - If you have space for it, you can install a woodburning kitchen cookstove and also use it to heat the house in an emergency. These stoves usually cost more than a parlor woodstove, from $1,000 to up in the stratosphere, but there are many rural families that still use and enjoy these reminders of yesteryear, at least until hot weather arrives! (That's where the old "summer kitchens" came from. In hot weather they either cooked outdoors on a campfire or on a small woodstove in a well-ventilated building away from the main house.)

One nice feature of some wood cookstoves is a built-in container that keeps water warm for washing or bathing and provides healthful humidity in the house. You can also do this on a parlor woodstove by keeping a large pot filled with clean water on top of the stove whenever it is in use.

Now that you see what is available on the market in cooking appliances, you can appreciate the wide variety in applications and prices from which you can choose. Perhaps the easiest way to approach providing for these crucial functions is to choose one basic fuel for heating, lighting and cooking, if possible. For instance, if you choose the propane cannisters, you can use a propane dual cooker-heater and a propane lantern, and stock up on the cannisters or bulk tanks. If you go for the solar battery recharger, and rechargable batteries for a lantern, you could also use the Sierra stove which has a battery-powered blower to assist the fire. And if you use kerosene lanterns, you would also use a kerosene stove, and so on...keep it as simple as possible.

Whatever system you choose it would be a good idea to shop around, as prices can vary widely, and there are some bargains out there. G*et these items as soon as possible, as production may not keep up with demand as time grows short.*

FOOD PREPARATION

Once you have chosen a stove, and purchased, produced, preserved, and stored your emergency food, you also have to know how to prepare it. Cooking during an emergency situation is a bit different than your everyday kitchen routine. You will be using different foods on a different stove, and you will have to make some adjustments. It's best if you practice preparing these foods during a weekend "campout", so when the time comes you won't be under the pressure of having to produce meals under unfamiliar conditions. Many prepackaged food programs talk about eating just like you always have, but this is a bit unrealistic, given the likely kitchen setup. Basically, forget about complicated recipes or dishes; this is no time to use a lot of cooking utensils due to restricted fuel and water supplies.

The type of stove you choose for cooking will largely determine the type of cooking that you can do. Each of the stoves listed above has a unique combination of size, fuel and type of heat produced, and it varies a lot:

1) If you have to cook on a solid fuel or gel stove, or over a candle,your best bet is to prepare quick, easy-cooking dishes (heating MREs, soup and one dish mixes, warming canned foods, etc.).
2) If you decide to use one of the smaller one-burner camping stoves, you'll be limited to cooking one-pot meals, but you can regulate the cooking flame for more precise heat.
3) If you try to use a fireplace, cooking on a grill takes some practice and skill, because it's hard to regulate the heat from a wood fire.
4) If you cook on your woodstove, or one of the charcoal "cookers" such as the Pyromid or Volcano, or outside on a charcoal or LP grill, you'll be unable to control the heat very precisely, and will probably have to settle for slow-cooked Dutch Oven meals.
5) Solar cooking brings in a whole new dimension, but is usually also confined to one pot at a time.
6) About the only stoves that will offer you a similar cooktop to your kitchen stove are the two or three-burner camp stoves that burn bottled propane or butane.

This doesn't mean that you can't prepare delicious foods, but it does mean that they will have to be simple dishes. So you'll need to know what you are doing in order to provide ample, nutritious meals.

COOKBOOKS

There are a large number of books that can teach you about using stored foods and cooking under your new circumstances, and you should learn about and practice ahead of time for the type(s) of cooking you'll be doing. The list below is just a sampling of what's available; most catalogs contain many more. And if you're on a budget, check your local second-hand bookstore for these titles:

CATALOG CODE **BOOKS ABOUT COOKING**

1) COOKING WITH STORED/DEHYDRATED FOODS

BA,SU ***"Cooking With Home Storage"*** - Vicki Tate - Over 700 food storage recipes and historical tips on pioneer living, home remedies, personal care, survival, and more - $15.

CF,MA,NP, RM,SC ***"Cooking With Home Storage"*** - Peggy Layton - Over 550 home storage recipes, information on home remedies, household cleaners, survival tips - looseleaf - $15-$16.

NP ***"Dehydrated Food Cooking"*** - Stan Smith - Walks you through rehydrating and using your dried foods for great meals - $7.

CF,MA,RM ***"MRE Excellence Cookbook"*** - Vicki Walters - Your guide to making ordinary "meals-ready-to-eat" extraordinary - $17.

RM,SU ***"The TVP Cookbook"*** - Dorothy Bates - Complete details on how to rehydrate and use the meat substitute, TVP (textured vegetable protein) - $7-$8.

2) ONE-POT MEALS

NP ***"Dutch Oven Cooking"*** - Dick Stucki - Complete instructions with award-winning recipes - $15.

NP,SU ***"Dutch Oven Secrets"*** - Lynn Hopkins - A complete guide to Dutch oven cooking by a veteran world champion cook - $10-$11.

SU ***"One Pan Gourmet"*** - Fresh foods easy for campers or others cooking simply - $13.

3) SOLAR COOKING

CF,CG,KW,LE, NP,RG,RM ***"Cooking With The Sun"*** - Beth & Dan Halcy - How to build and use solar cookers, plus recipes - $8-$11.

SU ***"Solar Cooking"*** - Harness the sun's power to cook food, also plans for building a solar cooker - $9.

LE,RG ***"Solar Cooking Naturally"*** - Guide to using the sun, with recipes - how to choose a pre-built oven, plus plans for building your own - $12.

4) WOODSTOVE COOKING

CG,LE,RM ***"Woodstove Cookery - or At Home On The Range"*** - Jane Cooper - How to buy a wood cookstove, set it up, fuel it, maintain it, and cook delicious food on it - $13-$15.

LE ***"American Woodheat Cookery"*** - Inventive ways to use your woodtove for cooking delicious meals - stove care, wood tips, and more - $9.

COOKING APPLIANCES AND UTENSILS

My father used to tell me that the right tools make all the difference, and this is certainly true when you're a cook! It took me years, but I finally got my kitchen supplied with all the necessary (and not-so-necessary!) appliances and utensils that I thought I needed, and it has made cooking easier, and more enjoyable. There are several items that you can add to your present kitchen to assist you in preparing meals during the Y2K:

MANUAL GRAIN GRINDERS

People have been grinding grains for food for millennia; I recently saw a show on the History Channel about a Native American mummy found with deformed toes and arthritic knees and elbows, probably from years spent squatting over a big stone, grinding grain!

If you'll be preparing meals using grains and beans during the Y2K, you'll definitely need a grain grinder. Today, grinding flour is a little easier than it was on early people, but using a manual grinder still takes some elbow grease. If you think it would be too much for you due to health conditions, you might consider simply purchasing flour prepackaged for long-term storage. However, whole grains store much better than flour, which tends to go rancid rapidly and is best ground fresh when needed. So don't try to store whole-grain flours over a couple of months without proper low-moisture packaging.

There are several good reasons to grind your own flours, even without an emergency: Fresh-ground flours have about 26 valuable nutrients, including the germ and bran, compared to store-bought all-purpose white flour with only 3-6! They also contain no additives, preservatives, bleach or other chemicals, and they taste *soooo* much better.

Although I don't advise trying to bake yeasted breads under crisis conditions, (unless you have a working oven in a propane-fueled cookstove, or a woodstove, and the experience to use it), there are a lot of delicious unleavened breads - corn and flour tortillas, chapatis, and pita breads - that can be made instead. And you can even make biscuits and cornbread in a Dutch oven! So you will want some way to prepare your stored grains for breakmaking.

Actually, you don't even need a grinder: in a pinch, you can put grains to be ground into a coffee can and chop them up using a piece of metal pipe, but this is doing it the hard way! It's much easier to use a hand grinder: Basically, all you do is place the grain or other food to be processed into the "hopper" of the grinder, and turn a handle or wheel. The food moves between the grinding surfaces and is broken up into smaller pieces or ground entirely into a fluffy flour.

There are two kinds of grinding surfaces (called "burrs") used in today's grain mills - stone and metal, and each has its advantages and disadvantages: The steel burrs are usually less expensive, but produce a coarser flour than the stone burrs. The stone burrs grind flour finer than the steel burrs, but they can glaze over when grinding oily foods such as nuts or soybeans, and they also introduce a small amount of grit into the foods that has been flaked off from the stones. This is generally harmless, but can sometimes feel "gritty" when eaten. Some native peoples, eating a diet of breads made from flour hand-ground on coarse stones, have worn down the ends of their teeth from this grit! Some grinders come with both kinds of burrs that are interchangable.

There are many different types of grinders, from large, heavy table models that must be permanently mounted, to small, slim ones that clamp onto a table or counter edge when in use, and can be stored in a drawer. Several all-electric models are available, but get one that can be converted to manual, or is made especially for hand-cranking only. Many manual mills can be converted later to electricity. Read about them carefully and choose the model and burr type you think will best meet your needs. Be sure the mill you select has a money-back guarantee. (Note: The Lehman's catalog has helpful information and a chart that compares several of the grain mills.)

1) **STANDARD FLOUR MILLS** - These mills can be adjusted from coarse (for cracked grains), to fine (for flours), and some even make nut butters and grind coffee:

CATALOG CODE	ITEM
CG,CL,LE, MA,NP,PP, RM,SA,SU	a) ***BACK TO BASICS GRAIN MILL*** - Uses unusual cone-shaped steel grinding burrs for very fine flours. Table-mounted, sleek design, can be stored in a drawer. Adjusts to grind grains, seeds, nuts, beans, herbs, etc. Can be motorized - two-year guarantee - $48-$90.
	b) ***CORONA HAND MILLS*** - The classic cast-iron hand mills with rust-proof finish, large crank handle. Fine or coarse grinding of grains, coffee, nuts, and seeds - table-mounted.
NL	* ***CORONA*** - Metal burrs only - $50.
CL,NL,SU	* ***CORONA KING*** - Two sets of burrs, steel for coarse grinding, stone for finer flour - $75-$99. Dehulling attachment (CL) for sunflower seed, oats, barley, rice, etc. - $34. (Great if you grow your own seeds or grains.)
LE,PP,SC	* ***CORONA-TYPE "Universal Mill"*** - Low-cost import - doesn't grind very fine - $45-$50, replacement burrs - $15.
CG	* ***QUAKER-CITY STYLE MILL*** - stone or steel burrs, cast iron body. Adjustable grind, will do nuts. Imported - steel burrs only - $59, stone and steel burrs - $113.
LE,RM	c) ***"OUR BEST" GRAIN MILL*** - Adjustable, burrs convert from stone to steel - grinds all dry grains but will clog with

oily materials. Grinds finer than similar hand-crank mills. Bolts or clamps to surface - cast aluminum body, rust-proof, disassembles for cleaning. Five-year warranty on body, one year on burrs - $150-$180, converter burrs - $39.

d) ***MANUAL FLYWHEEL MILLS*** - These heavy-duty mills have a large metal hand-cranked flywheel, which takes less effort to use.

CL,NP, RM,SU * ***COUNTRY LIVING GRAIN MILL*** - Grinds all dry grains fine to cracked, bolts or clamps on surface. Can be motorized, 20 year-warranty on all parts, one year on grinding plates - $300-$375. Optional nut and bean auger - $23. Optional Power Bar, increases torque - $23. Nut & Large Bean Auger grinds nuts, beans, soft grains and coffee - $30.

CL,LE * ***DIAMANT GRAIN MILL*** - Large, heavy, (58 lbs.) permanently mounted with extra large (5 1/4") iron burrs, and very large wheel-like hand crank. Grinds fine flours to cracked corn - doesn't clog from oily materials. Can be motorized - with standard burrs - $495-$529. Extra burrs - $65, extra-fine burrs - $60, extra coarse burrs - $65.

e) ***CONVERTIBLE ELECTRIC MILLS*** - In the absence of electricity, these mills can be converted to manual by adding a hand crank.These are usually harder to use as they are not made for manual grinding.

CL,NP * ***GOLDEN GRAIN GRINDER*** - Box-type mill - will not grind nuts. Am. made, 10-year warranty - $399-$420. Hand-crank bar - $8, fly-wheel hand-crank - $65.

CL * ***GOLDEN NUGGET*** - Smaller manual version of Golden Grain - very easy to crank - man-made stone burrs, adjustable grind, can be motorized - American-made - $275.

CG,LE * ***POWER MILL*** - Large mill - special alloy burrs grind everything from coffee beans to bones and roots. Am. made - $299-$365, extra fine burrs - $29-$42, hand crank - $28.

CG f) ***GRIST MILL*** - Best for grinding animal feed or coarse meals - cone steel burrs, counter-balanced crank, cast iron body. Adjustable, produces about 10 lbs. per hour - permanently mounted - $165-$209.

NOTE: For those who are interested, the Cumberland General catalog has several large, professional models of grain mills that cost from $1,000 to $7,000.

2) **SPECIALTY MILLS** - These dual-purpose units will flatten grain to make rolled flakes, such as oatmeal, or crack it for hot cereal and granola.

CL,LE a) ***FAMILY GRAIN FLOUR/FLAKER MILL*** - Easy to operate, manual base, flaker and flour attachments - $196-$219. Motor base - $160, vegetable grater/slicer attachment - $94.

CL,LE, PP,RM b) ***MARGA HAND GRAIN ROLLER/GRINDER*** - Three hardened steel rollers turn easily to flatten grains. Italian-made - clamps to any surface - $70-$79.

COOKING UTENSILS

There are several types of specialty utensils that can make the job of cooking during an emergency a little easier:

1) **CAST IRON UTENSILS** - Any heavy pot or pan will do in a pinch, but for outdoor or "primitive-style" cooking, nothing beats cast iron cookware. If you haven't tried cast iron cooking, you will be pleasantly surprised at its many good features:

* ***Advantages*** - This cookware can be found in most hardware stores and many flea markets and second hand stores, and it is relatively inexpensive. Be aware that there are varying grades of quality, the best usually being American-made. This cookware is almost as good as Teflon if it is "well-seasoned" by rubbing with a fat or oil and heating before it is used. Re-season any second-hand piece that shows any sign of rust. I have my grandmother's 12" skillet which she purchased and seasoned over 70 years ago, and it still cooks better than any Teflon skillet I've ever used. It's hard to burn anything in cast iron as it's so heavy. It retains heat, allowing you to continue cooking after the fire is off, (thus saving fuel), and it's almost indestructible when used under outdoor or primitive conditions.

* ***Disadvantages*** - As mentioned above, it must be seasoned before use; however, if done properly at first, it only requires infrequent renewals. If you suffer with arthritis or weak wrists, a pot can simply be too heavy for you to lift when filled with food. It has been known to crack when dropped from a height, and is definitely dangerous if it lands on your foot!

There are several books devoted exclusively to cooking with cast iron:

CATALOG CODE **BOOKS ON CAST IRON COOKING** (*also see book section above*)

CG ***"Black Magic - 100 Years of Cast Iron Cooking"*** - John Folse, Ed.

- A compilation of recipes from chefs across the country, plus historical information about this cooking style - $15.

CG,LE ***"Cast Iron Cooking"*** - A. D. Livingston - Complete directions for seasoning and care plus 75 recipes - $13.

LE ***"Camp Dutch Oven Cooking" VIDEO*** - Diane Thomas - as seen on ABC's "Home" and NBC's "Today" show, every step of this cooking method is clearly shown - free recipes - 20 min. - $14.

While there is a huge variety of cast iron utensils to choose from, I'm going to concentrate on Dutch Ovens and a couple of other items in this listing. If you want to purchase more cast iron utensils, several of the catalogs have a pretty complete selection. There are two types of Dutch Ovens: those with a domed lid, and those with a flat lid which allows you to heap coals on them and surround the food with heat. The "camp" versions have short legs so you can set them over the coals, and have wire handles that allow them to be hung from a campfire trivet or other hanger.

CATALOG CODE	ITEM
CG,LE,MA, NP,RM,	a) ***DUTCH OVENS*** - Glass lids are available to fit some of the ovens so you can watch the food cook. Models with domed lids in 5 to 10 quart sizes - $25-67. Camp versions with flat lids and legs in 2 to 12 quarts - $15-$163.
CG,RM	b) ***KETTLES*** - These smaller pots with a round bottom and legs also could be used for one-dish meals - sizes from one pint to 6 quarts - $13-$45.
CG,CM,LE, MA,NP,RM	c) ***GRIDDLES*** - Great for making flat breads, hot sandwiches, etc. - must have a 2-burner stove - $13-$48. Also a square one-burner griddle-skillet - $15-$18, or round griddle - $18.

2) **PRESSURE COOKERS** - These large pots seal tightly and allow you to cook foods quickly under high pressure. These cookers can be found in any department or hardware store, and in many cookware catalogs.

* ***Advantages*** - Pressure cooking saves some nutrients and shortens cooking time - some up to 1/3 - with only 70% of regular energy use. When first introduced, they were the microwaves of their time, and still save fuel by allowing you to make fast, delicious one-pot meals, especially when cooking grains and beans. The old problems with pressure cookers exploding have largely been eliminated, and if you follow directions, they can be used safely.

* ***Disadvantages*** - They need high heat to build up pres-

sure, and probably won't work well on stoves without any way to control the flame. They come in both aluminum (which are less expensive) and stainless steel models. Since aluminum has been implicated in several serious health conditions, including Alzheimer's disease, I wouldn't advise using any utensil made from it. Compared to ordinary pots and pans, pressure cookers are expensive, but many consider the time and fuel-saving features to be worth it. Most use rubber sealing gaskets which must be replaced occasionally, so you'll have to stock up on them, or you'll end up with a very expensive but ordinary cookpot!

CATALOG CODE	ITEM
NL,CL,RG	a) ***STAINLESS STEEL PRESSURE COOKERS*** - Several well-known brands offered - hold 2-12 quarts, $115-$300. Extra lid gaskets - $12-$26, glass lids available.
CL	b) ***DUROMATIC PAN SET*** - Includes a 5.25 quart pressure cooker, a frypan, a pressure lid and glass lids to fit both, - $199.
NL	c) ***SILIT SICOMATIC ENAMEL*** - Works even on a woodstove - two cooking levels - enameled surfaces and completely sealed design cooks about 10 minutes faster than standard pressure cookers. Easy to clean, patented valve system - 3 to 8 quarts range from $199-$269. Extra gasket rings - $9.50, glass lids - $24.

Here's a book that can help you with pressure cooking:

CF ***"Cooking Under Pressure"*** - Lorna J. Sass - How to cook using a fast and easy pressure cooker - $23.

OPTIONAL ACCESSORIES

There are lots of other items that you can buy to make cooking with your campstove easier: there are firestarter bars, fuel filters and fuel can nozzles for safe pouring, grills, special cookware; and for fireplaces, there are ash buckets, tongs, grills, and so on...

CATALOG CODE	ITEM
	1) **CAMP OVEN** - These little ovens sit atop a campstove or woodstove and allow you to do some baking. Of course, you can also learn to use a Dutch oven for most baking needs. You probably won't be baking that much during a crisis, although hot biscuits can be very comforting on a cold morning, and cornbread on a wintry evening...and if you just have to bake bread, this might work. Practice using it before you have to.
CG	a) ***THE EFFICIENCY OVEN*** - Operates just like a regular

oven. Works on gas, electric, campstove, fireplace, camp fire, and gas grills - $31.

CM,LE,SU b) ***COLEMAN CAMP OVEN*** - Made of heavy steel, sits atop a Coleman full-sized campstove for baking. NOTE: other stoves might not produce enough heat for it to work properly - $40-$80.

CM,SU c) ***OUTBACK OVEN*** - Works on any single-burner adjustable camp stove. True temperature oven, can bake almost anything. Comès with 12-inch baking pan and lid that doubles as a skillet or popcorn popper - sizes to serve 1-4 - $32-$70.

2) **OUTDOOR AND FIREPLACE COOKING**

CG,CM,LE, NP,RM a) ***TRIPOD*** - Cast iron tripod with chain for hanging a pot over an open fire - 43" high - some have adjustable height - $20-$48.

CM,LE,NP b) ***GRILLS*** - Small grills, some with folding legs for cooking over a wood or charcoal fire, or even a large three-wick pillar or survival candle - $8-$19.

RG 3) **CIRCULATING FAN** - Small battery-powered fan can be used to circulate fresh air for ventilation when cooking and heating, and for warm weather relief. Runs over 300 hours on one set of four "D" batteries - *good safety item* - $22, with AC/DC adapter - $11.

The most important thing to remember during the Y2K crisis period is that you will still need to eat, (preferably three times a day), and that you will be providing food under different and perhaps difficult circumstances. Therefore, anything that you can do to ease this situation, and to provide simple, delicious meals with high nutrition, is worth some preparation. If you struggle to maintain the old kitchen routine when everything else is changing, you may end up working very hard and still experience frustration. So make it easy on yourself and set up a simple and efficient cooking system before you have to use it. *(See Appendix A - Food, for some ideas for nutritious supplements.)*

SANITATION AND CLEANING
Chapter 8

Information in this chapter:

WHAT WASTE ???

Nobody wants to think about this subject, yet dealing with our waste is one of the most important considerations in any emergency planning. In most western countries with modern sewage systems, we simply flush it all away, and don't think about it. We depend on our garbage pickup for waste removal, and not enough of us recycle. But the issue of what to do about our waste will definitely have to be dealt with in an emergency situation! If the water and sewage plants go down, even for a short time, we will have to provide sanitary alternatives for waste disposal. *It will be important not to use the toilet facilities if you suspect that there is any problem with the water supply, or if you can't flush for any reason.* And if garbage pickups cease, we will have to learn to deal with household waste, as well.

One of the biggest problems in urban areas during a weather emergency or period of social unrest is garbage piling up and creating a breeding ground for disease. Did you know that New York City creates *15,000 TONS* of garbage every single day? And the waste dump where they put it is 50 times the volume of the Great Pyramid! What will we do with all this refuse if our collection systems falter or go down completely?

Fortunately, as with lighting and heating, people for centuries have dealt with garbage and waste disposal without high-tech solutions. How did they do it?

Well, for starters, they didn't use as much packaging - paper, plastic, cardboard, etc. - so they didn't have as much to dispose of! Most people composted their kitchen garbage, and burned and buried their trash and human waste. The country outhouse has a long and honored history, and people dealt with human waste in other innovative ways, such as composting toilets. Some of these practices probably won't work too well now for those of us who live in crowded city conditions, but there are several solutions (although none of them are ideal). We'll all just have to do the best we can under the circumstances until our normal sewage and garbage systems are back in place.

WASTE MANAGEMENT

Below are several books that discuss the subject of waste management:

(Note: Catalog Code refers to catalogs listed in Appendix D. Also, if you are on a budget, check your local second-hand bookstore for the following titles.)

CATALOG CODE **BOOKS ON WASTE MANAGEMENT**

BA ***"Don't Waste Your Waste - Compost 'Em"*** - Bert Whitehead - Covers the basics of composting wastes - $11.

MA ***"How To Shit In The Woods"*** - Kathleen Meyer - Endorsed by "Outside" magazine, "USA Today", and many others, and has over 300,000 copies in print. Essential and explicit information about primitive waste management - $10.

LE ***"Humanure Handbook"*** - Learn how to safely recycle human waste without chemicals, technology or environmental pollution - $17.

RM,SU ***"The Toilet Papers"*** - The classic book about recycling waste and conserving water - plans for a compact privy and waste-water systems - $11.

LE "***The Vanishing American Outhouse"*** - Humorous history plus practical plans and sanitary design - illustrated - $17.

URBAN

If there is no sewage service or sanitation pickup for some time, and if you live where you have no yard in which to burn and bury waste, you will have to store it in tightly-closed heavy plastic bags, preferably inside a plastic pail, metal garbage can or barrel, with a tight-fitting lid.

A simple way to set up an emergency toilet is to place a heavy trash bag in the empty toilet bowl and use a disinfectant in the bottom in a small amount of water. If you don't have disinfectant, use a little soapy dishwater with a small amount of kerosene or oil in it to kill some microbes and odors. Tie the bag off and take it outside to a storage barrel when necessary.

Here's a list of the best types of indoor emergency toilets. You can also find these at most sporting goods and outdoor stores.

CATALOG CODE **ITEM**

CM,MA,SC, 1) **PORTABLE FOLDING CAMP TOILET** - Comes with plastic bags - $11-$15,

SS,SU extra pkg. of bags, $3-$4.

MA,NP, SC,SS 2) **HASSOCK PORTABLE CHEMICAL TOILET** - A 3-gallon polyethylene pail with lid - $30-$42.

CF,EE,MA, NP,SC,SS 3) **"LUGGABLE LOO" PORTABLE TOILET KIT** - A 6-gallon bucket with a snap-on hinged seat and cover - with heavy plastic liners and BioBlue packet - $18-40.

SC 4) **POTTY-TIME COLLAPSIBLE TOILET** - Can be set up and used like other portable toilets - $50.

NP 5) **PORTABLE ECO-TOILET** - Heavy cardboard, folds open for use - supports up to 500 lbs. Biodegradable - includes 3 liners - $13, replacement liners - 12/$3.

MA 6) **PORTAPOTTI 135 -** A 2.6 gallon fresh-water holding tank plus a 2.6 gallon waste holding tank. For those with plenty of water - simply add disinfectant to water and use as regular toilet - $109.

EE,NP 7) **DELUXE WATER/SANITATION KIT** - Store 5 gallons of water in a metalized plastic bag inside a sturdy box. When water is used, insert the sanitary toilet bag into the box and use as a toilet! Includes enzyme deodorant, toilet paper, tape, instructions - $7-$10 each.

8) **DISINFECTANTS/DEODORANTS**

MA,SC, NP,SS a) ***BIO-BLUE TOILET DEODORANT*** - 12 pkgs of pre-measured non-formaldehyde, 100% bio-degradable deodorant - $9-$11.

MA b) ***BIO-GREEN DIGESTER*** - 12 5oz. pouches that break down all solid waste in your toilet or holding tank - $10.

EE c) ***ENZYME DEODORANT*** - 10 pack - $6.

NP 9) **RED HAZ-WASTE TOILET LINERS** - Use with most portable toilets - heavy-duty hospital grade hazardous waste bags - 12/$7.

Determine how much toilet tissue you use every week, and be sure to stock enough. Your grocer will probably order it by the case for you. If you're using a composting toilet (see below), it's best to use plain white paper; and some grocery stores now carry unbleached and recycled toilet paper and paper towels. It's also possible to purchase biodegradable camping toilet tissue, but it is somewhat expensive, and most ordinary white tissue will degrade also, just more slowly.

Use large heavy-duty garbage bags for waste and garbage disposal, and store the filled bags outside your living area in a garage or similar space, in tightly closed, heavy-duty garbage cans. *Check periodically to be sure the bags aren't leaking or available to rodents.* Keeping the rodent population down is an important part of sanitation, as they can carry serious diseases; so you may want to have some traps on hand. If municipal garbage systems don't come back up right away, some entrepreneur will probably begin a garbage pick-up service that you can use. If you have a vehicle and enough gas, you can take the bags to the city dump yourself.

SUBURBAN

You can use the camping toilet systems offered under the Urban heading, or if you have a yard and access to soft dirt, or sawdust from a local lumber mill, consider making your own composting toilet: Instead of using chemicals in the toilet, just keep a pail of dirt, sawdust, or peat moss, and a scoop, by a toilet bucket, and cover deposits with that. We lived in the country for ten years with this system, and never had any trouble with odors or sanitation, as long as everything was carefully covered up. You'll need to get a load of dirt or sawdust, or several large bags of peatmoss, ahead of time, and keep it covered with plastic sheeting so that it stays dry. Bring it into the house in a bucket.

It will be necessary to set up a compost pile in the backyard in which to deposit the waste. It will take almost a week for two adults to fill a six-gallon bucket, so you only have to empty it infrequently. If you don't have someone strong enough to lift a full pail, just empty it more often. I prefer sawdust or peat, as sawdust smells good, and both are lighter and more absorbent than dirt. Sawdust is probably cheaper than peatmoss, (if you can get it by the pickup load). You can find peatmoss at most lawn and garden shops in package sizes ranging from several pounds to fifty-pound bales.

Just empty the used toilet pail into a defined area (use wire, bricks, wood, etc.) next to the dirt or clean sawdust pile, and be sure it is all covered with more dirt or sawdust. Then scrub the pail out thoroughly using a disinfectant, before refilling with a small layer of dirt or sawdust to get started again. As long as everyone in the family is reasonably healthy, this system works fine. After a time, you'll have a nice pile of compost to use on your yard or ornamental plants! People in the Orient have been using this system for centuries, never wasting such valuable soil nutrients. To set up this innovative yet practical toilet system, you'll need:

CATALOG CODE **ITEM**

MA,PP,SC 1) **FIVE OR SIX-GALLON PLASTIC BUCKETS** - $7-$12 each. (These can sometimes be obtained free from restaurants, bakeries, and warehouses.)

2) **SOFT DIRT, CLEAN SAWDUST, PEAT MOSS** - I don't know an easy way to figure usage on this, but I'd have at least one large pickup load of soft dirt or clean sawdust, or several large bags of peatmoss, depending on the number in your group. If you don't have access to a pickup, see if the lumberyard will deliver, or fill a lot of large plastic bags for you. If carrying the large bags of peat is a problem, just get more of the smaller ones.

3) **GARDEN TROWEL or KITCHEN SCOOP** - A large metal one is preferable.

CF,SC 4) **TOILET SEAT** - Any toilet seat will work, but you can also get the polyethylene SNAP-ON SEAT, which fits most 5-6 gallon buckets - $11-$12.

If you're using a camping toilet, (and for other waste and garbage disposal), here's a fairly sanitary method to use: Set up a 55-gallon metal barrel or large metal garbage can in the backyard and carefully burn paper or cardboard trash in it on windless days. Once you have a supply of ashes, dig a trench in the backyard. Take the contents of any non-composting toilet you are using, place them in the trench, cover with the ashes, and then with soil. If you don't have any ashes, you can use powdered lime (available from any hardware store) instead. You'll have to bag and store any plastics until garbage pick- up is resumed. If you have the space indoors, you can also set up a purchased composting toilet (see below).

RURAL

If you want to do it the simple and inexpensive way, yes, you can dig a hole in the ground and put a shack up over it, but have you ever used an outhouse in the dead of winter? Not fun. Almost any other solution would probably be preferable, although our ancestors did it for centuries. If you just want to see what it's like to sit on a frozen toilet seat, give it a try...and you can get your exercise running back and forth to it in the blowing snow...But most of us would still prefer something inside where it's warm...

Any of the toilet systems listed under the Urban or Suburban headings will work for those in rural areas, and you'll probably have the extra dirt to use for a composting toilet. If you have time and money, and your sanitation codes allow, you may wish to set up a purchased composting toilet. These are a major investment, but are a good long-term ecological solution to waste-management in rural areas.

CATALOG CODE	ITEM
LE	1) **CHEMICAL INDOOR TOILET** - (capacity 6 gallons) - A more permanent installation than the camp toilets listed above - a toilet seat on a box that utilizes a chemical deodorant and a vent pipe to dispell odors. Environmentally safe, just bury the waste. - $111.
	2) **COMPOSTING TOILET** - There are a number of non-electric compost toilets. These install inside the home, use a vent pipe and produce odorless, dry, dirt-like compost. They evaporate liquids, carry vapors up through vent pipe for odorless dispersal, then use heat, oxygen, and organic materials to break down the remaining solids.
CG,BS,KW, RS,RM,SU	a) ***SUN-MAR and CENTREX N.E.*** Compost Toilets - Non-electric, vents through roof pipe - $900-$1300. Product video available for $10, $9 rebate with purchase.
KW,RS	b) ***EXCEL*** - Non-electric, uses natural draft to pull air into the unit and up the stack - $900-$940.

WASHING CLOTHES AND DISHES

I'm really going to date myself, but I remember my mother telling me how she washed my diapers in the bathtub using a toilet plunger, because they hadn't yet gotten one of those new-fangled electric washing machines. It was hard work, but I guess if it Mom did it, then we can also wash our clothes that "old-fashioned" way. If you've already filled your bathtub with water to save for bathing and washing, then you can use a washtub for doing the laundry. There are biodegradable laundry detergents that allow you to refilter the water and reuse it, and then pour the used "greywater" outside without any problems for your lawn or soil (see below).

If you believe the crisis will only last a short time, it's best not to waste valuable water washing dishes. Stock up on paper plates and bowls (not styrofoam) and disposable tableware, and only wash the cooking utensils. I'm aware that it's not ecological to use all those trees for paper plates, but during the crisis, clean water will be hard to come by, and you can burn the paper stuff later. If the crisis lasts for a long time, and you've secured a good source of water for washing, you can go back to using your usual plates and utensils.

If you have a good supply of water, such as a nearby pond or river, then you can wash to your heart's content, but *never use this water for washing dishes or even clothes (depending on the source), until you have filtered or purified it!* If you are using a stored water supply, you should conserve it by reusing "greywater" from bathing and dishes by first filtering and treating it (hence the vital importance of a good filter!). This "greywater" can be reused a number of times if you carefully treat it each time it's used. Another method of purifying greywater (if you have a steady source of heat like a fireplace or woodstove), is to boil it first for ten minutes to sterilize it, strain it through a cloth, and allow it to cool it a bit before reuse. Once you've used the water several times, you can pour it on your yard or houseplants, if you've used a biodegradable soap or detergent. They'll love it, and you won't be wasting valuable clean water on them.

CATALOG CODE	BOOK
SU	***"Create An Oasis With Greywater"*** - How to use water that doesn't go down the drain anymore - very important info. in low water situations - $7.

Unless you're sure about the drainage from your sinks, don't use them - they could overflow and spill contaminated water all over your bathroom or kitchen. Use a plastic dish pan in the sink and the biodegradable detergent mentioned above, and treat the water or pour it out. If you live in an apartment or high-rise with no place to pour the water, then you'll just have to take a chance on the drains. You can get the biodegradable washing products at any natural foods store or warehouse, or by catalog.

As to laundry, considering the other problems you'll be dealing with, who's going to worry about being spick and span? Under the circumstances, you won't be able to wash clothes very often, or perhaps not at all. I know... kids run through clothes like a hot knife through butter, but the main thing is to keep the underwear clean. Think about stocking up on inexpensive cotton underwear and socks and only wash them every week or so during the crisis. We did that one very cold winter in Chicago, when we were trapped inside by a blizzard and couldn't get to the laundromat. No matter what else we wore, we always felt fresh with clean underwear. If the crisis only lasts a few weeks, you may not have to wash at all during that time! If you do have a lot of laundry, consider using the nifty little hand clothes washer listed below that does up to eight or ten shirts at a time using very little detergent, and looks a bit like the Android R2D2 from the Star Wars movies! Be sure to have some way to hang the clothes inside if the weather is bad - over the shower-curtain rod, the towel rods, a line strung in the bathroom, garage or basement, or a wooden folding clothes dryer. *Don't hang the laundry near any open flame!*

Here are some washing supplies that you'll find helpful:

CATALOG CODE　　ITEM

1) **BIODEGRADABLE CLEANSERS**

RG　a) ***OASIS BIOCOMPATIBLE LAUNDRY DETERGENT*** - no phosphates - 1 quart $6.95, one gallon - $17.95 Many other non-toxic and disinfecting cleaners.

HA　b) ***SEVENTH GENERATION CLEANSERS*** - All these cleansers are also available by the case. They also have many non-toxic cleaning products: non-phosphate dish liquid - 64oz. - $4.95; liquid laundry detergent - 64oz., 2/$16.95; concentrated laundry powder with enzymes - 48oz. ox, 2/$9.95.

NL　c) ***NATURAL LIFESTYLE CLEANSERS*** - Hypoallergenic, biodegradable cleaners.
- ***EARTH-RITE DISHSOAP*** - tough on grease, yet mild - 22oz/$4.
- ***AUBREY'S ORGANICS*** - All purpose cleaner - Can do everything from dishes to floors to laundry - pure and simple ingredients - 32oz./$6.

SU　d) ***"BAKING SODA"*** - This small book deals with using inexpensive and biodegradable baking soda for over 500 household cleaning purposes - $7.

HA,RG　2) **ANTISEPTIC CLEANING CLOTH** - Made for NASA astronauts - kills most household bacteria for up to one year - good for wiping up around the kitchen and bath - $19-$20.

NP,SC,　3) **LIQUID OXYGEN TREATMENTS** - This process, called "Aerobic 7" or "ION", and Oxy-Stabile, destroys harmful microorganisms by releasing oxygen into water. Completely non-toxic - use to cleanse produce and food preparation surfaces and for any sanitary purpose. Concentrated, one ounce A-7 or Ion treats 55 gallons for storage - $18 per bottle, 2oz. Oxy Stabile treats 110 gallons - $19 *(also listed in Chapter 3 - Water Purification).*

4) **HAND-WASHING SUPPLIES**

CG,LE　a) ***WASHER/PLUNGER*** - Specially made for agitating clothes in a tub - looks like a toilet plunger - used for over 50 years - $9-$10.

LE,CG b) ***WASHBOARDS*** - Old-fashioned washboards in tin, brass, and glass -for serious scrubbing - $10-$20.

CG c) ***WASHTUBS*** - These large galvanized tubs make laundry easier - you can also bathe in them (*see next section on personal care*) - $25-$100. You can also get these locally at a farm supply store, or use plastic tubs from a local general merchandise store.

LE d) ***DUAL WASHTUBS*** - This is a set of 15.5 gallon tubs with drain hoses, in a heavy steel frame on casters - $145, extra hoses - $11.

LE e) ***HAND WRINGER*** - Use with the wash tubs to wring out the water in laundry - metal frame, rubber rollers, waxed, wooden bearings - $139.

LE f) ***JAMES HAND WASHER*** - This is a large stainless steel tub on legs with a paddle-like hand operated agitator - holds 15 gallons, gets clothes really clean - $298, with wringer - $408.

CG,HA,LE,RG g) ***DRYING RACKS*** - Collapsible wooden or metal racks for drying laundry - $13 to $75.

EE,HA,LE 5) **WONDER-CLEAN WASHING MACHINE** - A pressurized, hand-powered, tumble-washer that washes up to eight or ten adult shirts (about 5 lbs.) with about two minutes of cranking, using only a few quarts of water. Polymer body with no moving parts to break. Good alternative to hand washing - $46-$49. (People have also been known to churn butter in one of these machines!)

6) **NON-ELECTRIC IRONS** - I personally wouldn't bother with ironing during this period, but some may need to...I'm stocking up on sweatsuits! The Coleman-style irons use a liquid fuel to produce heat for ironing. This can be dangerous, and burns are common with either type, so be careful!

LE a) ***COLEMAN-STYLE*** - Based on same design as the lantern, uses Coleman fuel (white gas). Operates 12 hours on a full tank - $169.

LE,CG b) ***SAD IRONS*** - Old-fashioned, heavy flat-irons heated over a fire or on a wood stove, one with wooden handle - $20-43.

PERSONAL CARE

There's nothing like a good hot bath, but don't expect to get one during the crisis if you're using stored water supplies! Fortunately, there are other ways of staying fresh without using a lot of water. Remember, in the old days on the farm when all water was hand pumped and carried, people only bathed once a week, on Saturday night! If you want to bathe more often than that during the Y2K, you'll have to plan on washing smarter, not wetter.

Actually, a pretty good cleaning can be had with just a small pan of warm water, soap and a washrag. I remember when I was a child and was sick, how much better I felt after just a "spit bath" with a wet washrag and some body powder. And I have a friend who swears you can take a pretty good bath using a gallon jug of water: pour a bit over yourself to get wet, soap up, and pour the remaining water in the jug over yourself to rinse.

For those really luxurious hot showers that you'll be missing, you can rig up a makeshift version using a heavy plastic garbage bag and a gallon or so of warm water. Tie the bag filled with warm water at the top, hang it up over a washtub or in your bathtub or shower, poke a hole in the lower part, and stand underneath the water. You'll have to wash fast, as you can't control the water flow this way, but it works. But the good news is that there are camping showers with water-flow controls that work great and produce their own hot water!

Stock up on medicated body powder, or preferably cornstarch-based, that will help with rashes and such, and use a good skin conditioner. (Be aware that the talc in many powders, when used in the vaginal area, can migrate into the ovaries, causing problems.) Use deodorant and disinfectant soaps. Make everything you use during this time do double-duty. Also be sure you have enough shampoo, deodorant and toothpaste, with extra toothbrushes, dental floss, etc. Have you tried the new deodorant crystals? They last a long time, and many people swear by them. Here are some interesting personal items to make living easier during the crisis:

CATALOG CODE	ITEM
	1) **NO-WATER WASHING** - There are several no-water hand washing substances on the market. They might be very good to use with small children when water is scarce. I saw one called Purell by GoJo, at a local hardware store. Ask around at sporting goods and outdoor stores.
CM	a) ***NO-RINSE*** - Skin and hair products that require no water - non-irritating, no alcohol, biodegradable - shampoo, hair conditioner, body bath - $4 ea.
SC	2) **CLEANSING TOWELS** - Get the small, wet-wipe towelettes that can be found at most drug and department stores, and in infant departments, or use larger specialty towels:
	a) ***TRAVEL BATH*** - impregnated with a no-rinse cleanser, emollients and humectant to cleanse, nourish and moisturize your skin - 8.5" x 8.5" - 8/$5.
	b) ***DIAMOND WIPES*** - Pre-moistened 8" x 10" towels delicate enough for a baby's skin. 6/$2
HA,RG	3) **DEODORANT CRYSTAL** - Made from mineral salts that attack odor-causing bacteria - lasts for about a year - hypo-allergenic, no aluminum. Found in most natural food stores - $8-$10.

4) **SHAVING**

HA a) ***RAZOR SAVER*** - Resharpen used razor blades and get 50 or more shaves from any disposable blade. A real money-saver! - $12.

LE b) ***HANDPOWERED SHAVER*** - Guys, if you just have to have a clean shave, try this! Neil Armstrong took one to the moon. One pull on the cord spins an internal fly-wheel that sets three blades spinning at 20,000 rpms for about 30 seconds per pull. Self-sharpening blades - $40.

6) **SHOWERS**

CM,MA,NP,RG, a) ***SOLAR SHOWERS*** - These heavy black plastic bags go by several names, but they all work very well. Fill with water, place outside in the sun, and in just a few hours, even in winter, the water heats up to give you a wonderful warm shower. Bring it in, hang it in the bathtub or over a wash-tub and enjoy. Use the on/off hose to get wet, turn off the water, soap yourself, and then rinse. There are bags large enough to give up to four showers at a time, but the smaller bags heat up faster. Prices range from about $10-$35 and for the money, are probably one of the best things you can acquire for the Y2K. I wouldn't be without one in an emergency!

EE,NP,RM,SU b) ***HOT SHOWER*** - If you're heating with an open fireplace, or even a woodstove, you can use this to heat your bath water. The unit consists of a copper coil connected either to a heavy plastic shower bag or plastic tank. Slip the coil into the fire, and in 15-20 minutes, it heats the water to over 100 degrees. Hang up the bag or tank for a shower, or pour the water into a basin for bathing. - plastic 3 gal. bag/$30-40; plastic 3-gal. tank - $60. There's also an Ultimate Extreme System that utilizes a stainless steel tank that sits on your stove and heats 2 gallons for a hot shower - $110; with detachable propane burner and heating stand - $130.

The best thing to do in any emergency situation such as the Y2K is to keep as clean and sanitary as possible under the circumstances, and don't worry about maintaining your usual routine. You will have to be flexible with your household and personal cleaning activities and not expect life to go on as usual. Simply being willing to adapt to a new and simpler daily schedule will relieve a lot of the stress that such emergencies can produce.

LIGHTING AND GENERATING ELECTRICITY
Chapter 9

Information in this chapter:

Y2K PROBLEMS WITH ELECTRIC UTILITIES

Unfortunately, electricity production in most countries is a delicately interwoven web of generating stations and power plants, interconnected to provide backup supplies for each other, depending on consumer demand. Various power grids draw on each other for peak usage needs, and if one grid goes down, many others dependent on it will also suffer. So there is a genuine concern in the electric industry that a cascading outage effect could occur, rippling across the country as each grid goes down. (Fortunately, most utilities are able to isolate themselves from the grid, but then they are faced with producing their own power locally.)

The U.S. electric industry is working on the problem, but unfortunately, many power plants are behind schedule. Rick Cowles, Y2K program manager for Digital Equipment Corp., is a 17-year veteran of managing information systems in electric utilities, and director of a website dedicated to Y2K problems in the electric industry. He reports that two surveys held in 1997 found that between 32 and 45 percent of utilities questioned had not yet begun a Y2K analysis and repair program, and of those who had, 37% were behind schedule! Not only that, but the utilities have been focusing on their generating plants and *haven't even begun to address testing the embedded microchips in the 100,000 transformer stations, located across the country!*

Here are some recent quotes:

According to Joe Weiss, Year 2000 project leader of the Electric Power Research Institute (EPRI), "Despite the industry's best attempts, there will probably still be problems that will not be resolved, necessitating some degree of emergency/disaster planning." A report from the EPRI stated: "The problem facing the power industry is unique because of grid interconnections and links. Any problem in the chain has the potential to adversely impact all."

6/12/98, AP Headlines: *An informal survey by a Senate Panel of 10 of the nation's largest utilities serving 50 million people found that* ***"NONE has complete contingency plans in case their computers "fail because of the Year 2000 problem."***

Rick Cowles, quoted in The Trenton Times, 5/3/98: ***"It doesn't take more than one or two small companies having significant problems before you will have problems across the entire grid."***

Electric utility officials acknowledge that the entire industry badly needs upgrading and increased capacity in order to deal with growing power demands. Even in normal times, there are frequent brown-outs and outages due to peak overloads. So it doesn't seem alarmist to conclude that there is a real possibility that we will be without electricity for a time during the Y2K crisis, and that we could even suffer low power supplies for months afterwards. ***And if our electric power does go down, it doesn't really matter what else we do have that's compliant, because almost nothing in our society can function without it,*** except some isolated generator-powered emergency facilities.

If you want to get a good idea of the possibilities of the Y2K problem, just walk around your house and note how much of your life is assisted and made comfortable by electricity! How would you do without it? Well, our ancestors did, and millions of people around the world still do. And we can learn from them, and make our transition through the crisis much easier.

Just two generations ago, people solved the problem of living without electric lights - they went to bed at dark and got up at dawn! I still remember childhood summers spent with my Uncle Jim on a small farm in central Texas. Try as I might, I could never get up early enough to beat him! He would already be outside feeding the chickens when I staggered into the kitchen every morning. I was too used to the city way of life. He would rise before sunup, work hard all day, and be ready for bed at sunset. He never missed electric lights or other such amenities.

Unfortunately, most of us are no longer so Spartan in our habits, so if the electricity goes off, we will want to provide some form of indoor lighting to use after dark. There are some innovative battery-operated lights and there are also older, more traditional methods. Some groups of people in this country, such as the Amish, still live without electricity, and light with the old-fashioned oil lamps and lanterns by choice. So fortunately, there is still a wide variety of lighting fuels and lamps to select from.

(Catalog Code refers to catalogs listed in Appendix D.)

CATALOG CODE ***BOOK***

CL,SU *"What To Do When the Power Fails"* - A Country Wisdom booklet - $3.

LIGHTING WITH FUEL

SOME CAUTIONS: Whenever you use any flame-producing light or heat source, you must observe some safety cautions:

1) Keep any open flame well away from drapes, furniture, children and the elderly, and never leave it unattended. Never set any burning candle or lamp where it can be knocked over and spill fuel or touch flammable materials.

2) Never go to sleep and leave any flame burning in the house. There is always a danger of fire, and it also wastes your fuel. If you think you'll need a night-light, keep a flashlight handy.

3) Never burn any flame in an enclosed space without providing a source of fresh outside air, even if just by cracking a window nearby. Remember, all flames consume air, and you risk death by carbon-monoxide poisoning, which is odorless and undetectable without a carbon monoxide alarm - which you should have in any room where you are using flamable fuel for cooking or heating.

4) Always have a working smoke detector in each room where you will be using any open-flame heating or lighting device. Check the batteries often.

(Note: The Catalog Code refers to catalogs listed in Appendix D - Catalogs .)

CATALOG CODE	ITEM
	1) **CANDLES** - You probably already have a supply of decorative candles in the house, and they are are very useful - two are enough to read by, three provide enough light for sewing, and you can light a medium-sized room with six to eight. You can even cook over a multi-wick candle, and heat a very small space! But most ordinary candles burn down rapidly, and unless you stock a very large supply, you will quickly run out if you rely on them for most of your lighting needs. What you really need are some of the big multi-wick pillars, or some of the slow-burning emergency candles made especially for long-term use. If you are working with limited funds, go to garage sales, flea markets and wedding and bakery shops for a good source of used candles. Candles are probably one of the most economical lighting options, *but remember they can be hazardous and require constant monitoring.*
CM,KW,MA, NP,RM,SC,SS	a) ***NUWICK CANDLE*** - A three-wick canned candle - burns 120 hours for $10-$13. Another canned three-wick burns for 44 hours - $6-$8. If you have a grill to sit these under, you can also cook, or at least heat food over them. (You can also use the large multi-

wick decorative candles for this.)

SC b) ***THE SURVIVAL CANDLE*** - Also with 3 wicks, burns for up to 36 hours - $8.

BA,SS,SA,SU c) ***CANNED CANDLE*** - A one-wick candle that burns for 50 hours - $5.

CM,MA d) ***JAR CANDLES*** - 50-hour emergency candles in a jar - about $2 each, or 12/$18.

EE e) ***EMERGENCY "CANDLE"*** - A 100+ hour liquid paraffin candle - burns smokeless and odorless - $4.50

MA f) ***LIQUID CANDLES*** - Burns 40 hours, in a can with screw-cap and large wick - 3/$7.

CM,SC,SS,SU g) ***LONG-BURNING SINGLE CANDLES*** - To use in the candle lanterns listed below, from 5/$1.75 to $3 each. Usually also available at any camping or outdoor store.

SC h) ***UTILITY CANDLE*** - Small round "tea" candles in metal container, long burning - used in small backpacking stoves - 6/$3.50.

2) **CANDLE LANTERNS** - If you decide to light with candles, try using one of the lanterns made to hold and protect a candle or multiple candles. They are safer than carrying around an open candle flame.

CM a) ***THE UCO CANDLIER*** - Uses three candles - provides a flat top surface for heating food or water - $30-$33.

CM b) ***THE UCO DELUXE*** - One-candle version with a spring-loaded feature - fits in the palm of the hand - $14-$20.

CM c) ***THE UCO MINI-LANTERN*** - Uses small flat tea-candles - $9.

SC d) ***CODE 1 EMERGENCY CANDLE LAMPS*** - Small liquid candles - provide 50 hours of light per lamp - two for $12.

SS e) ***ALPINE CANDLE LANTERN*** - $6.

SC f) ***CANDLE LANTERN*** - An improved telescoping design in several colors - $17.

3) **OIL LAMPS** - Simple versions of these have been around since before the time of the Pharoahs, and they still work well. These are the familiar lamps seen in many movies about the last century when they were in almost universal use. Just like candles, you can still get these lamps and lamp oil almost anywhere, and many people stock them now for use during power outages. They can be as simple as a wick in a jar, or as elaborate as Swiss-made brass lamps with etched glass shades, but most are inexpensive to purchase and use.

Often these lamps can be found at garage sales or flea markets, and aren't really "antiques", so watch prices. Be sure all the parts are working, or that you know where to obtain replacements. They burn either "ultra-pure" oil (paraffin) or kerosene. The more poorly made, inexpensive models can flicker and don't actually produce the best light. And depending on the quality of the fuel used, they can smoke and smell bad. Some lamp oil is scented to alleviate this problem.

These lamps use a base, either metal or glass, to contain the fuel. A heavy glass base allows you to see how much fuel remains, and is more stable and unlikely to tip over. A cloth "wick" is inserted into and absorbs the lamp fuel and is then run up through a hand operated "wick adjuster" to the point of flame. You must use a wick of the proper thickness for the adjuster, and it must be trimmed to a rounded shape that allows maxmum light and burn. The shape of the chimney also affects the light: Tall, straight chimneys produce a tall, thin, very bright flame, while bulbous chimneys produce a wider flame that may actually give more total light. Be sure to stock up extra glass chimneys and the proper-sized wicks. Most hardware and general merchandise stores carry these parts.

To light the lamp, remove the glass chimney, turn the wick up a bit and light it. Replace the chimney, and after the glass clears up, turn the wick down just enough to prevent it from smoking. Extinguish the lamp by holding your hand behind the chimney and using your palm to direct your breath down into the chimney as you blow. A quick puff should do it. All these types of lamps produce heat so be careful not to touch the chimney while the lamp is in use...it's very hot! *It's said that there are two kinds of lamp users: those who've been burned on a chimney, and those who will be, so use caution when handling these lamps.*

Remember, any liquid fuel lamps or stoves can be dangerous around small children. I have a friend whose home burned down when her toddler knocked over an oil lamp. *So be sure to keep these well away from children and pets. And be careful to provide an outside air source at all times.* Just to be safe, the oil probably should be stored outside along with other fuels.

Here are the oil lamps available in the catalogs:

CATALOG CODE	ITEM
CG,LE	a) ***FLAT-WICK*** - Old-fashioned oil lamps that give the lowest-cost lighting, - come in a large variety of shapes and designs, some with etched glass shades, in table or wall-mounted styles - $5-$50.
CG,LE	b) ***FRENCH ROUND-WICK*** - About three-times brighter than flat wicks - use both oil or kerosene. (A specially designed burner forms the flat wick into a circle at the point of the flame that aids in combustion.) Solid brass table models - others can be hung or wall-mounted - $50-$150.
CM	c) ***THE CANDLEOIL*** - Small oil holder combines the design of a candle and uses lamp oil fuel - $10.

EE d) ***EMERGENCY CANDLE*** - Liquid paraffin candle (listed above under "Candles") - burns 100 hours - $4.50.

LE e) ***MASON JAR LAMP KIT*** - Makes an oil lamp from a canning jar - $3.50.

LE f) ***BOTTLE LAMPS*** - Turn any bottle into an oil lamp with a ceramic "cork" and wick burner that fits into the neck of a bottle - $5-$10.

CM g) ***CANDOIL*** - Fits most candle lanterns - converts them to oil - $10.

CG,LE,NP h) ***LAMP OIL*** - High quality lamp oil distilled from paraffin - burns cleanly - no odor or smoke - $2-$4.50 per quart, to about $62 for a four-gallon case of really high-grade oil.

CG,LE i) ***LAMP ACCESSORIES*** - There is a wide variety of replacement parts available. *Be sure to buy enough lamp oil, wicks, and repair parts to last for at least a year.*

4) **KEROSENE LAMPS/LANTERNS** - The wick lamps listed above, and the mantle lamps and lanterns listed below can burn inexpensive liquid kerosene (or high quality ultra-pure oil), and have been used for over a century. Styles vary from the oil-burning lamps described above, to simple, rugged railroad or "hurricane" lanterns, to the well-known camping lanterns, to the exotic and expensive "mantle" lamps still used in non-electric homes.

Kerosene is less expensive and burns brighter, but with more smoke and smell, than scented or odorless lamp oil. If possible, use "number one" water-clear kerosene, as lower grades can gum up the wick and cause smoking. DON'T MIX THESE FUELS! Also, store kerosene outside in metal cans. The instructions for using simple kerosene lamps are the same as that given above for oil lamps. Other types of kerosene lamps are:

CG,LE,MA, NP,RM,SU a) ***ALADDIN LAMPS*** - Aladdin Lamps became popular around the turn of the 20th century, and are still widely in use. They use air pressure to volatize the kerosene, and a burner that creates a unique blue flame to superheat a "mantle", causing it to glow white-hot. This provides a briliant white light six times brighter than common kerosene lamps. Because of complete combustion, there is hardly any odor or soot buildup. However, they use about twice as much kerosene as a standard lamp, burning approximately 12 hours on one quart, and you have to replace the mantles frequently.

Also be aware that over the years, Aladdin has produced a variety of models, and some parts are not interchangeable, nor are the parts from imitation lamps. There's an extensive list of replacement parts and special accesories available in the catalogs. *Be sure to get an Aladdin with a kerosene filler plug on the base so you don't have to take the lamp apart each time you fill it with fuel.*

Despite any problems, and the relatively high cost, the Aladdin remains the choice of many who use one or two for reading and other close work, and other types of candles or lamps for general illumination. These come in a wide variety of styles, both table and hanging, with beautiful decorative glass shades. Prices range from $50-$200.

NOTE: if you use any mantle-type lanterns, be sure to stock a good supply of extra mantles and replacement glass globes. If you've never used one of these lanterns, read the directions carefully and practice using it. There's a certain skill needed to ignite the lamps or lanterns and care for the mantles.

5) **OUTDOOR LANTERNS -** When we see "Kerosene Lanterns" most of us think of the familiar camping lanterns (with mantles) that can be purchased from any sporting goods store or camping catalog. *CAUTION: IT'S NOT ADVISABLE TO USE THESE KEROSENE OR PROPANE LANTERNS INDOORS, AS THEY GIVE OFF A LOT OF CARBON MONOXIDE AND ARE VERY SMELLY.* But they can be very handy to have for any outdoor activity. If you have to use them indoors, use very high grade clear kerosene and be very sure to provide adequate ventilation.

LE a) ***COLEMAN LANTERN*** - Model #639, a kerosene single-mantle lantern - puts out the equivalent of a 300-watt bulb, at about 1/3 the cost of propane lanterns - $80.

CG,LE,MA,NO, NP,SA,SU b) ***DIETZ OR HERITAGE LANTERNS*** - There's a large line of inexpensive "railroad"-type or "hurricane" mantle-less lanterns that are all-weather and very sturdy. These are pretty safe to use and come in about ten models, ranging from $8-$55.

LE c) ***OFFICIAL RAILROAD LANTERNS*** - A line of more expensive original "official" railroad lanterns that range from $60-$100.

MA d) ***COLEMAN GAS LANTERN*** - A gasoline lantern said to be very bright and economical - $70. (*NEVER use any gasoline lantern indoors*!)

6) **PROPANE LANTERNS** - These Coleman-type lanterns sit atop a small 16oz. propane bottle, or with adapters, on a bulk 5-gallon tank, and eliminate any danger of spilled fuel. Light can be regulated from dim to high. Burn time on one 16oz. bottle is approximately 16-18 hours on low, and 7 hours on high.

CM,MA a) ***DUAL MANTLES*** - This version has two mantles - $20-$40.

CM b) ***ELECTRONIC IGNITION*** - Lights automatically - $30.

SC c) ***MAX LIGHT PORTABLE BUTANE LANTERN*** - Up to 10 hours of light - built-in igniter - $60.

CM d) ***GAZ CAMPING BIVOUAC 270*** - Ultra-light lantern uses Gaz resealable fuel cannisters with a propane-butane mix. Burns 5 1/2 hours per cannister - $30.

7) **DUAL FUEL LANTERNS** - There are several models of lanterns that use both standard camping fuel or unleaded gasoline. *The same cautions about indoor use of gasoline fuel apply to these lanterns as to heaters - DON'T USE INDOORS.*

CM,MA a) ***DUAL-FUEL 2-MANTLE LANTERN*** - Burning time approximately 14 hours on low, 7 hours on high - $50.

MA b) ***DUAL-FUEL POWERHOUSE 2-MANTLE LANTERN*** - Provides more light and holds more fuel with same burn times as a) above - $50-$70.

CM c) ***PEAK*** - A small backpacking lantern - burns camp fuel or unleaded gasoline - burn time per tank - 3.5 hours - $50.

NP 8) **MULTI-FUEL LANTERN** - Petromax lantern will burn on kerosene, mineral spirits, lamp oil, diesel, white gas, gasoline, lighter fluid, aviation fuel, and napatha. *Do not use indoors with any fuel except kerosene or lamp oil!* One tank of fuel burns at full brightness for about 8 hours, 32 hours per gallon. All-brass construction, chrome exterior - provides 500 candlepower. In use worldwide since 1922. Two models, $135-$175. Use only spare mantles sold with lamp - 12/$15. Carrying case available.

NOTE: Whatever fuel you decide to use for a light source, be sure to coordinate it with your heating and cooking fuels, so you don't have to stock and store too many different kinds.

LIGHTING WITH BATTERIES

1) **SOLAR BATTERY RECHARGERS** - Before we talk about battery lighting, I want to emphasize that ***one of the most essential pieces of equipment you can obtain, along with a good water filter and a heater -cooker, is a solar-powered battery charger.*** With this amazing device, plus a good supply of rechargable batteries, you can keep flashlights, radios, lanterns, tape/CD players, toys, and many other household appliances going almost indefinitely. It will charge AAA, AA, C, D sizes, and some will charge the new flat prismatic batteries.

Get the best charger you can afford, as it is likely to get a lot of use. *If you plan to use a lot of batteries, get two or more chargers,* as these chargers work more slowly than the electric-powered ones. And be sure to stock enough batteries to have at least one set charging while another set is in use. In fact, I'd get three sets for any vital application: one set in use, one in the charger, and one fully charged and ready to use. *Caution: Do not leave these rechargers outside overnight or where they can be rained on* - they're not weather-proof! Best to put them in a sunny window.

Note: If you have a solar auto battery trickle-charger that keeps your car's battery charged, and a small battery recharger that you can plug into the car's cigarette lighter, you could have another renewal option for your batteries! (*See Chapter 14 - Transportation, for the auto battery charger.*)

I'd recommend that *anyone in an urban setting with little fuel storage space, and any family with small children, elderly members, or teens suffering from the "clumsies", plan to use battery-powered lighting if possible.* It's much safer than relying on any flammable light source.

Almost every survival catalog lists these solar chargers, so you can choose from several models:

CATALOG CODE	ITEM
CM,KW,SS	a) ***SMALL CHARGER*** - A small solar charger that revitalizes only "AA" batteries - $10-$17.
BA,CF,KW,NP,RG, RM,RS,SC,SS,SU	b) ***STANDARD SOLAR CHARGER*** - Charges AAA,AA,C & D sizes. One model with blocking diode - prevents discharging when there's no sunlight - $18-$35.
EE,MA,NO,NP	c) ***DELUXE SOLAR BATTERY CHARGER WITH METER*** - Charges 11 popular battery sizes, including new prismatic flat batteries. Equipped with charge meter - indicates how much solar energy is available, charge time for each battery size, and any shorts. With blocking discharge diode - $15-$25.
RM	d) ***LARGE SOLAR FLASHLIGHT BATTERY CHARGER*** - Charges 8 "D" batteries in one day, for those running numerous battery-operated appliances - charges AAA, AA, C, D, and 9-volt - $160.
KW	e) ***BUTTON BATTERY CHARGER*** - Charges button batteries used in hearing aids, cameras, calculators, watches, games, etc. - holds one battery - $17.
KW	f) ***NINE VOLT CHARGER*** - Recharges one 9-volt battery - $24.
KW,NP,RM	g) ***SOLAR FLASHLIGHT/BATTERY RECHARGER*** - Dual-purpose gadget keeps itself recharged - recharges two AA, and one also does C, or D batteries, either regular or nicads - $27-$37.
RS	h) ***12-VOLT NICAD BATTERY CHARGER*** - Can be plugged into auto battery to recharge AAA,AA,C,D, and 9-volt Nicads - automatically sets proper current - $20.

HA,LF,RG

i) ***NON-EMERGENCY RECHARGING*** - State-of-the-art *electrically-powered* charger for regular usage. First model to recharge both standard and rechargable batteries, even 9-volt! Over the years, will save lots of money, and spare the environment, *(see information below)* - $54-$80.

2) **RECHARGABLE BATTERIES** - Every year, U.S. consumers discard over 3.5 BILLION batteries, which are thought to account for over a third of the deadly mercury pollution released from land-fills into our water and soil. So using these rechargable batteries is a good idea at any time. *Over its lifetime, a single rechargable battery can replace up to 150 polluting alkaline cells, and save you a bundle of money!*

For instance, if you have a Walkman requiring 2 "AA" batteries your estimated annual usage of standard batteries will be 146 batteries. You will need only 2 rechargables, *saving you approximately $600 over a three-year period!* Using 4 "D" batteries for a motorized toy can save over $200. So the high initial cost of these batteries is soon repaid.

Some cautions in using these batteries: They will last longer if you deeply discharge them (run them completely down), and recharge them as soon as possible. *Be sure that the batteries you buy are the new alkaline "renewable" ones that can be recharged and set on the shelf for up to five years without any power loss,* and provide a better quality, longer-lasting source of power. There is no way to estimate the life of these batteries, as it depends on the usage, but they will usually last for years if used and recharged properly.

These can be bought at any hardware or general merchandise store, and prices vary somewhat. If they seem expensive, *remember that you won't be buying fuel*, which may cost more, and could become unavailable in the future. If you need to order them, they're available from the catalogs listed below - note the wide diversity in prices:

CATALOG CODE **ITEM**

HA

a) ***EVEREADY RECHARGABLE BATTERIES*** - claim to have a running time 33% longer than any other rechargables -

AAA - $11.00 C - $13.50
AA - $20.00 D - $13.50
A - $10.50 9V - $13.50

RG

b) ***GOLDEN POWER NICADS*** - Identical in power to Evereadys except that these offer a more powerful AAA size -

AAA - $2.25 C - $4.75
AA - $2.25 D - $6.75

CF,EE, RS,SU

c) ***REGULAR NICADS***- Standard rechargables. No "AAA" size listed for SU,EE -

AAA - $2.00-$2.20	C - $4.50-$5.95
AA - $1.95-$3.00	D - $4.50-$7.50
9-volt - $7.50-$8.90	

3) **STORAGE BATTERIES** - Also, there are some new long-storage batteries that don't activate until you use them, and are said to keep for up to 20 years. After activation, their available energy is similar to a standard heavy-duty battery, but they're not rechargable.

CATALOG CODE	ITEM
SS	a) ***"CODE RED" EMERGENCY BATTERIES*** - 2 "D" cells - $5.
MA,SC	b) ***ENVIROTRON BATTERIES*** - 2 "D" cells - $12-$13, price goes down with quantity purchase.

NP,SC — 4) **BATTERY ADAPTERS** - Adapts "AA" batteries to fit a "C" or "D" cell battery slot, or "C" to "D" size. Mix and match any "AA", "C" and "D" battery - never be without a matching set of batteries again - Excellent to use with single-size solar battery chargers - $5-$8/pair.

5) **BATTERY LAMPS** - *These provide adequate lighting and are safe to use around children.* There are lanterns that use "D"- size rechargable batteries. (*NOTE: Be aware that some battery-powered lanterns use the large, square 6-volt lantern batteries which are NOT rechargable.)* Most of these lamps can be found in the camping/survival catalogs and sporting goods stores. Realize that the light from battery lamps is not going to be as bright as that from a good Aladdin mantle lamp, and that it will dim as the batteries get low, but they will suffice for most general lighting purposes.

CATALOG CODE	ITEM
SC	a) ***COLEMAN FLOURESCENT LANTERN*** - Uses 8 "D" batteries and features a night light and adjustable output and run time - $60.
CM	b) ***COLEMAN TWIN-TUBE FLOURESCENT LANTERN*** - Runs on 6 "D" cell batteries - $20.
SC	c) ***TABLE LAMP*** - Small table lantern that uses 4 "D" cell batteries and produces approximately 20 hours of continuous light - $15.
SC	d) ***COMPACT SPOTLIGHT/AREA LAMP*** - Uses 4 "D" batteries to light a room or, can be focused to a narrow spotlight - bright krypton bulb - Adjustable table stand/handle - $11.
RG,SC	e) ***WATER-RESISTANT FLOATING LANTERN*** - Small compact lantern uses 4 "D" batteries - great for use near water - $20-$25.

NP 6) **SALT WATER GENERATOR** - Possibly the most innovative item that I've found, this unique generator looks like a kid's lunchbox and is actually a 12-volt battery that requires only salt water to work! It uses plain table salt and replacable magnesium anodes to produce 400 mAmps at 4 watts, and can run for 10-12 hours before the salt needs changing. An anode set lasts up to 60 hours before replacement. You can run radios, lanterns, cell phones, small 12-volt TVs, and more - $99, replacement anode set - 8/$13. Buy several 50 lb. bags of salt and have power! There's also a twin-bulb florescent lantern with adaptor to use with the battery - $23.

7) **FLASHLIGHTS** - There's an almost endless variety of flashlights available from most stores, so I'm going to mention only a few unusual ones:

CATALOG CODE	ITEM
CF,LF	a) ***THE STARLIGHT*** - Perhaps the most innovative flashlight around - uses no batteries at all! The Starlight utilizes a magnet and an LED diode to create a bright light, and is virtually indestructible. It is expensive, but probably worth it - $79-$99.
NP	b) ***SOLAR BRIGHT L.E.D. FLASHLIGHT*** - Flat flashlight with solar panel on body - 1 day of sunlight = 4 hours of light. 3 amber L.E.D.s provide 50 candlepower, bulbs give nearly 200,000 hours service! Unbreakable, all-weather housing, built-in replacable NiCad batteries - $36, 3/$33 ea.
BA,CF,EE,MA, NP,SA,SC,SS	c) ***HAND-GENERATED FLASHLIGHT*** - Inexpensive battery-less flashlights use hand-power - called "The Russian Pumper", The "Dyna-Lite", or "The Dynamo" - has a built-in dynamo generator that activates and produces light when you pump a handle. They don't stand up too well under constant use, but kids love these! $6-$16.
BA,KW	d) ***FREEPLAY SELF-POWERED LANTERN*** - User rotates winding handle for 30 seconds which activates a constant-force spring, driving a generator to produce light for up to 2 hours. Also has internal AC/DC rechargable battery for 6 hours usage - $63-$70.
EE,SC	e) ***FLASHLIGHT/LANTERN*** - Use as either a standing lantern or a hand-held flashlight. Takes 4 AA batteries - $8-$15.
EE	f) ***HEADLAMP/FLASHLIGHT*** - Straps fit the light on head for hands-free walking or reading. Adjustable narrow or wide beam, uses 2 AA batteries - $30.
CM,MA,NP,SU	g) ***HEADLAMPS*** - Wide variety offered - handy for reading or any activity that requires focused, hands-free light. All use AA batteries - some have krypton bulbs - $7-$70.
NP	h) ***NITE-WRITER PEN*** - For writing in the dark or low light -

soft green LED light at end of pen powered by watch battery, black ink - $17.

8) **SOLAR RECHARGABLE LIGHTS**

CATALOG CODE	ITEM
CF	a) ***SOLAR RECHARGABLE LANTERN*** - 3 types of light, flourescent, torch incandescent, and blinking. Uses solar power, alkaline batteries and AC/DC current with adapter. Solar cell has built-in blocking diode - protects against battery discharge - $70.
RM	b) ***SOLAR CHARGED LANTERN*** - Similar to above, 3 types of light - up to 4 hours light on one charge, high/low switch, blinking control - $100.
SU	c) ***SOLAR POWERED RECHARGABLE LANTERN*** - Flourescent lantern recharged entirely by the sun. Includes solar panel plus accessories for recharging from wall outlet or vehicle - no batteries required - $99.
KW,RM	d) ***SOLAR FLASHLIGHT/BATTERY RECHARGER*** - Dual-purpose gadget keeps itself recharged, plus recharges two AA, C, or D batteries, either regular or nicads! - $32-$37 (*also listed above under Battery Rechargers*).
MA,NO,SC	e) ***SOLAR FLASHLIGHT*** - Rechargable in sunlight or uses two "AA" batteries - waterproof - also a red LED signal or warning light - $15-$35.
NP	f) ***THIRD GENERATION*** - Solar AM/FM radio/flashlight uses four power sources - solar, built-in Nicads, hand-crank, and "AA" batteries - charges in about four hours - $35.

GENERATORS

1) **ELECTRIC GENERATORS -** Gasoline or diesel-powered electricity genenerators, like woodstoves, are a major investment. If you decide that you don't want to do without the amenities of electric living, and if you have the space to safely store a LOT of fuel *(see Chapter 14 - Transportation),* you might consider purchasing a generator. Many people in severe climates find that they are a real life-saver in winter storms. However, there are some drawbacks: First, these generators are noisy, inefficient, and use a lot of fuel and oil. So if there is a shortage of gasoline or diesel fuel for several months, and if you exhaust your supply, and haven't made other preparations for living without electicity, you could be unable to provide heat and cook food. Also, the gasoline you use needs to be fresh, so you must use a stabilizer if you store it for even short periods *(see Chapter 14 -Transportation).* Electricity generators are very expensive, prices for new models ranging from several hundred to many thousands of dollars. Low-cost ($300-$500) domestic generators are poorly made and will probably need repairing and/or replacement after a

short time. Some Japanese camping models are the best-made of the low-cost generators, are fairly quiet and light-weight, and will power a couple of appliances. Be sure that you get a model with a "low-oil shut-off" feature, as these machines use a LOT of oil, and can easily run out, ruining the motor. You'll also have to store a lot of motor oil.

Recently, a woman wrote on an Internet Y2K newsgroup about her experiences in a major winter storm in the fall of 1997 in Omaha, Nebraska. She stated that the news reported people being rushed to the hospital, overcome from carbon monoxide fumes leaking into the house from generators operating in their attached garages. But the problem was that if people put the generators outside for saftey, they promptly got stolen! So it seems that in some situations, unless you have a safe place for both you and the generator, it won't do you much good to have one!

However, if you feel that you do have a safe place to operate the generator and store enough fuel and oil, and you've weighed the cost against the convenience, you may still want to use one. It's best to purchase one locally, as they are heavy and can be costly to ship. You can find them at most hardware and farm supply stores. Be sure you know how to set one up and keep it operating, (and make repairs!), and follow instructions carefully. *Do a test run before you have to use it.*

CATALOG CODE	ITEM
MA	a) ***USED MILITARY GENERATORS*** - Two models - $550-$750.
MA,NO	b) ***PORTABLE/NON-PORTABLE GENERATORS*** - Large selection, featuring Honda and Coleman - $400-$8500.

2) **HAND-CRANK GENERATOR**

CATALOG CODE	ITEM
MA	a) ***PORTABLE MILITARY GENERATOR*** - As long as someone is hand-cranking this, and you have an AC/DC converter, it puts out enough DC power to run a small household appliance. You might be able to watch a taped movie on your TV/VCR if you're willing to work for it! - $129. Good price.

So there are your choices for lighting without electricity. Fortunately, there is enough variety to choose from to satisfy everybody. Our ancestors lived without bright electric lights, and so can we. Who knows, we might even learn to enjoy firelight and candlelight again!

FIRST AID AND HEALTH
Chapter 10

Information in this chapter:

THE PROBLEMS IN OUR HEALTH CARE SYSTEMS

Keeping healthy during a crisis is complicated by the problems inherent in a lack of sanitary facilities and shortages in critical medical supplies. In no other area of the Y2K crisis are the possibilities for human suffering so great as that of medicine and health care. The medical industry in most countries is enormous, affects millions of people, and is dangerously dependent on the effective functioning of its computers and embedded systems.

According to the London Times, 5/3/98, *"Hospitals are having to postpone operations because their computer systems are already being hit by the Millennium bug..."* And a study by the British National Health System has found that computers are already failing to provide doctors and NHS staff with correct information. *Unless the bug is eradicated, it could make NHS computers read information incorrectly and cause problems with critical equipment such as life-support machines and kidney dialysis units."* And this problem is not confined to the British health system, but is applicable to almost all systems worldwide...

It's hard to be too pessimistic when it comes to the effects of the Y2K crisis on the healthcare industry, as the ramifications of failure in any part of its systems are so devastating. We can't really over-exaggerate the problems that will be faced by our medical facilities if the utilities fail, and deliveries of food, water, medical supplies, and fuel for hospital generators are erratic or non-existant. *Our own government has warned us to avoid two places during the Y2K crisis - airplanes and hospitals!*

Some realistic worst-case health scenarios could include:

1) Areas with no 911 or emergency medical service due to phone and electric power outages.
2) Failures in water treatment plants *(see Chapter 3 - Water)* causing delivery of polluted water, with resulting cases of chemical poisoning, dysentery or other water-borne diseases.
3) Failures in sewage and waste-pickup systems leading to build-up of uncollected

waste, and outbreaks of severe dysentery, cholera and other serious plague-like diseases.

4) A major flu epidemic or invasion of deadly opportunistic bacteria and viruses resulting from people's lowered immune response due to stress, crowding in shelters, hypothermia (being too cold) lack of food and water, exhaustion, etc.
5) Inability of clinics and hospitals to deliver care due to failures in vital equipment, and loss of electricity and finally emergency power. Also, shortages of medicines, first aid supplies, food, water, etc., due to failures in their normal order/delivery systems.
6) Already overloaded hospital systems unable to deal with a large in-flux of patients from a serious fire or other disaster.
7) Severe shortages or non-availability of many critical and life-saving drugs due to shutdowns in the pharmaceutical and shipping industries.
8) Problems with staffing medical facilities when their employees are overwhelmed with providing basic necessities for themselves and their own families, and unable to get to work due regularly due to winter weather, lack of public transportation, and low gasoline supplies.

And the list could go on...but I'm sure you've got the idea by now. Unfortunately, there is no way for us to cover all of the possible health-care problems in this small book, so we'll just have to concentrate on two areas most likely to affect you at home during the crisis: personal health and personal first aid. But you should contact your local health-care and public first aid officials and see what they are planning in order to deal with the Y2K crisis.

STEPS YOU CAN TAKE

Of course, the ideal situation is for you and your family to get healthy and stay that way. Understandably, there will be situations where that isn't feasible, such as family members with chronic conditions, or sudden illness, or accidents with children. But if you begin now, at least you will have some time to work toward geting your health and medical affairs in order.

1) **CHECK-UPS** - First of all, get you and your family's medical history updated with check-ups, and tend to any needed treatments right away. This includes dental work, eye exams, hearing tests, and any optional surgery you've been postponing.

2) **RECORDS** - Be sure that you get copies of any important medical-dental records, including x-rays, and keep them in a safe place at home. If your health care facility loses these, you can help them reconstruct your records later.

3) **MEDICATION** - If someone in your care suffers from any chronic illness that requires medication, now is the time to begin investigating ways to stock up on it (*see below*). Also, see that the children have any needed immunization shots, and that all adults are vaccinated against tetanus and flu.

4) **TRAINING** - Be sure that you or someone in your family or group knows advanced first aid and even EMT procedures. Study a good emergency first aid book or

manual and stock up on adequate supplies (*see books listed below*).

A NIGHTMARE SCENARIO

Just to give you a feel for the possibilities of problems in Y2K healthcare, suppose that you are one of the millions of insulin-dependent diabetics who must take daily injections of this perishable drug... Here's a nightmare scenario that you need to be aware of: Did you know that *seventy percent of all insulin is made at a single manufacturing plant in the Netherlands?* Undoubtedly, this plant is automated and computer-dependent in order to produce such huge amounts of this drug. This means that nearly three-quarters of the world's diabetics are betting their lives on the proper functioning of the plant's computers and embedded systems, and also on the performance of thousands of others that control the entire distribution and shipping network. Now it's unlikely that any system this complex will continue to function as usual during the Y2K crisis, so we're looking at a medical disaster of truly monumental proportions unless doctors and hospitals themselves stockpile the medication ahead time. Are you willing to bet your life or the life of your loved ones on that...and on the possibility that the drugs will remain effective for long periods of storage? (Note: *according to my pharmacist, insulin will store, when kept in a dark place, for approximately a year or more from date of manufacture.*)

It's likely that this scenario will be played out in other drug production facilities as well, so you can see the importance of addressing these situations now, as there are certain to be shortages in many critical supplies. So what can you do?

PREPARE FOR SPECIAL CONDITIONS

If you or anyone in your family or group has a special medical/health condition, then you will need to take that into consideration when you prepare your supplies. There are three basic areas to consider:

1) **PHARMACIES AND MEDICATION** - ***Plan to store at least a six-month's supply of any vital, non-perishable medication on which you or your family is dependent***. And if you must keep any medication under refrigeration, you'll have to purchase and use one of the small propane-powered ice-chest refrigerators *(see Chapter 4 - Food Storage)*. If the medication is not highly perishable, and you live where it's feasible, you could pack it in a moisture-proof container, dig a hole several feet deep in the ground, and store it where the temperature is usually around 55 degrees.

   Talk to your doctor and see if he or she will write the prescriptions, and to your pharmacist and see if he/she is prepared to supply those prescriptions. Ask your pharmacist to go upline to his suppliers and find out what their preparations are to keep medications available for the Y2K. **DO THIS NOW! *This is too important to put off!***

   Get a copy from your local library of the article from Fortune Magazine, dated April 27, 1998, that deals with the problems in the manufacturing industry, and have your doctor and pharmacist read it. If the doctor won't agree to provide the prescriptions, and if you're in an insurance program that forces you to use a specific physician, have your lawyer write a letter to him, reminding him of the consequences of restricting a necessary medication to a patient. This should get his attention! You still might have to locate another doctor in order to obtain a supply of the medication. If the medication is highly perishible, wait until the last minute to refill it, and at least get an extra pescription to refill as soon as possible after the Y2K.

If you expect to have to deal with major injuries or health problems, there's are websites listed in Appendix B - Internet Links, with lists of supplies that will equip you to deal with most anything (*also see the **ACTION CHECKLIST** for a fairly comprehensive list).* There is a mail order pharmacy in Britain that can supply some drugs (such as antibiotics) that aren't available in the U.S.without prescription:

* **International Anti-Aging Systems, P.O. Box 337, Guernsey, Channel Islands, Great Britain; email is: iasltd@attmail.com.**

Do whatever you have to do, as you can't afford to ignore this problem. The classic book listed below could also help you:

(Note: Catalog Code refers to catalogs listed in Appendix D.

CATALOG CODE	BOOK
CF,NP,SS,SU	***"Survivalist's Medicine Chest"*** - Ragnar Benson - For those interested in obtaining medicines and treating serious illnesses themselves - $10-$12.

2) **SPECIAL MEDICAL CONDITIONS -** If you are caring for someone with special needs - the elderly, chronically ill, handicapped, etc., be certain that you have stocked any special equipment and supplies that your patients may need. You will need to conference with the attending physician and make plans for continuing treatments. Some conditions to consider are:

a) Those with acute or chronic respiratory illnesses such as asthmatics, and those with emphysema, who need oxygen.
b) Those dependent on regular medication, such as diabetics, those with serious heart conditions, etc.
c) Anyone dependent on dialysis, tube feeding, chemotherapy, catheters, or intensive-care therapies.
d) Those with colostomies, pacemakers, tracheotomies, and other in-body devices.
e) Those dependent on medications for severe pain and similar conditions - arthritics, etc.

3) **PERSONAL MEDICAL DEVICES -** If you're caring for someone dependent on a

personal medical device, such as a pacemaker, oxygen equipment, various health monitors, and other life-support equipment, you will have to contact the manufacturer and get their assurance, *in writing*, that the device will function correctly at the Y2K. If they can't give you this assurance, then shop for a supplier that can, and replace the device. *(Dont expect the doctor or hospital to do this for you, except in the case of a surgically emplanted device - they've got their own Y2K problems!)* But do check with the attending physician to see if there are any options available in case of an electric or mechanical failure, or any alternatives to the currently-used device. If the physician indicates that there are no alternatives, then you will have to take all precautions to supply a back-up power source if needed, such as solar panels and batteries, or a generator and a large stock of fuel. Several catalogs have extensive information on the use of solar panels to generate electricity - look in CL, KW, & BW catalogs *(see Appendix D - Supply Catalogs).*

If you fear you won't be able to care for a seriously ill family member, work with your physician to have special-care arrangements made before you need them. According to the Federal Emergency Management Agency, *anyone requiring any type of life-support using electricity should register with their local FEMA office.*

4) **CLINICAL MEDICAL DEVICES -** If anyone in your family is dependent on clinical treatment devices, then you must contact the health facility and obtain assurances, also in writing, that their equipment has been tested and will be Y2K compliant. Don't worry about feeling like a fool for making these inquiries...*the life of your loved one(s) is at stake*...If the hospital or clinic cannot give you the assurance, then contact your lawyer as soon as possible, and see what can be done to force them to test their equipment and become compliant. Most facilities are already doing this, but some may not see the need until time has run out and it's simply too late. *(If they aren't ready to TEST the compliance upgrades and embedded systems by January, 1999, then they're already too late - these things take time!)*

Some of the medical devices and equipment that could be affected include:

a) Many laboratory diagnostic systems.
b) MRIs, CT, PET scans, and other sophisticated diagnostic equipment.
c) All Emergency and Intensive Care systems - infusion pumps in intravenous drips, heart defibrillators, monitors, etc.
d) All health maintainence systems - dialysis, chemotherapy, radiation equipment, etc.
e) All surgical machinery with embedded systems.
f) All hospital or clinic monitoring and control systems, including heating, air conditioning, lighting, safety equipment, etc.

With even this brief rundown, it's easy to see how serious the problem could quickly become in case of electrical, computer, or microchip failure. Most likely, there will be a combination of these, but even the smallest problem could put a vital system out of order for some time. With so much at stake, it is up to all of us to insure that this doesn't happen. As more and more people insist that our health-care systems become compliant, the public pressure will be the best insurance we have against such nightmare scenarios. But it all starts with you...***don't wait!***

FIRST AID & EMERGENCY CARE

In case your local health care facilities are not able to deal with your personal health needs, then you will have to provide them as best you can; It's always a good idea anyway to back up their efforts with your own first aid and emergency care program. The following suggestions can be of help:

1) **GET TRAINING -** Nobody wants to think about performing first aid on a loved one, but it is always worth the trouble to be prepared for this possibility. If communications break down for a time, transportation is difficult, and medical facilities are basically non-functional, you may have to attend to your and your family's own health needs. In light of this, it would be a good idea for at least one member of your family or group to have advanced First Aid training. Contact your local Red Cross chapter to see when classes are held. Many hospitals also hold classes. If you're really serious, and have family members who might need advanced medical assistance in an emergency, someone can take EMT training. Even better, locate a wilderness school that teaches survival first aid skills. These classes are more detailed and can include techniques for working under primitive conditions. They may take a while to complete, so you should get started on them right away. This training can always come in handy even in noncrisis situations, so it's worth whatever time and effort you expend.

2) **STUDY -** Even if you can't take any first aid training, you can still prepare yourself: Purchase several comprehensive books on emergency medicine. Study this material carefully - *the time to learn this is now, not during the stress of dealing with an accident or illness!* There are dozens of excellent first aid and emergency books available in the catalogs, at online bookstores (such as www.amazon.com), or any regular bookstore. The list below is only a sampling, but they can help you to decide what kind of supplies you'll need for your particular preparedness program.

CATALOG CODE	BOOKS ON FIRST AID
SC	***"The American Medical Association Handbook of First Aid and Emergency Care"*** - Comprehensive, step-by-step guide to dealing with injuries, illness, and medical emergencies - $14.
RM,SC	***"Emergency Medical Treatment"*** - Handbook technically reviewed by the National Safety Council. Flip-open quick-reference design - $8-$13.
SC	***"Emergency Preparedness and First Aid Guide"*** - Billed as America's #1 guide for emergency situations. Includes survival supplies checklists, medical and property profile forms - $13.

NP,SU ***"National Safety Council's First Aid Handbook"*** - NSC & Alton Thygerson - Detailed chapters in full color on every first aid subject - $11-$15.

MA,NP,RM ***"U.S. Army Special Forces Medical Handbook"*** - Glen K. Craig - An updated version with over 600 pages. Info. on diagnosis, emergency surgery, and paramedical skills - $11-$26.

CF,NP, RM,SU ***"Where There Is No Dentist"*** - Murray Dickson - Detailed and well-illustrated information on care of teeth and using dental equipment - $9-$17.

CF,NP,RM, SC,SU ***"Where There Is No Doctor"*** - David Werner - Latest edition of the classic written as a guide to those with no medical training living in third world countries - illustrated - $17-$30.

FIRST AID KITS

You can use the books above to make your own list of first aid supplies, or use the basic First Aid Supplies checklist. Also check out the *Appendix B - Internet Links* under First Aid, and print out the lists found at those addresses. If you have the time to study and do the shopping, it will probably be much less expensive and more appropriate for you to compile your own first aid kit. Or, you might purchase a kit and then personalize it with other items that you know your family will need. You can find a lot of the ingredients at general merchandise and drug stores, and even the surplus-freight "dollar" stores. Just be sure that any products you purchase are in good condition and unopened.

If you have someone in your family or group with special medical needs, (such as asthma, diabetes, etc.), be sure to include those supplies and any necessary equipment on your checklist.

There are a number of First Aid Kits available, from the simplest single-person ones, to those capable of helping you set up a field hospital. Most survival and camping catalogs carry first-aid kits, as do many sporting goods and outdoor supply stores. These kits include a variety of bandages, adhesive bandages, gauze, cotton, antiseptics, prep pads, towelettes, swabs, gloves, instruments, and over-the-counter medicines. But many of these kits are deficient in the real medical supplies sometimes needed in treating a serious illness or injury. So try to include all the possibilities when stocking up on first aid supplies. *Compile or purchase the best kit you can afford, as it's much better to go overboard on these supplies than not to have them when needed.*

There is a wide variety in these kits: some are based on the number of people using them, some are called "72-hour" kits (which often contain many other emergency supplies in addition to first aid), and some kits are based on the type of emergency, such as earthquake, mountaineering, etc. And there are also many "specialty" kits for burns, surgery, etc. So it is almost impossible to list them all and to make any comparisons, as each catalog has its own kits and packages. You'll note that there is a large difference between prices for the same or similar items in the catalogs, so you'll want to choose the kit(s) and supplies closest to your needs that offer you the best value for the cost. This is going to take a bit of study and time to decide what you need, but there's really not an easier way to insure your family's well-being!

CATALOG CODE	TYPE OF KIT
	1) **GENERAL KITS**
BA,CM,EE,MA NP,SA,SC,SS	a) ***PERSONAL, CAMPING, BACKPACKING and OUTDOOR KITS*** - (1-10 people) - Stocked with standard first aid supplies and bandages, prices range from around $5 for simple one-person kits, to deluxe kits for up to $60.
BA,NP,RM, SC,SS	b) ***TEAM KITS*** (up to 25 people) and **GROUP-SIZED KITS** - (25 and over) - Also stocked with standard first aid supplies - $25-$250.
EE	c) ***MEDIC'S FIRST AID KIT*** - Over 175 pieces of general first aid equipment, including burn products - $79.
MA	d) ***THE MEDIC*** - Similar to *Medic's* above - $60.
	2) **PROFESSIONAL KITS**
NP	a) ***COMPREHENSIVE AQUATIC KIT*** - Developed for those needing first aid while on the water - 3 versions - $145-$210.
NP,RM	b) ***COMPREHENSIVE AND COMPREHENSIVE PLUS KIT*** - Dental, rehydration, wound management, burns, trauma, infection control, medical instruments - and more - $150-$155.
MA,SA	c) ***EMT MINI*** - Professional EMT-designed medical kit for wilderness or emergency use - $220-$229.
NP,RM	d) ***FIRST RESPONDER EMT/MOUNTAIN MEDIC KIT*** - A comprehensive, professional trauma kit, chosen for Atlanta Olympic Games paramedics and EMTs - $345-$350. Also comes in a First Responder Kit - $446.
SU	e) ***RESCUE KIT*** - A general first aid kit with airway management, dressings, bandages, medications, burn care - $225.
RM	f) ***RESCUE RESPONSE KIT*** - Designed for use by first responders, contains essential emergency products - $260.
SU	g) ***SURVIVAl RETREAT MEDICAL KIT*** - Over 800 items in 55 categories from band-aids to surgery kit - complete emergency care - $575.
RM	h) ***TRAUMA MANGEMENT KIT*** - Includes infection control, dressings and bandages, basic EMT equipment - $400.
	3) **SPECIALIZED KITS**
EE,MA	a) ***BURN KIT*** - Sterile Kit for dressing burns - $20-$30.
EE,CM,MA,	b) ***DENTAL KITS*** - Kits for dental repair and trauma

NP,RM,SC treatment - $16-$30.

NP,SU c) ***EMERGENCY CHILDBIRTH KIT*** - $19-$25. (*Combine this kit with the book on childbirth listed next.*)

NP,RM,SU * ***"SURVIVAL CHILDBIRTH"*** - Written as a manual for midwives, its 39 chapters cover every phase of pregnancy and childbirth - $9-$11.

SC d) ***HERBAL KIT*** - Bandages, wound care, oils, homeopathics, extracts, herbal medical guide - $52.

SU e) ***HOMEOPATHIC FIRST AID/HOME REMEDY KIT*** - 35 proven remedies with instructions - $75. *(Combine this with a book on homeopathy from the list below under Home Health and Self Care.)*

RM f) ***INDUSTRIAL BURN KIT*** - Sterile dressings for serious burns - $90.

EE,MA,NP, RM,SA,SC, SS,SU g) ***SURGERY/SUTURE/SYRINGE KITS*** - Field kits for closing wounds - from simple to field-hospital equip ped - $18-$69.

SC h) ***WATER-JEL BURN KIT*** -Recognized as an authority in emergency burn care - $64.

MA,SU i) ***WOUND TREATMENT KIT*** - Sterile kit for treating serious wounds - $19.

4) **MEDICAL SUPPLIES & EQUIPMENT**

NP,RM a) These two catalogs carry a large stock of medical supplies and surgical instruments that can be bought individually. Many supplies possibly not available elsehere: stethoscopes, scapels, splints, syringes, a thermal blanket for newborns, and much more... Customize your kit with these items.

SC b) ***ELECTRONIC CPR VOICE PROMPTER*** - Talks you through every step of CPR for adults, children and infants. Requires 4 "AA" batteries - $100.

MA c) ***AIR LEG SPLINT*** - For fractures, inflatable splint encases leg - $10.

LE d) ***MEDICAL EQUIPMENT STERILIZER*** - Lehman's catalog has information on how to utilize a pressure canner to sterilize medical equipment - call and ask for #L-MS for free literature.

HOME HEALTH AND SELF CARE

As discussed above, one of the problems during any crisis is that most doctors and health care professionals will be overworked and possibly unable to serve all their patients. Stocks of medicines will be short and probably reserved for the very ill. If the electricity to hospitals and medical facilities goes out, and backup gasoline generators run out of fuel or malfunction, serious healthcare crises could result. You should be prepared to take care of yourself and your family for most minor ailments and conditions.

There is a great wealth of information available about the many alternative health care approaches being utilized these days. These may prove more helpful during a crisis than western allopathic medicine, especially if utilities are down for an extended period.

Below are some of the many books available on natural healing:

CATALOG CODE	BOOKS ON NATURAL HEALTH AND HEALING
SU	***"Doctor's Book of Home Remedies"*** - Over 2,000 safe, drugless ways to alleviate or cure 138 common illnesses - $7.
SU	***"Doctor's Book of Home Remedies for Children"*** - Hundreds of safe techniques and tips for kids - $28.
SU	***"Handbook of Alternatives to Chemical Medicine"*** - Jackson & Teague - A compliation of herbal and other all-natural drugless remedies - $11.
SU	***"Practical Encyclopedia of Natural Healing"*** - Hundreds of natural remedies from the editors of Prevention Magazine - $13.
NP,SS,SU	***"Survival Medicine, Nature's Way"*** - Marilyn Moore - Complete guide to preventative and curative natural techniques using herbs, fruits, and vegetables - 60 pgs. - $12.
SU	***"Treasury of Natural First Aid"*** - James Kusick - Natural remedies for most kinds of illnesses and accidents - $11.

Many of these seemingly "new" therapies are really very old, and have been in use continuously in so-called "primitive" countries for millenia. They must have positive effects, or people would have quit using them long ago. It's up to you to decide what you want to learn about and use. Here's an alphabetical listing of just a few of the methods:

1) **AROMATHERAPY** - This practice is an old healing method that has recently become popular, and uses essential oils and other substances to stimulate the body via the sense of smell. Everyone knows that smell can be powerful: ever smelled a pumpkin pie and been transported to your Grandmother's Thanksgiving kitchen? The theory is that certain smell receptors in the brain stimulate body responses that can be effective in promoting healing. Also, European research has shown that many oils have antibacterial effects, similar to that of garlic. There is a growing body of anectdotal evidence as to their effectiveness, and the oils smell wonderful!

CATALOG CODE	BOOKS ON ESSENTIAL OILS
RM	***"The Essential Oils Book"*** - Stephanie Touries - Recipes for the

use of herbs, roots, flowers, and oils, with properties and applications of over 20 oils - $13.

SU ***"Illustrated Encycolpedia of Essential Oils"*** - Julia Lawless - A complete guide to the use of oils in aromatherapy and healing - $19.

BA,SU ***"Australian Tea Tree Oil"*** - Cynthia B. Olsen - The healing oil with over 101 uses, called "first aid kit in a bottle" - handbook - $3, guide - $7-$8, one oz. oil - $10.

Young Living Essential Oils - Many oils are diluted and impure... for top-quality oils and information call 801-236-6200, or go to: www.youngliving.com. Use reference #163571 for orders.

2) **BODY WORK/ACUPRESSURE** - Massage and acupressure have come into their own and there are many licensed schools training excellent therapists. Many medical doctors now prescribe massage and other bodywork for their patients. You can learn simple techniques for relaxing and soothing muscles, relieving pain, and stimulating beneficial circulation throughout the body. If you haven't used them, you'll be glad when you do!

CATALOG CODE **BOOKS ON BODY WORK**

SU ***"Applied Kinesieology"*** - T & C Valentine - Bodywork to assist in healing - $8.

SU ***"Body Reflexology"*** - Mildred Carter - Healing at your fingertips - how to relieve many ailments using massage - $5.

SU ***"Finger Acupressure"*** - Pedro Chan - Do-it-yourself treatment for many common ailments using massage - $5.

SU ***"Reflexology Today"*** - Dorothy Bayley - The technique of stimulating the body's healing forces through foot massage - $9. Foot massage is much more effective than you might realize, and has been used with good results for many years.

SU ***"Vital Touch - Japanese "Do-In" -*** exercises for energy and healing - $12.

3) **HERBS** - This field of study is well-documented and researched. There is no doubt that herbs do affect the body, and there is a large volume of information available about their healing properties. *Consult a good reference before using any herb or herbal product.* My experience in working with herbs for over twenty years has shown that the tinctures and liquid extracts are more efficacious than the dried capsules or tablets. I take them in a strong-flavored hot tea to disguise the sometimes *unique* tastes!

CATALOG CODE BOOKS ON HERBS AND HERBAL HEALING

CL,RM ***"The Complete Medicinal Herbal"*** - Penelope Ody - More than 250 remedies for common ailments with full color photos of 120 medicinal herbs. How-to section, case histories, and making an herbal first aid kit - $30-40.

SU ***"First Aid With Herbs"*** - John Heinerman - Tried and true health care for emergencies and minor injuries - $3.

NP ***"Herbs To The Rescue"*** - Kurt King - An herbal first-aid handbook for home, travel, survival - author has over 25 years' field experience - $9.

RM ***"Identifying and Harvesting Edible and Medicinal Plants"*** - How to find and prepare over 500 different plants for health and nutrition - 260 drawings - $18.

SU ***"Natural Healing With Herbs"*** - Humbart Santillo - The complete reference book on the use of herbs - $15.

SU ***"Today's Herbal Health"*** - Louise Tenney - Compares herbal treatments to that of prescribed medicines - $13.

4) **HOMEOPATHY** - This system of treatment is older than our modern "allopathic" medicine, and is based on the use of minute dilutions of certain healing substances. It is considered a "holistic" system that treats the entire body, not just isolated symptoms. It has a long and effective history, with the singular benefit of almost no recorded side effects. Many countries in Europe have more homeoathic than allopathic practitioners. There are many good references available, and treatment is simple and inexpensive.

CATALOG CODE BOOKS ON HOMEOPATHY

SU ***"The Complete Book of Homeopathy"*** - Weiner & Gross - A comprehensive manual of natural healing - $10.

NP ***"Homeopathic First Aid"*** - Marilyn Moore - Covers most common ailments and their appropriate remedies - $11.

SU ***"Homeopathic Treatment of Children"*** - Use this safe and natural way to treat children's ailments - $19.

SU ***"Homeopathic Medicine"*** - Dr. Tevor Smith - A doctor's guide to remedies for common ailments - $11.

5) **NATURAL ANTIOBIOTICS -** Silver has a long history of usage for medicinal and preservative purposes. People in the Middle Ages used silver eating utensils to

protect them against plagues. Early American settlers put silver coins in their water barrels to keep their drinking water potable. And only a couple of generations ago, people put silver coins in unpasteurized milk to help it last longer in the old "iceboxes" then in use. Until recently, silver nitrate eye drops were put in newborn babies' eyes to protect them from venereal diseases transmitted by their mother.

Today, modern processes of making "colloidal silver" provide a product believed to be effective against virtually every bacteria, virus, and fungus, used both topically and internally. The pathogens are unable to mutate and become resistant to the silver solution as they are to other treatments. Because of certain requirements when using the silver, it is important to educate yourself in the proper usage for maximum effectiveness, although it is completely harmless. Several companies, listed below and in the Catalog Index, can supply you with the silver solution, or the equipment to make your own colloidal silver. Some wholesale natural food warehouses also carry the silver solution (*see Appendix A - Food*).

CATALOG CODE **BOOKS AND ITEMS**

SV ***"Making and Using Colloidal Silver"*** - Instructions on making this antibiotic yourself - $12.

CF,CS,SU a) ***COLLOIDAL SILVER SOLUTIONS*** - The completely non-toxic, broadspectrum natural antibiotic - $3.50-$4.

b) ***COLLOIDAL SILVER GENERATORS*** - This equipment allows you to produce a non-toxic silver-based antibiotic product that is said to kill over 650 bacterial/viral/fungal/parasitical pathogens with no side effects, and has a large body of positive anectdotal evidence.

CF,RM * ***COLLOIDAL SILVER GENERATOR*** - $75-$76, colloidal silver - $85/gallon.

* ***SILVER SOLUTIONS*** - Generator uses 3 9-volt batteries - with instructions, accessories - $80, AC/DC Silver Gen erator - also plugs into wall outlet - $130, You-Build DC Generator - Kit to build your own - including instructions, equipment - $60. Call: **800-505-6005.**

* ***CS PRO SYSTEMS*** - Rt. 2, Box 510GG, San Antonio, TX 78264 - Sells AC and DC systems, testing services, and steam distillers - 210-626-2546, **www.csprosystems.com**.

MA,RM c) ***KATADYN MICRO-PUR*** - Keeps pre-filtered water fresh and drinkable for up to 6 months. Safe, non-toxic, and tasteless, contains a simple *silver compound that prevents bacterial growth without the need for chlorine, iodine or other chemicals.* Shelf life - 5 years from date of manufacture - Treats 250 gallons/$12-$13, 2,500 gallons/$25, 12,500 gallons/$75. (*Also listed in Chapter 3 - Water.*)

Another powerful, all-around anti-microbial product - grapefuit seed extract - kills dozens of bacteria, fungi, and other harmful pathogens. The active ingredient is called *Citricidal* (a trademark), and is used worldwide by healthcare professionals.

CF d) ***GRAPEFRUIT EXTRACT PRODUCTS*** - Excellent disinfectant, kills bacteria, fungi, and other harmful organisms. Many forms - liquid extract, capsules, tablets, skin spray and ointment, ear drops, nasal spray, dental gel, non-soap skin gel and cleansers - $5-$18.

MA e) ***TRAVELER'S FRIEND*** - Contains a highly potent extract of grapefruit peel, pitch, and seed, diluted with deionized water. Certified non-toxic, effective against more than 50 pathogens, including Giardia, e.Coli, and Salmonella. No iodine, no off taste - one bottle treats 10.5 gallons untreated water, 16 gallons of filtered water -$12/3 bottles. *(Also in Chapter 3, Water)*

6) **MISCELLANEOUS TREATMENTS** - There are a large number of alternative treatments that many people swear by, such as the ancient use of French green clay and other earth products, which are quite effective when used appropriately.The use of magnetic healing is gaining in popularity, as well. There are many more holistic methods and products that you can explore if this field interests you.

CATALOG CODE **MISC. HEALING BOOKS**

"***Biomagnetic Handbook***" - Philpott & Taplin - Detailed discussion of magnetism and its effects on the human body by an M.D. Includes preventative and theraputic techniques - $20. Obtain from bookstore.

"Magnet Therapy" - Holger Hanneman - Clear, practical discussion of magnetic therapy by a Swiss naturopath. Documents sucsessful techniques with full color illustrations - $10. Obtain from bookstore.

SU ***"Our Earth, Our Cure"*** - R. Dextreit - A book of natural remedies with emphasis on French green clay therapies - by one of France's foremost healers - a classic - $16.

BA,SU ***"Oxygen Therapies"*** - Ed McCabe - Information about using oxygen, hydrogen peroxide and ozone for healing - $15.

SU ***"Parasites, The Enemy Within"*** - Hanna Kroeger - Many otherwise "incurable" conditions respond to parasite cleansing treatments - $5.

7) **NUTRITION** - There are a number of high potency nutritional substances that can

be used to prevent illness and promote healing, vitamins and minerals being the most well-known. This subject is covered in more detail in Appendix A - Food.

8) **EXERCISE** - ***TRAMPOLINE REBOUNDER*** - If you don't have any exercise equipment in your home, and want to keep in shape while you're waiting out the Y2K, consider getting a small exercise rebound trampoline; they usually can be found at garage sales and flea markets, and they don't cost that much new, around $20-$40. These confer several beneficial results from daily use: jogging on them for at least 12 minutes a day conditions the lungs and heart, and also aids the lymph system in eliminating toxins. Your muscles will stay toned, esecially if you add small hand weights for the upper body, and it makes a pretty good all-body workout. If you've never used one, or if you're out of shape, start out slow, about five minutes at the beginning, and work up to about 15 minutes. More than that is unnecessary. If someone is too ill to exercise, you can simply sit them on the rebounder, stand beside them, and and jog for them! Even that much movement has been shown to benefit their muscles and lymph system. It's also a great way to help kids use up some of that high energy!

My philosophy about all this is simply that when I'm ill, or nursing someone who is, it seems best to do something active and positive for the patient. Over the years, I've seen the methods suggested in this chapter work in many situations. So if the treatment does no harm, and if there's a chance that it may help, I'll use it.

Because there is no way for me to address the health care issues of thousands of readers, all I can do is present sources for you to use to educate yourself about your individual health needs and treatments. Yes, it takes some time and attention, some study and financial committment, and the shouldering of personal responsibility, but it's worth it, because as a wise person once said:

"He who has health has hope, and he who has hope has everything."

Arabian Proverb

FOR PARENTS ...
Chapter 11

Information in this chapter:

PREGNANCY
INFANTS
YOUNG CHILDREN
SAFETY
HEALTH
HOME SCHOOLING

Those who have infants and children will need to make a few extra preparations for the Y2K period. Dealing with children is often stressful in normal times, and can be even more so during times of crisis.

Mothers who are nursing infants will have to store extra water and food for themselves to insure adequate milk production for the child. Parents of small children will be dealing with the problems of keeping children safe and occupied during what could be a long period of unusual living conditions. Children usually fare pretty well under situations of change, but parents have to cope with both a crisis and the everyday stresses of parenting at the same time, and this can become overwhelming.

Physical and mental preparation can make all the difference between a very difficult time with children and one that is at least tolerable. Listed below are some ideas for keeping children busy, and some items you can store to help you deal with parenting during the Y2K.

PREGNANCY

Those who are expecting and may deliver during this time should take all precautions to be prepared for this major event. It would be advisable to have the services of a midwife secured just in case the physicians and hospitals are unable to assist you. You may have to deliver at home. Don't worry... people were all brought into this world at home until very recently, and it can be done! There are several books you need to have to educate you and your partner about all the details of childbirth *(see Chapter 10 - First Aid and Health)*. Learn as much as you can so you can assist your midwife and make the experience as easy as possible. Any classes you can take during your pregnancy will be helpful, also. Do anything necessary (exercise, diet, etc.), to keep yourself as healthy as possible and increase your chances of a safe delivery.

Here's a book and a kit to help you through childbirth:

CATALOG CODE **BOOK**

NP,SU ***EMERGENCY CHILDBIRTH KIT*** - $19-$25. (*Combine this kit with the book on childbirth below*).

NP,RM,SU ***"SURVIVAL CHILDBIRTH"*** - Written as a manual for midwives, its 39 chapters cover every phase of pregnancy and childbirth - $9-$11.

INFANTS

Taking care of infants won't be much different during the Y2K than any other time: lots of love and attention! But if you're also dealing with a change in your living routine and diet, and the other stresses of such a time, you will have to take care to be very organized and get plenty of rest, if possible, in order to be able to give that attention. If you're totally occupied with securing the basics of survival - heat, water and food - and you've made no other preparations, things could get pretty difficult for you and your baby. If you're nursing, you want to insure that you continue to produce plenty of milk for your child. That should take priority. So being prepared for the Y2K is especially important for anyone with an infant or baby to care for.

1) **FOOD** - If you are nursing, you will have the problem of food taken care of, but as mentioned above, you should be careful to store extra water and food for yourself, to be sure that you always have enough milk for the child.

   Otherwise, you can store canned or powdered formula, available at most grocery and general merchandise stores, and mix it up as needed. Store it tightly sealed, in a cool place. The powdered formula that I found costs between $6-$7 per can, and should make about 25 four ounce bottles. You will have to figure out how much you think you'll need for your storage period, and also store enough water for formula preparation. *Always boil AND filter any water before using it for formula, and follow directions carefully when reconstituting it.*

2) **DIAPERS** - Diapers are a real problem. I have talked to several mothers (and had little ones myself many years ago!), and we can't come up with a really satisfactory solution that will allow you to deal with this situation as usual. Most parents in western countries have gladly embraced the use of disposable diapers, for many reasons - there's always a nice clean pile of fitted, no-leak diapers waiting to use, and little clean-up afterward! There's no rinsing out dirty diapers, no stinking diaper pail to deal with, and no time spent washing, drying and folding. Mothers in primitive countries have solved this in another way, however - they simply allow the child to go without diapers and eliminate as they wish, usually on the ground or a dirt floor. Since this isn't a very sanitary or desirable alternative for those of with hardwood floors or carpeting, what can you do during the Y2K to provide diapers for your infants?

   There are only a couple of answers that we know of: stock A LOT of disposable diapers, or plan to use cloth ones and try to deal with washing them under low-water conditions. This will probably be impossible using stored water, because it requires so much, but if you have access to a pond or river that's not frozen over, you might try it. Past weather disasters have shown that one of the first items to be sold out are disposable diapers, *so the time to purchase them is well in advance of the Y2K!*

If you use disposable diapers, get a Diaper Genie pail, or one similar, in which to store the soiled diapers. These clever gadgets compact each diaper into a small roll for easy disposal. When it's full, empty the contents of the pail into a large garbage bag and treat it like any other waste. You can store these bags in large garbage cans until normal sanitation pickups resume. Infants usually use between 8 and 10 diapers per day, so you can figure how many you'll need by multiplying by the number of days you expect the crisis to continue. I'd over-stock, or have a supply of cloth diapers on hand, just in case. Disposable diapers have the disadvantage of being rather expensive, bulky to store, and also of using a lot of paper products. You'll just be buying a two-year supply of diapers all at once, or more quickly, but the cost could be a consideration.

If you have a reliable water supply *(see Chapter 3 - Water),* your least expensive option is to use cloth diapers and plan to wash them yourself. This will involve a tub large enough to hold a batch of diapers, a lot of filtered water, detergent (and disinfectant), a plunger or other type of agitator, drying racks or lines, (*see Chapter 8 - Sanitation and Cleaning*) and the time and strength to do this much washing by hand. Also, if your home is unheated except for the space you're living in, it could take some time for the diapers to dry.

You are the only one who can decide which way to go. If the crisis proves to be severe, stocks of disposable diapers will be gone, and none will be manufactured until the plants and distriution systems return to normal. So perhaps a combination approach would be best: stock several months of disposable diapers, and then if it becomes necessary, you could use the cloth ones. Hopefully, that also would give you time to locate a supply of water for washing.

3) **CLOTHES** - Infants grow rapidly, so it would be a good idea to stock enough baby clothes to last at least a year. These can be bought inexpensively at any second-hand store, or obtained from relatives with older children. And be sure to have enough warm "bundling" blankets and sleeping clothes.

YOUNG CHILDREN

1) **FOOD** - Children who are weaned, or are in the process, can eat regular baby food in the jars, but it will take a lot of space to stock enough to last for any reasonable period of time. If this would be a problem, an easy and perhaps healthier solution is to simply get a baby food grinder and prepare their food from your own. Almost any simple grain, vegetable or fruit dish can be mashed up in a grinder and fed to a young child. Prepare your child's food before you season it for the adults, as lots of spices can be hard on a child's digestion. Also, grind up some sprouts and add to the food to provide vital nutrition. Baby food grinders, or "mills", can be found in many grocery and general merchandise stores.

(*Note: Catalog Code refers to catalogs listed in Appendix D.*)

CATALOG CODE **ITEM**

LE a) ***BABY FOOD MAKER*** - Developed by a doctor, meets FDA requirements - hand-cranked mill grinds adult foods into soft baby food using stainless steel blades. Plastic body, holds 4oz. at a time - $12.

2) **TOILET TRAINING** - If your child is close to being ready for toilet training just before the Y2K, you might want to give this some attention, as it will greatly simplify your problems in dealing with dirty diapers (see above). However, don't make it such a big deal that the child feels pressured. You could use any camping or other special toilet that you plan to use during the Y2K for training, and the child would then be used to it when the rest of the family begins using it. This would make it easier on you, so you don't have to also accustom the child to a strange toilet when you're busy dealing with a lot of other problems.

If you have slightly older children, who are already toilet trained, it would still be a good idea have them begin using the Y2K sanitary facilities ahead of time, and make it fun...perhaps during the "indoor campout" that you hold for Y2K preparedness training. That way, they'd know what to do when the new toilet system has to be put to use.

3) **CLOTHING** - As with infants, children grow out of their clothes and shoes very quickly, so be sure to have some larger sizes on hand, in case you can't obtain them for a while. It may not be the height of fashion, but second hand stores and garage sales are a great way to stock up on useful and warm clothing for kids. They usually don't care if clothes have been worn before, and it will save you a lot of money that you will need to use for essential supplies.

4) **KEEPING KIDS BUSY** - This may be the hardest part of any Y2K situation with kids! They need positive stimulation and ways to discharge their abundant energy. Realize that if the electricity goes down, there won't be any TV, videos, computer games, or other electronic fun available! And realize that any small hand-held battery-operated games will eventually run out of juice and be abandoned. Even if you are using solar-charged batteries, you'll probably need them for other appliances. Many parents will find this a great opportunity to reintroduce their children to the joys of reading, family games, and other creative activities. Just be sure that you have stocked up enough interesting and educational toys, books, and games to keep them busy for quite a while. And don't bring them all out at once - ration them so they continue to be new and interesting. Many books, games and puzzles can be found very inexpensively at garage sales and flea markets. Here's some ideas:

a) Huge jigsaw puzzles are great all-family activites - stock simpler puzzles for little ones.

b) Specialty card games are fun, and you can also obtain a book on card games and learn to play many new games with a regular deck. Other board games can be played by the whole family, and games such as Scrabble are always "new", and can serve as a way to develop various learning skills.

c) Paper dolls, coloring and activity books can keep children busy, but also stock creative art supplies, such as lots of blank drawing and construction paper, crayons and water colors, cardboard, modeling clay, scissors, glue, etc.
d) Musical instruments, such as rattles, a small drum, whistle, harmonica, small bells to string, etc. can make a "band" with lots of dancing and fun.
e) Give an older child an inexpensive polaroid camera and lots of film, and have them document the "Y2K family adventure" for a family photo album. (Because electricity to run VCRs, and film developing may not be available for a while, it's best not to use standard photo film or video recorders.)
f) Sort out all those family photos you've been wanting to get organized, and put them in albums.
g) Have poetry and story-writing/telling contests, with small prizes of new toys or treats for winners (and losers).
h) Read to each other, and enjoy introducing the children to any of your favorite childhood literature and poetry.
i) Begin to collect a trunk or box full of costumes that you've acquired at flea markets and garage sales...let your imagination take over and buy all the outrageous stuff you would have used as a kid...jewelry, hats, feather boas, fancy shoes, etc. Then let the kids play dress-up. A fun game is to have lots of unusual hats and headgear, and ask the kids to put them on and tell a story about who they are when wearing each hat!
j) If you have a solar battery charger (or two), and a battery-powered radio/tape deck, or a hand-cranked one, (which you should, as part of your communications supplies), as a special treat, you can have "radio nights". Gather the family around the radio and play one of the great old-time radio shows now available on tape from many tape catalogs or music stores. These were made for listening, and many are still fresh, and funny, and scary, decades after they first aired. The children will be amazed and interested in such a "new" activity!
k) Don't forget exercise equipment, if you're stuck inside during bad weather. A stationery bike will suffice, but kids get bored on one pretty quickly. A small indoor trampoline is better - it's safe for any child with good balance, is a great indoor energy-user, can be used to music, and lends itself to all sorts of innovation and fun (*see Chapter 10 - First Aid and Health*).
l) A big bag or bags of blocks, either store-bought or home-made, cut in many sizes and shapes, (or a lot of Leggos) can be used for a thousand construction projects...building doll-houses, castles, space stations, and more...
m) Don't forget to let the child help you with cooking, growing

sprouts, cleaning up, and all the usual household chores. If you present this time as "an indoor campout" they will go along...

n) If weather and location permit, include some outdoor activities. Plan nature walks to identify birds, insects, trees, etc. Inexpensive nature guides can be found at local bookstores.

I found the following books at a local general merchandise store; if you're on a budget, check your local second hand bookstore:

"Child's Play - 200 Crafts and Activities for Preschoolers" - Probably a mother's life-saver - $11.

"Discovery Play" - Ideas to keep kids busy and constructive - $12.

"Games Babies Play" - Vicki Lansky - How to play with your infant and teach them developmental skills - $9.

"Parents' Little Book Of Lists" - Jane Bluestein, PhD. - Lots of ideas for parents to use in keeping kids occupied - $11.

That should give you some idea of how to keep kids busy during a long winter period without the usual electric gadgets. After all, until the last couple of generations, kids always managed to find lots to do if the parents provided the supplies. Don't underestimate their creativity!

CHILD SAFETY

I've tried to emphasize safety throughout this book, because during times of change and stress, it's very easy to forget our normal safety habits. We can get distracted for a moment in an unfamiliar situation, and that's all it takes for a child to get in trouble. And with normal emergency assistance or your physician perhaps not even available, you don't want to have to rush your child to a hospital that may not be able to admit or treat them. So as a parent, you will have to be prepared and well-organized, and remain extra-vigilant to insure your childrens' safety.

It's possible that you will be heating and lighting with open flames, and unfamiliar fuels, and you can't be too careful around these. Emphasize to the children how important it is to stay away from any open-flame lamp or cookstove. *Never give children under teen years (maybe not even teens!) a candle or open-flame lantern to use as a night-light.* There are small flashlights available everywhere, and "miners' lamps" that can be worn on the head, that can be ordered from the catalogs *(see Chapter 9 - Lighting)*. Kids love these, and the colorful "lightsticks" that give enough light to allow them to move about at night or to feel safe:

CATALOG CODE	**ITEM**
EE,MA,	*** *LIGHTSTICKS*** - Small sticks that glow when flexed to activate

NP,SC chemicals inside a soft plastic tubing. Available in several colors and varying light intensities. Some burn for minutes, others up to 8 hours. Non-toxic, waterproof, completely safe - 5-30 minutes - $.99-$2.19, up to 12 hours - $2-$11, 10/$18.50.

Hold family fire-drills before the Y2K so that everyone knows exactly what to do in case of a fire. Fire extinguishers and smoke hoods for everyone would be one of your best investments (*see Safety chapter*). Nobody ever thinks that a disasterous fire could happen to them or to their children, but it can, and you don't want to deal with this along with everything else. *Realize that the fire department may be unable to respond in case of fire.* Be aware that colloidal silver has been used with great success in treating severe burn cases, and aloe vera in treating milder ones. Also, a thin mixture of French Green Clay and sterile water is excellent spread on burns, even severe ones *(see Chapter 10 - First Aid and Health).*

HEALTH

Most of this subject is covered in Chapter 10 - First Aid and Health. A list of medications and toiletries will be included in the ***ACTION CHECKLIST***. Be sure to stock up on any needed prescription medicines well beforehand, and know that in the absence of other medications, homeopathic remedies are completely safe and effective for use with children, as are many herbs. Be sure to stock vitamins for the kids, as they may not eat as well as needed during a crisis. Add sprouts to their diet for live enzymes and extra nutrition! Also, before Y2K, occasionally cook a one-pot meal with some of the storage foods; it's a good idea to start accustoming them to these new foods before they *have* to eat them.

HOME SCHOOLING

If we suffer a breakdown in utilities and transportation, it is likely that the schools will not reopen for a while, until things get back to normal. This could be days, weeks, or even months. If you have school-age children, you will want to be prepared to give them some home-schooling on a daily basis, so they won't fall too far behind in their study habits. One good way to pass the time while the electricity is out is to hold "school" for several hours each day. Younger children can join in, coloring, drawing, and listening to the older children read to them out of the textbooks. It won't be quite the same as their regular classes, but it can remind the kids that learning goes on, no matter what!

Ask your children's teachers what they would recommend as a curriculum for the kids for the fall and spring of 1999-2000, and begin to stock up on supplies. The teachers can point you to their catalog sources, and there may be an educational supply store in your area where you can find all sorts of instructional materials. Check online for information about home-schooling *(see Appendix B - Internet Links).* There is also a source from one of the catalogs in this book:

CATALOG CODE	ITEM
CF	The multi-product Christian Family Resources catalog is published by parents who have home-schooled successfully for many years. They offer several books about home-schooling, reading materials, language arts, geography, a writing

program, and a phonics game. This should be enough to keep you busy for a while!

If the Y2K crisis forces your family to stay at home for a period, why not view this as an opportunity to get away from your daily routine and enjoy spending this time playing and learning together.

FINANCE AND PERSONAL RECORDS
Chapter 12

Information in this chapter:

I find myself putting off writing this chapter, as I don't really feel qualified to offer financial advice to anyone; there are literally hundreds of good books and Websites that can do that (*see Appendix B - Internet Links*). But there are some simple, commonsense actions that anyone, no matter how modest their income, can take to be prepared for the Y2K. So I'll confine my remarks to these:

PROBLEMS WITH THE BANKING SYSTEM

"Finance is the art of passing currency from hand to hand until it finally disappears." Robert W. Sarnoff, "Forbes Magazine"

It's likely that there will be disruption in our international banking systems due to the Y2K that will affect the stock market and even your local bank; although this seems a dire prediction today, (August,'98) with the market the highest it's ever been, and millionaires being made daily. But the problem with any system such as our fragile financial network is that it runs basically on the confidence and goodwill of its participants; and once that is gone, a serious financial crisis can result. The recent disasterous situation in Russia with the devaluation of the ruble is a perfect example of how volatile any nation's economy can become. In only six months, inflation in Russia has risen to 300% as their money continues to be devalued.

On April 4, 1997, the New York Federal Reserve Bank (which sets policy and issues money to the nation's banks), issued a "Year 2000 ALERT" in a circular (#10937), which warned that the problem is valid and vast, and that if any part of the financial world is not compliant by the year 2000, the entire banking system could crash.

In addition to their computer problems, it's possible that the banks will also have to deal with a run on their deposits: When people finally realize the implications of the Y2K problem on the banking system, and that their financial records could be lost or made unavailable to them, they are likely to panic and begin withdrawing their funds. Last year, *38 percent of computer industry executives worldwide said they might withdraw their personal assets from banks and investment companies just before the year 2000!* Someone said that's like seeing the pilot of your airliner heading for the door with a parachute... And try asking your friends what they'll do first if the computers go down at Y2K...when I have, without exception, they've all said, "I'd better get my money out of the bank!" Unfortunately, if everyone tries to get their money, the banks won't have the cash to cover the demanded withdrawals *(currently, they have less than $2 on hand for every $100 reportedly on deposit)*, and will have to freeze transactions or close; or the government will have to step in with stringent regulations. So the very thing that everyone has feared will be created, and it didn't have to happen! Ironically, the fear itself causes the very thing that is feared!

The person with major investments and financial assets will already know what to do to prepare for the Y2K, because they spend a lot of time dealing with such things, and will be well-informed about the dangers to our financial systems. And this is not the place to give specific advice about complicated financial dealings *(as mentioned above see the abundant financial advice on the Internet)*. But the average person, with perhaps a few shares of stock, a small savings account, and a couple of CDs, will be hard-pressed during the Y2K crisis to preserve what little they have managed to accumulate. Everything you've worked for all your life could be lost in the space of a day or two because of a crisis in our current monetary system, and because of the way it is now operating:

Once upon a time, our paper money was backed by gold or silver...something tangible that had real worth. Now our money is mostly bits and bytes in some computer's memory bank, and is not backed up by anything real and solid. It continues to be valuable because we all agree that it is...to do anything else is too horrible to contemplate. But even the most cursory investigation into the other "world-wide web" of current international banking and its increasingly fragile situation is enough to make anyone very pessimistic.

We can only pray that the banking system doesn't completely collapse, and that at the Y2K, some semblance of normality is restored in a reasonable period of time. If that doesn't happen, and if banks close, the stock market crashes, and our financial records are lost somewhere in cyberspace, then you can kiss your money goodbye. It's likely that governments will print up large amounts of paper money to try to stave off the inevitable, and thereby create rampant inflation (the Federal Reserve is now printing extra cash so the banks can supply it to their customers in order to "prevent panic".) Then nobody's money will be worth the paper it's printed on for a good long time. (In Italy, after WWII, money was so devalued that people had to take a wheelbarrow full of the worthless paper to the store to purchase a loaf of bread!)

GETTING YOUR MONEY FROM HERE TO THERE

Ric Edelman, CFS, RFC, CMFC, hosts "The Ric Edelman Show" on personal finance, and is the author of "*The Truth About Money*." He's also a faculty member at Georgetown University. He had this to say about the Y2K financial problem:

> *"As an investor, then, what should you do to protect your money from Y2K fallout? The answer is: nothing. Here's why:*
>
> *There's nowhere to hide. If you fear Y2K and sell all your investments, where will you put your money? You can't move it to money markets or bank accounts, because those are also controlled by computers. You*

shouldn't liquidate to cash, either, since paper currency could be of little value. If bank accounts are inoperable, the only way for people to get more cash is for the government to print more of it - resulting in hyper-inflation, which could destroy the value of your currency."

So how can we assure that we can pass over the bridge from now through the Y2K with even some of our finances intact? Many emergency books suggest that you have anywhere from a week to a month's worth of cash set aside, but that's for the usual disaster scenarios, where our basic infrastructure outside the disaster area remains in place, and the cash has value. In this case, since things could be very different, you might think about turning some of your money into something tangible again, something that will always have worth to everyone:

HARD CURRENCY

First, let me say that *the following is not meant as financial advice, but only as helpful information, and before making any decisions about your pesonal financial resources, you should always consult a reputable and reliable professional financial advisor.*

In none of the information below am I assuming you are investing in these metals for the purpose of increasing your portfolio, (although that can happen), but simply as a hedge against the instability of paper money during the Y2K. Please get professional advice for any other investment purposes. If you are interested in professional information concerning your personal financial situation, contact a local expert or call Resource Consultants, Inc., 800-494-4419, advisors with many years' experience in hard currency strategies.

With that said, here are some ideas to think about concerning the use of hard currency:

Many people are currently investing in gold, silver, gems and other precious metals. These things have always carried value through troubled times, and are likely to do so again. If you have a large portfolio, and you want to hedge your holdings against a Y2K crisis, many advise keeping *at least* 5%-7% of your total assets in precious metals, which you should keep at home or in your possession. However, there are some considerations inherent in this strategy relative to gold, silver and platinum:

1) Advantages of buying gold:

* Because of its stability, gold is usually purchased as a long-term holding strategy.
* It provides a hedge against both inflation and deflation in rising or falling markets, as it has always held value.
* Gold is an appropriate investment for those with a large portfolio, seeking to protect liquid assests during volatile times.
* Gold coins with collector's value appreciate faster than bullion, and throughout history, have been the only form of money with enduring value.
* Americans investors might consider foreign coins such as British soverigns, Swiss and French francs, as they are not subject

to possible Federal confiscation, as are U.S. coins.
* "Fractionals" - small gold coins, from 1/10 ounce to one ounce, are more practical than gold bars, but you must deal with a reputable supplier if you aren't knowledgable in this field.

2) Disadvantages of buying gold:

* Gold is best used for protecting large amounts of liquid assets during times of financial instability, and is expensive for the average person with only a small amount of money to invest.
* It's possible to lose your gold assets because they are subject to Federal confiscation during an economic crisis, at about 14% of its purchase price! This happened to U.S. citizens in 1933, when the government confiscated privately held gold supplies, and then raised the price by 69%!
* The Federal government *requires* anyone to report purchases of gold for cash in amounts over $10,000 during any 12-month period.
* Because of its high value, gold is sometimes impractical in a barter or hard currency economy, when you need smaller amounts for transactions. (Are you going to chip a hunk off a gold bar to buy a loaf of bread?)

Platinum is another precious metal that many use for long-term investments, and its value is tied to its uses in industry and jewelry-making. It is the most precious metal, five times scarcer than gold, and is usually not considered practical for the average investor with limited assets.

Silver is considered a good hedge and is more practical for those with limited finances. Its uses are similar to platinum, but it is more widely available.

1) **Advantages of buying silver**:

* Silver is less expensive for those with limited resources.
* Silver will always have some value due to its usage in industry and healing *(see Chapter 10 - First Aid, on Colloidal Silver).*
* Silver coins minted before 1965, (quarters and dimes which actually contain 90% silver), are useful for money transactions during times of financial crisis. You can always use them to buy basic supplies.

2) **Disadvantages of buying silver:**

* Inventories of silver buillon coins are lower than any time since 1950, and likely to get scarcer, so if you wait until the last minute, there may be none available.
* Silver's prices tend to be more volatile than gold, falling with

other commodities during a depression; but demand is currently exceeding supply, and the price is likely to increase dramatically until then.

* Some advisors feel that the smaller silver coins (quarters and dimes), are too bulky to store in any quantity, and suggest larger denomination coins.

But if you don't have a lot of money to put into hard currency, you might consider the smaller denominations of silver coins that were discontinued after 1965, when our money began to be alloyed with copper and other metals. Thoughtful people even then began to save them, and bags of these dimes and quarters are still available in small quantities at coin and pawn shops. You will pay about five times their face value now, and this will go up rapidly as time passes, but if I were you, I'd try to locate some right away, as this seems to be the most practical solution. But realize that *there is a limited supply of these coins, and when they're gone, they're gone...*

Ask a local coin dealer (*or see Appendix B - Internet Links)* for online dealers) about the availability of these coins, called "trash" or "bag" silver. You will have to decide how much to buy, and where to store them, but they will come in handy for small daily necessities. Whatever precious metals you purchase, don't put them in a safety deposit box, because you may not have access to it if the bank closes. There are some private safety deposit box companies, but probably only in large urban areas, and you'll have to check them out carefully. People used to put their coins in a can or jar and bury them, and to this day, these stashes are still found at old homesteads; so burying your money is always an option. And you might want to hide your valuables in several locations in case one is found. Or, if that sounds a bit risky, check the Yellow Pages for local merchants who carry affordable safes that can be permanently secured in a hidden location. Some can be installed into the floor of your home. Second-hand safes are usually available for about 40-50% less than new ones. Safety Central carries a small safe box:

CATALOG CODE	ITEM
SC	**BRABANTIA SAFEBOX** - The safe box locks into its own steel chassis that can be securely mounted to any out-of-the-way location in your office or home, car or boat. Once fitted, the box can only be removed and opened with its own key. By obtaining several chassis you can relocate your safe box if needed - $60, additional chassis - $24.

OBTAINING CASH FOR HARD CURRENCY CONVERSION

There are an endless variety of ways to raise money for the Y2k, from selling your skills and services, to selling unwanted property. Now is the time to convert into cash any items that you own that you aren't using or that you've been meaning to sell. This can be anything from household items to autos, to property. If you don't think you'll need it after the Y2K, then now's the time to get rid of it and replace it with something more useful.

Another consideration is to collect any debts owed to you well before the Y2K, if possible, and buy supplies or turn that cash into hard currency. The fewer financial obligations you have after the Y2K, either debts or accounts receivable, the easier your life will be!

BARTER AND TRADE

Another method of exchange that comes into use in almost any time of disaster or social unrest is barter. That exchange can be anything from your labor, skills, time, service, information, or hard goods. Our entire monetary system was developed in order to make barter easier. Hard goods are sometimes bulky and heavy, and in the case of livestock, difficult to carry around! So money was invented to represent the value of goods exchanged. It was light, portable, and uniform. It works, as long as everyone agrees that it has value, but in times of stress and unrest, when the value of money is disputed, people have always fallen back on the old tried-and-true system of barter.

Basically, barter is simple: you take something you have to spare or that you are willing to do without, and exchange it for something someone else has that you do want. It will rarely be an even exchange in actual value, but it's the perceived value here that counts. If you need it, it's worth whatever you want to give in exchange.

Entire books have been written on how to barter, and you might find these interesting as they introduce several concepts you might not have thought of - because there's barter and there's *BARTER*, and you need to know the difference. For instance, you can either exchange your store of supplies one-for-one for other items, eventually exhausting your supply, or you can set up a round-robin system whereby you can get what you need (along with everyone else in the system) for just one initial trade! So there's definitely some things to be learned about bartering...This system is too complicated to go into here, so if you're intererested, you can get more information from the book listed below:

CATALOG CODE	BOOKS ON BARTERING
NP,RM,SS	***"Survival Bartering"*** - Duncan Long - Complete manual for stockpiling items for barter and obtaining your needs in a cashless society - 56 pgs. - $8

It would be advisable to stock up on some barter goods - perhaps things that you could use later yourself if you don't trade them off. Ask yourself, what would I want that I can't produce myself? Here's some ideas for items to stock:

1) **FOOD ITEMS** - Salt, sugar, yeast, baking soda, spices, tea, coffee, cocoa, chocolate, candy, drink mixes, soup mixes, dry milk, pet food, baby food, formula, any canned or packaged foods.

2) **HOUSEHOLD GOODS** - Matches, candles, toilet paper (always needed!), facial tissues, other paper goods, detergent, unscented bleach (and other water purification products), aluminum foil, plastic wrap, canning jars and lids, blankets.

3) **PERSONAL ITEMS** - Shampoo, bath soap, deodorant, toothbrushes and toothpaste, razors, dental floss, sanitary pads, condoms, first-aid sup-

plies, aspirin, other over-the-counter medicines.

4) **MISC. ITEMS** - Straight and safety pins, sewing needles and thread, pens, pencils, various hand tools, chewing gum, open-pollinated seeds (likely to be worth their weight in gold someday).

5) **TRADITIONAL BARTER ITEMS** - Beer, hard liquor, ammunition, cigarettes, gasoline.

You get the idea...almost anything can be used for barter, depending on your supply and their need and vice versa!

Another caution: When arranging a barter, it's best to imply that the item in question is the only one you have. There's no sense letting anyone know that you have a large stock of goods set aside. Also, don't store everything in one place! Put your supplies away in mixed sets of food, household goods, fuel, etc. in several hidden locations, so that if faced with looters or marauders who take one set, you won't lose everything. Also, don't tell children under teen years about your storage plans, as they tend to "blab" to anyone at the worst time!

Even though this all sounds pretty depressing, the upside of it is that once you have taken care of your own family's needs, extra supplies can allow you to be of assistance to others and supply them with much-needed items. If everyone did this, we get through the crisis a lot easier.

PRESERVING VITAL RECORDS

One thing you will want to have in a fireproof safe, safety deposit box, or other secure place is a complete inventory of all your financial and personal records. *(The **ACTION CHECKLIST** will offer a list of suggested records to obtain.)* Some personal records, such as birth certificates, insurance policies, and land deeds, can be stored right away, but some, such as bank balances, accounts payable and receivable, medical information, and other dated records will have to be done at the last minute. This will take some preparation and coordination, so do what you can as soon as possible. Keep originals if possible, and good copies if that's all you can obtain. If you are using vacuum packing equipment for your food supplies, you can also vacuum pack important papers in heavy mylar bags, or include an oxygen absorber packet to keep them dry and safe in their box. (This would be a good idea even in normal times.) Another idea is to keep all your personal records in plastic covers inside a three-ring binder for easy access.

Hopefully, as things recover and banks and other businesses begin to rebuild their computer systems, you can help them by providing accurate records regarding your accounts. In some cases, this may be all they have to go on, so this could be one of the most crucial "storage" items that you need to deal with. Try to think of every kind of vital information about you and your family that could be lost in a computer, and take steps to save it in hard copy.

Hopefully, the Y2K crisis will be over in a short time, we won't lose too many vital records, and our financial life can get back to normal with only a reasonable amount of disruption. But in case this doesn't happen, at least you will be prepared for whatever comes.

PERSONAL SAFETY
Chapter 13

Information in this chapter:

The issue of personal safety in a crisis is fraught with problems: everything depends on your philosophy and religious and cultural beliefs, and therefore, no one line of advice will satisfy everyone. All I can do is present some options for you to consider:

SOCIAL UNREST

In areas of widespread utility outages with their resulting social upheaval, it's not unrealistic to suppose that there will be cases of looting, burglary, and worse. A recent Internet report on a winter storm blackout in a large Midwest city stated that there were an average of 10 house break-ins every hour! So, unless you have lived in your neighborhood for years, know all the neighbors well, and can pre-arrange some kind of cooperative protection system, you could find yourself defending your property or your family from someone intent on taking what they want at any cost to you.

It has also been speculated that the Y2K is a perfect opportunity for professional criminals and terrorists to strike; in fact, there are several movies with these themes, now in production , that are due out in 1999. This should prime the general public to an awareness of the dangers that can arise in this situation, but it won't help the average citizen with their preparedness plans. You'll still have to do that yourself. And in light of recent events worldwide, with bombings and terrorist threats, this doesn't seem so unlikely anymore.

GUNS

The question of whether to purchase and use a gun is an intensely personal one, and we won't go into it here. If you already own guns or are considering getting one, there is ample information available. Just be sure that if you do decide to purchase a weapon, that you take all safety precautions and get adequate training in handling it. *And keep all guns and ammunition safely locked up away from children.*

SELF DEFENSE

If you don't want to get into lethal weapons, there are other things that you can do to insure your safety: First, if you're in reasonably good health, you can enroll in a course for self-defense; they are now offered in almost every larger city. If you are planning to be with a group during the Y2K crisis period, then at least one, and preferably every able-bodied person in your group, needs to have this training. There are also several good self-defense books available (*see below.*)

SAFETY IN NUMBERS

There's safety in numbers: Probably the best defense is a group of united, supportive neighbors or relatives who can back each other up in any threatening scenario. Consider forming a neigh-borhood Y2K watch group, and develop a crisis contingency plan. Sharing the work and worry of preparation with a group of like-minded people can greatly reduce effort and expense. At first, it may take some skill to convince those who are reluctant to see any problem to join the group. And it also will take someone skilled at dealing with group-dynamics to keep it going until the situation becomes widely accepted by the general public. Unfortunately, by that time, it could be too late to put a lot of the critical contingency plans into effect, but any effort is ultimately better than none. If the group is up and going, then people can join as they become more Y2K aware. *If you build it, they will come..." Don't wait for someone else to begin this...you're probably IT.* Group work can be extremely frustrating, but it beats fighting with your neighbors over scarce supplies...

Here are some interesting books you might want to study:

(*Note: Catalog Code refers to catalogs in the Catalog Appendix.*)

CATALOG CODE	BOOKS ON PERSONAL SAFETY
SU	***"How To Be Safe In An Unsafe World"*** - A security consultant shows you how to protect yoursef and your home - $12.
RM,SU	***"Principles Of Personal Defense"*** - Jeff Cooper - New edition of the classic booklet teaches weapon-craft and mental conditioning for personal survival - $8-$10.
SC	***"Self Defense Pocket Guide"*** - Barry Davies - Compact, practical manual of self-defense techniques covers many scenarios - $7.50.
MA,RM, SS,SU	***"Street-Smart Survival"*** - Victor Santoro - What to do in high-threat situations, with real life scenarios and solutions - $15.-$16.
NP,SC,SS	***"The Urban Survival Handbook"*** - John Wiseman - How to

recognize, prepare for, and overcome the dangers of urban life - illustrated, 320 pgs. - $25-$27.

DEFENSIVE EQUIPMENT

If you would feel safer with some kind of defensive equipment, there are a number of non-lethal items that you can purchase. Just be sure that you first try them out and get some experience with them before you have to use them in an emergency situation. These products can also be found at many general merchandise, hardware, and outdoor supply stores.

1) **ELECTRONIC ALARMS** (listed alphabetically) - These are products that alert you to any intrusion and that use rechargable batteries.

CATALOG CODE	ITEM
SC	a) ***BARKING DOG ALARM*** - Portable, hangs on any doorknob. Vibration sensor detects attempts to enter a room - alerts with sound of barking dog or traditional alarm. Adjustable alarm timer, low battery indicator - $25.
SC	b) ***BODY ALARM*** - Ultra-loud siren activated by pulling a pin - attaches to belt, waistband or hold in hand - also has built-in flashlight - one 9-volt battery provides up to 2 hours continuous sound - $17.
SC	c) ***DAZER*** - Repel dangerous dogs up to 15 feet away - safe, silent, produces a high-frequency sound only dogs can hear - 9-volt battery - $40.
IM	d) ***DRIVEWAY MONITOR*** - Infrared sensor detects motion and transmits a radio signal to house - weatherproof - $200.
SC	e) ***GLASS WINDOW ALERT*** - Stick wireless device on any window or door and if disturbed, emits a loud alarm. Hidden on/off switch, low-battery indicator - uses one 9-volt battery - $15.
RM	f) ***INTRUSION DETECTION DEVICE*** - Seismometer with range of 30 yards in every direction from probe, can be used underwater. Powered by 6 "D" batteries, the control may be placed up to one mile from the probe - $215.
SC	g) ***KEY ALERT*** - Lightweight, loud keychain alarm with flashlight, activated by switch - one 12-volt battery included - $15.
SC	h) ***MOTION ALERT*** - Attach wireless device to any door and it will chime or alarm at any motion. Uses personal code to arm/disarm - uses one 9-volt battery - $35.
SC	i) ***PROTECT-ALL ALARM*** - Movement-sensitive alarm

attaches to any equipment, computer, TV, etc. Uses 9-volt battery - $14.

SC j) ***REX-10 BARKING DOG ALARM*** - Activate with key-chain remote that also turns on lights, or use the optional outdoor motion-sensor - sounds like a ferocious dog - $80.

SC k) ***SAFE & SOUND*** - Compressed air horn for emergency signaling - 40gm/$12, 4.5oz./$19, 8oz/$22.

RM l) ***The Ready Made Resources*** catalog also has several professional seismic and radar units.

2) **PEPPER SPRAYS** - These are personal safety products that fire a cone-shaped blast of pepper spray that impairs vision and when inhaled, restricts breathing. To use, simply point the device at the target and depress the activator button. In most cases, the subject will instantly be incapacitated. They do no permanent harm. *Note: These should be kept away from children, as they are not toys and should only be used in self-defense.*

CATALOG CODE	ITEM
BA,NP,SC	a) ***STANDARD PEPPER SPRAY CANNISTERS*** - Carry in purse or pocket, sprays either a fog or foam to coat the target - range from 8-20 feet, in 4-15 oz. - $9-$37.
BA,NP,SC	b) ***PEPPER SPRAY PAGER CLIPS*** - Looks like a pager, with belt clip, spray ranges from 9-20 feet - $15-$20.
BA,NP,SC	c) ***KEY RINGS*** - Keychain versions delivers spray up to 5 feet - for "close encounters" - $7-$30.
NP,SC	d) ***PEPPER GAS BRAND AUTO UNIT*** - Especially made to carry in an auto - attaches anywhere inside a vehicle - $12-$20.
NP,RM,SC	e) ***BIO SHIELD/BIOGUARD RESCUE*** - Neutralizers for tear gas and pepper sprays - FDA approved and non-toxic, used by U.S. Marshalls to safely recover from effects of chemical agents - 100 times more effective than water - 2-10 oz. - $8-$30, towelettes - $16.

3) **STUN GUNS** - Stun guns produce an electric charge that immobilizes attackers without doing any permanent damage. Contact can cause a dazed mental state, loss of balance and muscle control, and disorientation. Works through clothing, and effects wear off in 5 to 10 minutes.

CATALOG CODE	ITEM
SC	a) ***STUN GUNS*** - Three models provide a humane defense - requires 2 fully charged 9-volt batteries to be

effective - 100,000 volts - $70, 200,000 volts - $120, 300,000 Volts - $160.

LF b) ***THE MYOTRON*** - Developed for the FBI, not technically a stun gun. Emits pulse waves that intercept assailant's brain waves, incapacitating for about 30 minutes. Can be hidden in palm - with 20-year lithium battery - $150.

4) **AIR TASERS** - Most stun guns, although effective, require close contact with an attacker. Now the new air taser technology allows you to fire twin leads powered by compressed air and tipped with cloth-penetrating barbs, up to 15 feet away. These leads carry a unique, dual 50,000-volt current which jams the nervous system, rendering anyone immobile. Effects wear off in 10-15 minutes. Built-in probes also give back-up stun gun protection. Guaranteed that if you lose it in an attack situation, it will be replaced free. Endorsed by the National Police Chiefs' Association.

CATALOG CODE	ITEM
SC	a) ***AIR TASER DEFENSE SYSTEM*** - includes air taser, instructional video, practice target, 2 air cartridges, carrying case, strap, safety grip - $250.
SC	b) ***SPORT TASER*** - Smaller version comes with three launch cartridges and belt pack - $300.
SC	c) ***EXTRA AIR TASER CARTRIDGES*** - 2 for $60.

5) **MISCELLANEOUS SECURITY PRODUCTS** (listed alphabetically) - There are several other useful items that you can get for personal safety:

CATALOG CODE	ITEM
SC	a) ***THE BIG JAMMER*** - Heavy-duty steel rod slips under doorknob to jam door shut - use horizontally for sliding glass doors - $20.
RM	b) ***BODY ARMOR*** - A selection of bullet-proof vests - call for prices.
SC	c) ***BRABANTIA SAFE BOX*** - Heavy-duty portable safe, steel-plate construction, locks into a steel chassis for security - opens with a coded key - $60, additional chassis - $24.
SC	d) ***CHANGE-A-LOCK*** - Do-it-yourself re-keying set - complete instructions - change up to six single-cylinder locks. Specify brand of locks when ordering - $13.
SC	e) ***GARRETT SUPER SCANNER GS-1*** - Locates concealed weapons, using audio signal and visual alarm - $160.
NP,SC	f) ***HIDDEN WALL SAFE*** - Looks like ordinary electric wall plug - hide valuables - instructions included - $9-$11.

NP	g) ***CAN SAFES*** - Name-brand cans of household and garage products made into a safe place to hide small valuables. Bottom unscrews to reveal hiding place - $13.
SC	h) ***ID-2000*** - Invisibly mark valuables for easy identification in case of theft. Marks visible only under ultraviolet light - used by law enforcement - does 1200 markings - includes inventory sheet - $9.

FIRE SAFETY

The time to prepare for a fire is before it happens. Be sure that all members of your family or group know their part of the plan and how to exit in case of fire. Rehearse before you need to! There are several products that can increase your chances of surviving a fire:

CATALOG CODE	ITEM
HA,IM	1) **DUAL SMOKE/CARBON DIOXIDE ALARM** - Combines both functions and uses a 9-volt battery - $60-$65.
IM	2) **SMOKE DETECTORS** - Dual system, using ionization and photoelectric sensors for early fire and smoke detection - uses 9-volt battery - $40.
EE,MA, NP,SC	3) **GAS SHUT-OFF TOOL** - In case of utility failure, this steel tool helps anyone shut off the gas (and water) to your home (sometimes called an "earthquake key") - $5-$20, also a "four-in-one" tool - $15.
LE,MA, NP,SC	4) **SMOKE HOODS** - Each year 10,000 people die in fires, 80% of them overcome by toxic smoke. These hoods provide filtered air and greatly increase chances of survival. (Note: They are not a fresh air supply and are to be used only for evacuation, not re-entry into a burning building.) Styles vary from small hand-held masks to complete head-covering hoods. Adult and child sizes - $15-$70.
IM,SC	5) **ESCAPE LADDER** - A must for any multi-storied home or building. Carries over 1,000 lbs. - slip resistant rungs. Fits windowsills up to 10" thick - 15 ft.(2-story) - $50-$80, 25 ft. (3-story) - $75-$99.
SC	6) **QUICK-OUT FIRE BLANKET** - Cover fire and quickly extinguish it - no messy fire extinguisher clean-up - 2'x2'/$25, 4'x4'/$50.

RADIATION

EE,MA,NP, RM,SC,SU	If you live near a nuclear facility and are worried about leakage, many catalogs carry masks, thyroid tablets, filters, radiation detectors, and books with information on radiation safety.

TRANSPORTATION
Chapter 14

Information in this chapter:

During any crisis, a reliable form of transportation can sometimes be life-saving. It would be ideal if we could all just stay home and wait the Y2K crisis out, and if it only lasts a few days, perhaps we can. But if problems persist into weeks or months, it will be necessary for us to leave home and go to work, check on relatives, deal with medical emergencies, volunteer our services, and engage in many other activities. We will need a good way to get from here to there, one that uses little gasoline, which is almost surely to be scarce either through rationing or a breakdown in supply systems.

A GOOD VEHICLE...

> *A recent report discussed how the engineers testing the AMC Eagle found that the main processing unit, which controlled the car's ignition, power steering, fuel injection and drive train, failed during Y2K testing. The processing unit did not fail due to date calculations, but because the advent of 2000 caused a data buffer to overflow, thereby making the embedded processor fail."*
>
> Michael Maynard, *Newsbytes*

Many people haven't yet begun to investigate whether their vehicle is Y2K compliant, but as you can see from the above quote, it is more than a simple matter of whether all the onboard computers will function. It's whether all the systems can function together if the embedded systems haven't been checked out in a real-time situation. Unfortunately, I don't currently know of any mechanics who are offering this service, but I imagine that some will be doing so in 1999. However, that may be too late for you to make other arrangements for safe transportation during the Y2K. Remember, a functioning vehicle could make the difference between life and death for you or your family, because it is unlikely that many emergency services will be operating, or if they are, they will be completely overextended. If you live in a rural area, you will definitely need a way to get into a nearby town for aid or supplies.

So now is the time to begin investigating the type of transportation that you want to be driving during the Y2K crisis. Consider purchasing an older vehicle that doesn't rely on complicated computer systems and that can be repaired easily with hand tools by a local mechanic. There are still some around, (both vehicles and mechanics) and I'd start looking for both right away. *They are going to be worth their weight in gold someday*. Give some thought to the following criteria for a self-reliance vehicle:

1) The vehicle must get *very good* gas mileage, as gasoline is almost certain to be rationed or in short supply.

2) If the weather is severe, a four-wheel drive with a winch would be ideal. Otherwise, carry chains and a hand winch.

3) A sturdy, older vehicle, preferably a truck or van, can be easily repaired and can carry water and other provisions.

4) The vehicle needs to have enough power to get you out of any emergency situation you might meet on the road.

5) *The less conspicuous it is, the better.*

6) ATVs and similar vehicles can prove useful in some situations.

7) A Moped bike could come in very handy for short trips around the neighborhood, if it's safe.

8) Bicycles are the optimal fuel-free vehicle, especially if you live in an area where you can safely ride them. You can even pull a small two-wheeled trailer behind to carry supplies in.

Chances are that you'll find any vehicle you need locally, but one catalog does carry a couple:

(Note: Catalog Code refers to catalogs listed in Appendix D.)

CATALOG CODE	ITEM
NO	1) **MINI-CYCLE** - 3.5 HP engine, 10" wheels, small two-wheeled motorcycle - $700.
NO	2) **MOPED** - Larger two-wheeled motorbike gets 150 mpg, can also be manually pedaled. Meets Federal Motor Vehicle safety standards - free shipping - $825.

Whatever type of vehicle(s) you choose, realize that ***keeping it in top operating condition will be crucial.*** Have your vehicle(s) checked thoroughly and any needed repairs done well before the end of 1999. Lay in all necessary repair and replacement parts because they will likely be in short supply (*see* ***ACTION CHECKLIST***). Also, if anyone in your family or group can work on cars, be sure to help them stock up on all the necessary tools and mechanic supplies, including a bar to remove tires manually from the rims for repair.

BATTERY CHARGERS

There are several devices that use solar power to keep your battery charged and ready to go. They won't recharge a completely dead battery, but they prevent a working one from going dead, especially if the vehicle is not driven for a while.

CATALOG CODE	ITEM
NO,RM, SC	1) **SOLAR AUTO BATTERY CHARGER** - For auto and other deep-cycle batteries, - a *solar charger* that works even on cloudy days - extends battery life - $30-$99.
BA,NO, RG,RM,SC	2) **TRICKLE AUTO BATTERY CHARGER** - Plugs into cigarette lighter and keeps battery at peak charge - $30-$40.

GASOLINE

There is a lot of difference in opinion among experts concerning the safety of storing gasoline. It is a highly flammable substance and it deteriorates rapidly, so most don't advise the inexperienced to attempt to store gas in any large amounts. *Extreme caution is always necessary in storing and handling gasoline.*

With that said, however, if you have to drive during the crisis, you will need to store a supply of gasoline, especially if you can provide a safe place well away from any dwelling to keep it. Determine your vehicle's mileage, and from that figure how much gas you must store for your projected driving needs. Don't forget to figure in gas usage for lawnmowers, and power tools such as chainsaws, garden tillers, etc.

1) **GASOLINE STORAGE CONTAINERS -** To store gasoline, you will need metal cans or drums, or plastic containers *made especially for gasoline storage*. Gasoline will degrade ordinary plastic containers and it's not advised to use them for any length of time. You will also need to use a fuel additive to prevent deterioration. When gasoline is stored for any length of time, *butane will vent out of the gas within six months, making engine starting difficult, unless you use vapor-proof gas containers.* Even using a gas-saver doesn't prevent this. Always fill storage containers nearly full to prevent water condensation inside, which can contaminate the gas, and leave only about 5% space at the top for fuel expansion in hot weather. Gas cans are available at almost any hardware or general merchandise store, or by catalog. If you need to store a lot of fuel, you can use 55-gallon metal barrels, which are selling at our local fuel supply store for around $20. Check with your local farm or fuel supply store for these, or for a farm gasoline tank that holds several hundred gallons. These can sometimes be located second-hand at farm sales and auctions. Price on the new tanks runs about $1.00 per gallon of capacity, so purchasing and filling a 300-gallon tank could cost well over $500.

CATALOG CODE	ITEM
MA	a) ***THE EURO GAS CAN*** - Heavyweight quality 5-gallon steel can from French military - used, reconditioned and suitable for all kinds of fuel storage - heavy duty attached cap - $10. Special steel nozzle - $7.
MA	b) ***SUPER CAN*** - Stainless steel 7-gallon fuel drum with ma-

chined screw cap and handle - $25, flexible screw-on nozzle - $4.

RM c) ***VAPOR-PROOF GAS CAN*** - Super heavy duty plastic, uses standard spout - new/$33, used/$20.

NO d) ***FIVE-GALLON CAN*** - Metal - $22.

NO e) ***GAS CAN WITH PUMP*** - Set can on ground, pump fuel with 4 foot hose - also nozzle, pour spout - $25.

NO f) ***TOMMY PUMP*** - Transfer liquids, up to 90 weight oil - fits most cans - $16.

(It's also been suggested that you have a good siphon pump on hand if you have to get gas from any underground storage tank.)

2) **GAS SAVER** - Once you have your gas storage containers, you will need to obtain an additive to preserve the gasoline, as it is volatile and deteriorates rapidly. In the past, some preservers didn't work very well, but there are new products that are said to be tried and proven to extend storage life. Use them on any fuel that you intend to store for more than a few months.

There are two kinds: one for gasoline and one for diesel. Depending on the starting condition of the fuel and on the storage facilities - tightly sealed contain ers and a cool environment are ideal - the gas can be kept between five and ten years. The product is said to inhibit carbon deposits, increase engine efficiency, reduce emissions, lubricate and clean the fuel system, extend engine life, improve all gasolines, and prevent tank corrosion! For diesel, it also removes slime and sludge, controls moisture and inhibits gelling, and reduces smoke.

MA,SU a) ***PRI-G AND PRI-D*** - One pint treats 256 gallons of gasoline or diesel fuel - $20. One quart treats 512 gallons- $25-$30. Larger quantities available - 55-gallon drum, etc. Call the Survival Center for a quote on this.

MA b) ***GAS SAVER*** - Can be used on most fuels, diesel, heating oil, aviation gas, jet fuel, and gasoline. Prevents gum and lacquer formation, used extensively by military and all oil companies for years - Treats fuel for five years - 8 oz. treats 800 gals./$15, pint treats 1600 gals./$25.

NP c) ***FUEL SAVER PLUS*** - Said to prevent reaction of fuel with metal containers, and stop formation of gums and lacquers in carburetors. Rotation recommended after 3 years - one oz. treats 16 gallons - 16oz./$16, 32oz./$28.

CF d) ***BOUNDARY FRICTION CONTROL*** - Not technically a gas saver, this treats all metal surfaces with a chemical friction barrier to reduce wear and protect against corrosion. Includes oil - 1 qt.-5 gal. - $47-$480; extreme pressure grease - 16oz. - $5; spray lubricant - 1-5 gal. - $37-$140; and diesel fuel conditioner - 1-5 gal. - $68-$320.

If all electricity and gasoline pumping and delivery systems are down, even for only a short time, gasoline is likely to be rationed for military and emergency use only. After a crisis, the cost is going to be prohibitive, so ***store as much gasoline as you can afford and have room to keep.*** It can always be used for barter; and along with a good water filter, *gasoline (and any auto parts) could prove to be one of your most valuable storage items.*

COMMUNICATIONS
Chapter 15

Information in this chapter:

RADIOS
- *Hand Operated*
- *Multi-Powered*
- *Multi-Use/Multi-Powered*
- *Shortwave*
- *Antennas*

WEATHER BROADCAST RECEIVERS
TWO-WAY COMMUNICATIONS
BOOKS

One of the most difficult things about any emergency situation is not knowing what is going on outside our immediate surroundings; the feeling of being all alone in a crisis is frightening. We need answers: How widespread is the problem? How severe are the effects of it? How long can we expect it to last? What is being done to correct the problems? These questions occur immediately, and only compound our stress when they can't be answered.

Unfortunately, in a crisis such as the Y2K, our normal communications systems are likely to be down or only partly functional. At present, our entire local, national, and worldwide communications network is completely dependent on the use of electricity, computers, and other embedded microchip systems. It's not unrealistic to surmise that if we lose our capacity to generate electricity over widespread areas, that we will also lose our newspapers, TV, radio, Internet, and telephone transmissions.

The recent breakdown (Spring '98), of one of our pager satellites highlights the fragility of our entire satellite transmission system, which runs on embedded microchips. And there's the Post Office and the express package delivery companies that depend extensively on computers and computer-dependent airlines to provide their services. If we retain the electric grid, we can stay in touch via telephones, faxes, and the Internet, even if regular television and radio programming is down for a while. But if all our normal information channels become unavailable, how will we learn about the situation outside our local area?

In the old days, before the advent of electronic communications, word-of-mouth and letters delivered via the Pony Express worked just fine...but it sometimes took months to get the news! Unfortunately, we're not used to waiting that long for information, and aren't likely to be willing to revert to the old ways in a crisis situation. So what can we do do assure that we have some contact with the outside world?

We have several options: Most commercial radio sites are prepared to operate for a time with generator-powered equipment, and if we have a good solar or battery-powered emergency radio, we should be able to get some news at first, at least locally. The AM band will probably offer the best reception. If you have a short-wave radio, you can also pull in many stations from distant locations. Listening to the short wave radio is a fascinating hobby in normal times, and in a crisis like Y2K, can offer a larger view of the world situation. CB radios can give you an idea of what's happening from police and others who use them, but since none of the catalogs listed carry these, you'll have to get them locally.

If you have a bent for electronics, you might also want to investigate ham radio, but this takes a lot of study, equipment, and licensing, and is not really practical for the average person. However, if you know of a ham operator in your neighborhood, cultivate him/her! They could be a valuable source of information during the crisis. And if you think circumstances might separate you from your family or group, you can use two-way radios for communication within a couple of miles.

RADIOS

1) **HAND-OPERATED RADIOS -** There are several reasonably priced solar and/or hand powered radios manufactured especially for emergency use. They are inexpensive and should be on everyone's list. Nearly all the self-sufficiency catalogs carry them.

(*Note: Catalog Code refers to catalogs listed in Appendix D)*

CATALOG CODE	ITEM
BA,CF,KW, RG,RM,SC	a) ***BAY-GEN FREEPLAY RADIO*** - Wind it up with the fold-in hand-crank for 30 seconds, and it plays for 30 minutes or more - powered by a Baylis Clock-Work Generator. Produces good audio for AM, FM, and SW (shortwave) bands between 5.8 and 18 MHz. - AM/FM only - \$63-\$70, (with solar power - \$71-\$80), AM/FM/SW - \$70-\$129. SW antenna - \$20, and AC adapter - \$17-20 (solar option - \$20.)
	2) **MULTI-POWERED RADIOS**
BA,EE,MA, SA,SC, SS,SU	a) ***SOLAR HAND-CRANK AM/FM RADIO*** - Four power sources: solar panel, hand-crank generator, built-in batteries, and rechargable batteries - built-in telescoping antenna - \$22-\$38.
	3) **MULTI-USE/MULTI-POWERED RADIOS**
RG,SS	a) ***THE DYNAMO*** - Emergency AM/FM radio and flashlight can be powered by standard batteries or by charging it with a hand-cranked generator - \$35-\$50.
CF,EE,MA, NP,RG, SC,SS	b) ***4-WAY SOLAR RADIO/FLASHLIGHT*** - Two models offer AM/FM reception with flashlight/3-color strobe. Four power sources: solar panel, hand crank gener ator, built-in NiCad batteries and two "AA" batteries. DC backup jack, full swing antenna - \$30-\$50.

4) **SHORTWAVE RADIOS -** All Sangean models have AM/FM, plus stereo headphone jacks, signal and battery-strength meter, dual time display, sleep timer, buzzer-radio alarm, auto and manual scan, memory recall, rotary tuning, and 45 station presets.

KW a) ***SANGEAN SG 789A ANALOG TUNED*** - AM/FM (stereo at headphone jack, 8 shortwave bands, 13 meter bands and part of 90-60 meter band. Uses 3 "AA" batteries, has telescoping antenna, SW handbook - $39.

b) ***SANGEAN SW RADIOS -*** The digital shortwave radios are easy to tune and can keep up when stations change frequency.

CF,RM,KW * ***ATS-909 DIGITAL*** - Newest, high-performance with memories, preprogrammed, RDS capable, SSB tuning, includes AC adapter and portable antenna. Uses 4 "AA" batteries - $275-$290.

CF,RM,KW * ***ATS 818 DIGITAL*** - Deluxe model with most features. Has programmable cassette/recorder, tone control, AM wide/narrow filter, side band for some ham radio signals, timer for automatic recording, safety lock, SW handbook, and external AC adapter. Runs on 4 "D" batteries and 3"AA" batteries for memory backup - with cassette - $207-$240, w/o cassette - $167-$190.

CF,KW * ***ATS 808 DIGITAL*** - Smaller, lighter than 818 w/o cassette BFO, display light, AC adapter. Has stereo headphone, SW handbook, and case. Requires 4 "AA" batteries for radio and 2 "AA" batteries for memory backup - AC adapter - $10, radio - $135-$139.

RM c) ***GRUNDIG SW RADIOS*** - No information available in catalog except prices - Grundig YB-400 SW - $200, Grundig YB-305 SW - $170.

5) **ANTENNAS**

KW a) ***SELECT-A-TENNA*** - Antenna booster for AM radio. Simple to use, place near radio, tune in AM station, and turn knob on Select-A-Tenna until station volume increases. Can double daytime range, and helps with too-strong signals - $46. Model M for use inside metal buildings, basements - $55.

KW b) ***PORTABLE SW ANTENNA*** - Pocket-sized, with 23' wire antenna in compact reel case improves reception. Plugs for radios with jack, and antenna clip for telescoping antennas - $14.

WEATHER BROADCAST RECEIVERS

In case of inclement weather, and in the absence of other broadcast weather reports, you still might be able to receive warnings from the NOAA weather reports. These receivers are good to have anytime.

CATALOG CODE	ITEM
BA,SC	1) **WEATHER ONE** - Pocket-sized receiver tuned to NOAA broadcast frequencies, current forecasts and prediction 24hours/7days a week. Handheld or desktop - $30.
SC	2) **HOME EMERGENCY ALERT MONITOR** - Will begin broadcasting NOAA "hazard alerts" from any weather condition, floods, earthquake, hurricanes, tornados, etc. - built-in thermometer, portable - $70.

TWO-WAY COMMUNICATIONS

CATALOG CODE	ITEM
CM,SC	1) **TALK-ABOUT PLUS** - two-mile range, portable, palm-sized professional-quality radios, static-free 14 channels, 38 privacy codes, 30 hours on 2 "AA" batteries - $140-$160.
NO	2) **TWO-WAY RADIOS** - Large selection of these radios - from FM hands-free to deluxe 5 watts - $37-$150.

BOOKS

(*Note: If you're on a budget, check your local second-hand bookstores for these titles.*)

CATALOG CODE	TITLE
CF,KW, MA,RM	***"GUIDE TO EMERGENCY SURVIVAL COMMUNICATIONS"*** - Dave Ingram - Throughly explains all aspects of setting up and using various communications equipment. Highly recommended - $16-$30.
CF	***"PASSPORT TO WORLDBAND RADIO"*** - L. Magne - The TV Guide for shortwave radio - see at a glance all information about SW stations - $20.

In your Y2K preparations, you'll feel a lot better if you can keep informed about what is happening outside your immediate environment. Also make any arrangements you feel necessary to stay in touch with family and close friends. This will alleviate a lot of anxiety during an already stressful time.

AFTERWARD

ACKNOWLEGEMENTS

"OK, well, I'll just type something up and put it on the 'Net..." was my naive comment some months ago! As it turns out, nothing is that simple...It has taken many months of concentrated effort to produce this book, and I have several people to thank for their assistance:

* My most heartfelt thanks go to **Jeff Danks**, my husband, who has, in addition to a full-time job, shouldered many of my usual household chores, relieving me to sit at the computer for hours, and days, and months, when he'd much rather have been on it himself! And his willingness and ability to do the impossible on the computer, even when he wasn't sure how to, has my deepest admiration. This book is as much his as mine - he literally put it together - and my apreciation for his unconditional love and support can't be adequately expressed.

* My dear friend, **Merri Lu Park**, author of the excellent book, "*Menopause, Time For A Change*", (Alive Books, $16.95 U.S), now living the good life in Hawaii, who through the magic of the Internet slipped into my life again and took up the chore of editing as if she'd been born to it! Your input was intelligent, incisive, and most welcome, and your many, many long hours spent reading the *very rough* copy is gratefully acknowleged. Thanks, old friend.

* My mother-in-law, **Shirley Danks**, wise enough to realize what was at stake early on, who has been supportive and helpful throughout the process of creating this book. Your insight and input into the ***Action Checklist*** helped me finalize that project, and your teacher's eagle-eye stood you in good stead in the long job of proof-reading. All your efforts are appreciated!

* An old friend, **Lucy Pittard**, who gave the final copy a good inspection, and made me feel a lot better about sending it off to the the printer and the Internet. Thanks for being here when I needed you, and thanks for your time...

* My sister-in-law, **Kim Danks**, who gave me valuable suggestions about infant and child care, since my own kids have been grown for many years. Thanks, Kim, for taking the time from your two beautiful babies to sit down and bring me up to date!

* **"Doc" Thoma**, another "old friend" who helped me stay on course, and was always there with wise advice and suggestions. I appreciate you!

* **Becky Simpson**, a real wizard, who listened when no one else could, and always had time to help me work it out. Your presence is a blessing in my life...

* **Michael Akerman** - My "computer archangel", who was always there with a positive voice: "Yeah, we can do that"..."Don't worry, we're still on track"..."It's all coming together". Not only was your computer expertise invaluable, but your assurances that it

all could be done were crucial to my living through the last few weeks! Thanks.

* **GARY** - You didn't have to do it, but you did. The generous sharing of your time, advice and experience was more than I could have expected or asked for. Many thanks... I needed that!

And I want to express gratitude for the many others in my life, who, over the years, have added to my store of information and experience - you know who you are....Thanks, all!

ABOUT THE AUTHOR

Lia Marie Danks is a native Texan, now living the simple rural life on a five-acre farm in the south-central United States. She and Jeff, her husband of 25 years, have used most of the methods recommended in "Building Your Ark" for self-reliant living, and she has studied and collected information on the subject for the past 18 years. Lia is an organic, deep-bed gardener, producing and processing much of her family's food. She has heated and cooked with a woodstove, used a home-made composting toilet, and lived comfortably through several extended severe winter periods without power or outside contacts, thus gaining hands-on experience for many of the suggestions in this book.

Jeff has worked in the computer field for about 15 years, and this connection first spurred Lia's interest in the Y2K phenomenon several years ago. As she studied the situation, she became convinced that she needed to prepare for this Millinneum occurance, and began to make a preparedness list for her family to use. Then she realized that her friends would want a copy, so the ***ACTION CHECKLIST*** was born, and at their suggestion, this was soon followed by many months of work on **"BUILDING YOUR ARK".** Because of the lack of time before Y2K, it was decided to offer the book via the Internet first, in order to speed its dissemination to as many people as possible. Both online and printed versions are now available. See the order form at the back of the book for information on how to obtain more printed copies, and visit www.yourark.com for a download copy.

Both Jeff and Lia hope that many people will benefit from their efforts to share these ideas, and that they can be spared suffering and assist others during the coming Y2K crisis period.

APPENDIX A
FOOD & NUTRITION

Information in this Appendix:

BASIC NUTRITION
DETERMINING CALORIC REQUIREMENTS
FOOD STORAGE QUANTITY REQUIREMENTS
NURITIOUS SUPPLEMENTS
NATURAL FOOD WAREHOUSES

BASIC NUTRITION

When setting up your food program, it's important to have some idea of what we need to eat for good nutrition. This will help when you are making important decisions about what foods to include in your food plan.

At the most basic level, our bodies need only three things: proteins, carbohydrates, and fats. Everything we eat is ultimately broken down into these substances for use in our body's amazing chemical factory. Carbohydrates and fats provide us with energy, and proteins with the building blocks for our body's basic tissues.

Carbohydrates are broken down into simple sugars, which circulate in the blood as glucose, providing energy for our cell's activities. Fat is also an efficient fuel for our muscles, which demand most of our energy stores. Fat supplies more than twice the calories that carbohydrates do for the same weight. But whenever we eat more of any of these substances than our body needs, it is all stored as fat, to be broken down later for use wherever the body requires it. If fat and carbohydrate intakes are too low to meet our requirements, then protein from food or our body tissues will be broken down for energy, since this takes priority over tissue buiding. This is why we lose weight and muscle tone when we go without food for an extended time. So we obviously need a balance of these three basic substances to remain healthy.

A SIDE NOTE: A very popular book has recently discussed this issue, and the proper ratio of each nutrient to the other. You might want to obtain a copy of *"The Zone"* by Barry Sears, PhD. - $23. Just as with most diet suggestions there are those who swear by his system and those who criticize it. You will have to decide for yourself if it is approprate for you.

So the basic pattern is quite simple - we need just enough protein for growth (in children) and body repair and maintainence, and just enough calories to meet our needs for energy. These calories come from both complex carbohydrates and the fats that occur in all whole foods. And the key word here is "whole" - foods that have not been processed to the point that all they supply is empty calories, without crucial nutrients.

Also necessary for health are the dynamos - vitamins and minerals - which are usually called micronutrients. They are regulators, working with our hormones and serving as catalysts for most body functions. But, unlike hormones, they are not made in the body, and must be supplied from our diet: vitamins from the cells of the food we eat, and minerals from plants, which have absorbed them from the soil (hence the problem with the demineralization of our soils due to modern farming practices). When we eat highly refined foods, we can acquire deficiencies in these vital nutrients; but if your diet meets the requirements for these nutrients and calories from a wide variety of whole foods, then your body will be able to maintain itself quite well in most situations.

WHAT FOODS PROVIDE THE NUTRIENTS

Most foods contain a mixture of various amounts of the three basic nutrients, but some are better suppliers of each than others.

CARBOHYDRATES provide most of our energy because of the starch in them which is changed to sugar (glucose) and burned as fuel in our cells. Since the body needs fiber and certain vitamins to metabolize carbohydrates properly, eating highly processed foods without them causes a rapid infusion of sugar into the system. This is the "sugar high" and "crash" that we experience when eating junk foods. ***WHOLE GRAINS AND LEGUMES***, in all their forms, supply all the nutrients in their proper proportions for the body to slowly burn the carbohydrates as fuel and sustain energy. In fact, you can get almost all the calories and amino acids that you need from them, which is why they're the basis for any food storage program.

FAT serves us, (in spite of popular opinion!), by storing and transporting the fat-soluble vitamins and providing twice the amount of energy as carbohydrates when burned as fuel for the body. And fat also helps carry flavor, making most foods simply taste better, so we need to include it in our diets in small portions. However, most of us ingest much more fat than we actually need, much of it hidden in prepared foods. We need only about one tablespoon of almost any ***POLYUNSATURATED OIL*** per day to meet our fat needs. (Saturated fats are solid at room temperature, polyunsaturated fats - the recommended type - are liquid at room temperature). With a natural diet, you will get almost all your fat needs from ***WHOLE GRAINS, NUTS, SEEDS AND high-grade, cold-pressed, liquid VEGETABLE OIL.***

PROTEINS are actually clusters of amino acids, which are the building blocks of all living tissue, both plant and animal. Over half the body, excluding the water, is protein. Enzymes, hormones, and antibodies, which regulate most of our body's important functions, are mostly protein, as is DNA and RNA, which carry our genetic codes. Our rich diets currently supply almost 100 grams of protein daily, almost double what adults really need. Our body also has a very efficient protein recycling program that breaks down and reuses old proteins, so that little is lost.

What our body really needs are the amino acids from plant or animal protein to use in building its own tissues. To make new proteins for our body, all of the amino acids must be present in certain percentages, and there's plenty of all of them in breads, beans, and many vegetables. So a diet containing a wide variety of foods in combination can easily provide these. Since any good whole-foods diet actually can more than meet our protein needs, we needn't worry about a storage diet that is low in animal foods. The only times that your body might need extra protein for tissue building is during pregnancy, lactation, and major trauma, such as surgery - or if you're a growing child. And there are a number of easily stored sources for this extra protein, most of them ***SOY PRODUCTS*** such as protein powders, amino bouillon, miso, dried tofu, and so on *(see list below)*. And of course, ***FREEZE-DRIED AND CANNED MEATS AND FISH*** can be used if they aren't stored for too long.

VITAMINS cannot be made by the body and are absolutely essential for life, as they allow us to utilize our food. The foods we eat are basically passive until acted upon by vitamins, which are catalysts in every step of the body's digestive and chemical processes. Vitamins remain unchanged in these processes, like enzymes, of which they are a part. Most are soluble in water, and must be replenished daily, but a few, like A and E are fat-soluble and can be stored in the tissues. When a vitamin is absent from the diet, even though the needed food substances are present, the body's needs are not met because the biochemical processes it assists cannot occur. So *vitamins must be provided daily through our diet or via supplements*. Since many vitamins can be destroyed by cooking and other processing, our most useable vitamins (and crucial enzymes) are found in ***FRESH, LIVE, FRUITS AND VEGETABLES***. Thus the emphasis in storage food programs on ***SPROUTING SEEDS, WHEATGRASS, AND OTHER GREENS,*** as an easy, tasty, and inexpensive source for these vital elements.

MINERALS (both major and trace, organic and inorganic) are only needed in our body in minute quantities, but they play much more important roles than these quantities imply. Minerals are found as constituents of vitamins, enzymes, and hormones, as well as of cells and hard tissues such as bones and teeth. They make possible the contraction of muscles, the chemical balance of the blood, the activation of enzymes, and the overall functioning of most body processes. Due to the close integration of minerals in the body and their slow turnover, deficiencies can take a long time to show up, and then many times, as in osteoporosis, it's too late to do much about it. So we need to be careful to supply all our body's requirements. Minerals are found in ***MOST WHOLE FOODS***, in certain ***SEA VEGETABLES AND FISH PRODUCTS***, and can also be taken in ***SUPPLEMENTS.*** The only caution is not to get too much of any one kind, such as sodium from table salt. (Solar-dried sea salt, however, is recommended, as it can provide many needed micronutrients not found in regular table salt.)

Sources for all these nutrients will be suggested as we discuss each type of storage program in more detail in Chapter 4, Food Storage. As you probably know, there are as many diets out there as there are people willing to try them out. Many readers of this book have, at one time in their life, probably been on some special dietary regime or another, for weight loss or health reasons. Some of us have tried just about any diet you might imagine, and some you couldn't! *The purpose of this book is not to suggest any particular diet, (especially if you're already eating a medically-prescribed diet), but to give you some ideas about what kind of food intake might be the most optimum for you during the Y2K crisis period.*

As you read and study this material, you may decide to rethink some of your dietary habits, and see if you want to continue them under crisis conditions. It's important to have familiar foods in such times, but it's equally important not to expect to have your usual, over-abundant diet, probably too rich in many unnecessary ingredients! So consider developing simpler eating habits before the Y2K, and then eating a storage-food diet won't seem so bad!

AN INTERESTING THEORY...

One recent best-seller that I enjoyed is a book called *"Eat Right 4 (for) Your Type"* by J. d'Adamo - $23 - that suggests special food intakes based on the four basic blood types. It makes sense to me, as our blood is a chemical soup which carries all the nutrients to our cells for their nourishment. So there is probably a relationship in the reactions of our blood to the chemicals found in our foods. Dr. d'Adamo and his father investigated this premise for many years, and found that certain blood types metabolized certain foods better than others. They've constructed complete dietary suggestions for each type. Certain blood types, because of their cultural and genetic history do better with meat, some don't do well with wheat, or dairy, and so on. So these suggestions might influence the types of foods that you decide to store.

For instance, my husband is a type O, which doesn't do well with wheat (he's suspected this for years). So we are going to substitute other grains instead of the large amounts of wheat suggested in most food storage programs. Too much wheat is also harsh on children's digestion. There's no sense in adding further stress to our bodies from an inappropriate diet. So you might find this information helpful. Of course, if you aleady know of specific food allergies, you will have to take those into consideration when you plan your food storage.

Basically, if you provide an appropriate, whole foods diet of balanced carbohydrate/protein/fat intake, (with an occasional treat just for fun), you will probably be assured of adequate nutrition from your storage plan, especially if you are careful to include some live foods every day, and take high-quality, complete vitamin and mineral supplements. In the section on Nutritious Supplements below, I'll include some interesting foods that I've found that can boost your nutritional intake and that are delicious and fun to eat.

DETERMINING CALORIE REQUIREMENTS

In order to begin planning your food program, you'll need to determine how many calories per day to provide for each person. This is the criteria that many food storage programs use in their sales material, so you will need this figure. Here's how to estimate calories needed for a normal diet:

1) Take your actual/ideal weight and for each pound, figure:

   If you're under 45, women - 10 calories, men - 11 calories.
   If you're over 45, women - 9 calories, men - 10 calories.

   This represents your basic caloric needs.

2) Then take this figure and add 1/2 that number of calories to represent your daily activity, including moderate exercise. Add 3/4 if you're vigorously active or working under very physically stressful conditions.

3) This figure is your ideal normal daily caloric intake.

4) If you wish to lose weight, you can subtract 500 calories per day, but don't go below 1600 calories per day for a man or teenage boy, 1200 for a woman, or 1400 for an adolescent girl.

FOOD STORAGE QUANTITY REQUIREMENTS - (How Much To Store)

Before you begin calculating the amount of food to store for your family, you might want to get some helpful software:

CATALOG CODE **ITEM**

PP **FOODSTOR PLUS SOFTWARE** - Select recipes, enter number of months for which you wish to prepare, and SOFTWARE calculates ingredient amounts you will need; then enter what products you have on hand, and print out a shopping list - includes nutrition information - $15 intro. special.

(*Also, see the Links Appendix for another source of food storage software.*)

The following information is for ***the food storage requirements for an adult male for one year, consuming approximately 2500 calories a day.*** To figure amounts for other members of your family:

For an adult female, mulitply the weight of food by .75.
For children: ages 1-3, multiply by .3.
For ages 4-6, by .5.
For ages 7-9, by .75.

(Teenagers are considered adults when figuring food requirements.)

Simply figure the amounts needed for each member of your family and add them together to get the total amount of each food to store.

The weights given here are for foods (except oils and sugars) that are dehydrated dry weights from storage food plans, so if you're storing regular canned foods, you'll have to figure what the amount of dry vegetables and fruits you need would weigh if reconstituted with water. Talk to the folks at the food prepacking houses for this information.

1) **GRAINS - 300 lbs.** - This can include whole grains, rolled grains such as oatmeal, flours, pasta and noodles, popcorn, and grains stored for grinding into flours, such as "dent" (flour) corn for tortillas.

2) **BEANS & LEGUMES - 75 lbs. dry weight** - These include the many varieties of beans, sprouting beans and seeds, and legumes, such as split peas, and the important low-fat, high-protein soy beans.

3) **MILK AND DAIRY PRODUCTS (or substitutes) - 40-50 lbs.** - Dried milk powder can be reconstituted for drinking or cooking, or making cottage, cream or hard cheeses (get the "low heat spray-process fortified milk). Cheese and other dairy powders are available. Dehydrated whole eggs are the best-tasting egg product (*see Chapter 5 - Food Preservation, for information on preserving whole fresh eggs*). For those allergic to dairy, non-dairy milk products such as dried soy or

tofu milk are available at natural food stores.

4) **MEATS OR MEAT SUBSTITUTES - 10-20 lbs.** - Freeze dried meats and dehydrated soy meats weigh very little, so this can be a lot of meat! It tastes best used as filler in stews and soups, and to flavor bean and grain dishes. Fresh tofu packed in the sterile boxes will last for about a year, as will canned meats.

5) **FRUITS AND VEGETABLES - 10-30 lbs.(dry weight)** - Almost any vegetable or fruit can be freeze-dried, and most fruits are tastiest this way. Most vegetables are less expensive prepared by regular dehydration, rather than freeze-drying, and there's a wide variety available. You can also get a tomato powder and many vegetable blends for soups and stews.

6) **FATS AND OILS - 20-30 lbs.** - This category includes powdered butter, margerine and shortening, cooking oil, regular shortening, nut butters, and olive or other good vegetable oil.

7) **SWEETENERS - 60 lbs.** - This includes white sugar, honey, maple syrup, molasses, hard candy, jellies and jams. You can also find dried cane and date sugars at a natural food store.

8) **SPROUTING SEEDS - 20 lbs.** - Many seeds can be sprouted, including almost any grain, bean or legume. Alfalfa, lentils, and mung beans are the most common, but many others are equally delicious. (*See Chapter 5 - Food Production.*)

9) **MISCELLANEOUS FOODS - (weight varies)** - These include just about anything else you usually eat, inluding condiments, herbs, spices, seasoning sauces and mixes, cocoa and chocolate syrup, drink mixes, vitamins and protein powders, other cooking aids - baking powder, etc.

Once you determine the amount of food your family will need for the time period you've decided to prepare for, you can make your shopping lists and begin purchasing. *Remember, it's best to purchase any prepacked foods first, then bulk foods from warehouses, and then grocery items, as shortages will probably show up in that order.* Preserving any of your foods yourself will depend on the season the foods are available and your time.

NUTRITIOUS SUPPLEMENTS

Many of us think that the only way to get extra nutrition is via some kind of suppplement, usually the standard vitamin/mineral tablets. But there is a host of other sources for boosting your nutrition that can be easily incorporated into your regular diet and cooking habits. Some consider these sources to be superior to taking artificial vitamin supplements, as they contain many nutrients in a synergistic form which the body can utilize more efficiently. Some of them can be found in the Natural Lifestyle catalog, or at any natural food store or warehouse. Here are some I've learned about and used successfully over the years:

1) **AMINO ACIDS (protein)**

a) ***SOY PROTEIN POWDER*** - This can be quite expensive, but you can also buy it in bulk from the wholesale natural food warehouses listed below. You can pay from about 20 cents for Guisto's Soy Protein Powder in bulk, to $4.50 for a "designer protein supplement" for an amount that will provide enough powder to add 50% of daily protein requirements for a 2000-calorie diet. So buying in bulk offers a considerable savings. Some of these so-called nutritional products also include powdered milk, so be careful to read the labels if you're dairy-intolerant.

b) ***LIQUID AMINOS*** - Ask for Bragg's Liquid Aminos at any natural food store. This is a dark, tasty, bouillon-like liquid that you can use to season any soup, grain, or bean dish. It's extracted from soybeans and is not fermented. It's Kosher, and has no preservatives, coloring agents, alcohol or chemicals. It's said to contain 16 amino acids, and be a healthy, low-salt (5% sodium) substitute for soy sauce. It comes in pints for about $7 and quarts for about $11 (at my local store). It takes just a dash for flavor, and lasts a long time. It stores well unrefrigerated for several years. Add it to any main dish that needs salt; it adds extra nutrition and the flavor that salt would usually provide. (Hint: for a delicious snack, soak raw pumpkin seeds overnight in Bragg's and drain. Lightly toast in skillet or small toaster oven until seeds dry, get browned and some pop. Everyone loves these crunchy tidbits to eat out of hand or on salads, etc., and they're full of nutrition.)

NL c) ***MISO*** - This dark, salty, very intensely-flavored paste is a product of centuries of oriental food-science and has some amazing properties. It's made from aged, fermented soy-beans, and it provides not only predigested protein, but also essential digestive enzymes It's said to be useful in binding to and leaching toxic substances out of the body, and has many other healing properties. If you think that a diet rich in fibrous grains and vegetables might cause you digestive upset, a small amount of miso added to these dishes can help you deal with it. There have been many cases of children and the elderly, too ill to eat anything else, who could manage to digest a nutritious broth of miso.

There are many variations of miso which depend on the added ingredients such as wheat, barley, or rice, and which impart subtle differences in taste and texture. The making of miso is as much an art in Japan (and recently in America) as wine-making is in France. Try to get the naturally-aged product, as there are some lower-quality commercial varieties made with white rice and not aged properly. Since it's already fermented, miso stores well if simply kept covered, dark, and minimally cool.

Use miso dissolved in water as a bouillon and added to any main dish, or heated gently for a soup or warm drink. You can also get a dehydrated miso soup that is very tasty. A warm cup of miso with rice or barley in it provides a high-protein, easily digestable, lowfat snack or meal, even in the morning as breakfast. Never boil miso, as that kills the valuable enzymes; always add it after the dish to be seasoned has cooled a bit. Miso can be found at any natural food store and at many regular groceries.

NL d) ***DRIED TOFU*** - Although subjected to much derision as tasting like "unflavored styrofoam", this high-protein (53%), low-fat, long-storage product will absorb the flavors of whatever it is added to. It makes a nutritional addition to soups, stews, bean and grain dishes, and can be flavored by soaking in a marinade of your choice and drained before cooking.

e) ***RED STAR NUTRITIONAL YEAST*** - This is not a baking yeast, but a delicious, flaky, cheesy-tasting food that provides protein and valuable B vitamins. It stores well in a tightly closed container, and can be sprinkled on just about anything, from salads, to soups, to popcorn (especially tasty). It's readily available at any natural foods store. There are other brands available, but I've never found any others to equal the taste of the Red Star brand.

NL f) ***ALGAE*** - Before you get queasy at the thought of eating pond scum, know that dried forms of this highly nutritious green food has been used for centuries in Africa and South America, NASA has considered using it as an ideal food to grow on space stations, and Olympic champions swear by it. Now it's gaining popularity in America for good reasons: it is nearly 65% protein, (as opposed to about 20% in beef) and contains significant amounts of vitamins and minerals, phytochemicals (the stuff you get from raw greens and vegetables), and antioxidants, all necessary for good health.

There are three basic kinds of algae - Spirulina and blue-green algae are similar in nutritional and physical content and have cell walls that are easily broken down in digestion. They are said to have anti-viral, anti-cancer, and immune-stimulating properties, and to feed the vital friendly intestinal bacteria. These algae are largely produced in the U.S., (grown in special lakes, and also harvested wild), and are widely available at natural food stores and catalogs. Chlorella, also a micro algae, is highly nutritious, but has indigestible cell walls like green grasses, and must be preprocessed before ingestion. It is mainly produced outside the U.S. and imported.

Nutritionists tell us that we need a minimum of 3-5 servings per day of fresh fruits and vegetables to stay healthy, yet how many of us get that now, and what are the chances of our getting that under crisis conditions? Green algaes and the other grasses (wheatgrass and barley) offer a source of highly digestible vegetable nutrients in an easy-to-store form. Most are available in powders, capsules, and tablets in single form and mixtures, and provide a valuable addition to any storage food diet.

2) **MINERALS**

NL a) ***SEA VEGETABLES*** - "Seaweeds" are simple marine vegetables that have the advantage of absorbing and containing many valuable minerals and vitamins found in the sea. They rank second by weight to land vegetation in amounts of calcium and phosphorus, and first in magnesium, iron, iodine, and sodium. They also contain vitamins A, B1, B12, C, and E, as well as proteins, and easily digestible carbohydrates. A real power package! They are said to be significant in healing a wide variety of conditions, and have the added benefit of helping dissolve fat and mucous deposits in the body. In the intestines, they turn metallic elements into harmless salts that can be eliminated, and allow for better nutrient absorption. Overall, they are one of the best foods available.

They can be found in any natural food store and sometimes a regular grocery, and are usually sold dried in packages that will store well. After opening, store in a tightly closed container.There are many kinds, including the familiar kelp and dulse, that are available powdered in shakers to use at the table. There are many others with exotic names such as Arame, Wakame, Hiziki, etc., each with its own unique flavor. You might want to start with a milder variety such as Arame, if you decide to cook with it; simply crumble a small amount of the dried vegetable into your soup or stew. You'll soon find out how much is best for your taste. Sea vegetables have the added benefit of preventing flatulance when added to beans! They also impart a slightly salty flavor, but are usually unnoticable in a big pot of beans and grains. Some feel that they are an acquired taste, but it's worth it, because using even small amounts on your foods can impart a lot of extra nutrition.

b) ***MINERAL TEA*** - This is a process, used in exclusive European health spas for decades, that you can also do in your own kitchen. It is a tasty broth to use in place of any cooking water, for increased nutritional intake. Here's how you prepare it:

* Save any undamaged but unused portions of the vegetables that you prepare for salads or cooking. Store these in a zip-lock bag in your freezer. It doesn't take long to

fill up a large zip-lock bag if you make salads regularly.

* Use common sense when collecting the scraps; don't use anything that is the least bit moldy or rotten. But there are lots of vegetable parts that we normally throw away, from carrot and radish tops, to the ends of most vegetables, seeds and tops of peppers, any clean skins, and broccoli and cauliflower stems, (which also make great miso pickles when cut into small "carrot-stick" pieces, and stuck into a crock of miso for a few days).
* When you have collected a bag full, briefly rinse off the contents, chop up any large pieces, and put them into a large pot.
* Cover the contents with pure water, put a lid on the pot, bring it to a boil, stir a couple of times, turn off the heat, and let it steep covered, until cool. Strain and use instead of water in cooking.
* This process will extract the nutrients (especially minerals), from the scraps, adds delicious flavor to soups, grains, etc., and can be used in place of bouillion.

During the crisis when you'll likely be without refrigeration, and using stored foods, this process wouldn't be practical, but you might consider making it ahead of time, and storing it in the one or two-liter soda bottles in your freezer in addition to plain water. It's especially good used for miso soup with some sea vegetables added. If you're going to use water for cooking, it might as well be highly nutritious!

NATURAL FOOD WAREHOUSES

One of your best sources for good food in bulk at reasonable prices are the large, natural food, wholesale warehouses. These are scattered around the U.S. and usually have delivery routes through several states. These warehouses developed to serve the growing numbers of retail natural food stores and cooperatives, but anyone can buy from them if you meet their minimum order requirements, which can be rather high for delivered orders. To meet this minimum, people have joined together into buying clubs which split up large orders among their members. If you wish to join a buying club in your area, get the name of a local contact person from the warehouse. Or, if you think you'll have an order large enough to meet the warehouse's minimum, you can see if they will deliver your order to a natural food store nearby, or along with an order for a local buying club, where you can pick it up. They will usually work with you to see that you get the food. However, some will not deliver unless you set up an account (usually free) and order regularly. If this is the case, you will have to pickup the order at the warehouse. Pickup orders usually have a much lower minimum requirement, so, if you live within driving distance, it would be worth it to drive to the warehouse to get the order yourself. Before you place an order, call the warehouse near you and talk to their routing coordinator to determine if they deliver near your location, and what their specific ordering requirements are.

Also, get a catalog, and ask for any product information they can provide. Some warehouses have books or pamphlets that explain their products in detail. These are worth studying in order to learn about the products and prices. Call their customer service department if you have any questions about products.

These warehouses are great sources for inexpensive bulk grains, legumes, herbs, spices, soup mixes, TVP, biodegradable washing and cleaning soaps, natural personal care items, and a host of other foods and products. If you know of a warehouse that I've missed, please email me with the address and phone number. Here are the ones I've located so far:

AZURE STANDARD - 79709 Dufur Valley Rd., Dufur, OR 97021
541-467-2230 (orders)
Minimum order - $300 delivery, also will ship via UPS.
States served: AK,(northern)CA,HI,ID,MT,(western)ND,OR,WA

BLOOMING PRAIRIE - 2340 Heinz Rd., Iowa City, IA 52240
319-337-6448 800-323-2131 (orders)
At present, they discourage single orders, but they will deliver for a regular customer for $750 minimum, or you can pickup for $250.
States served: IA,IL,IN,KS,MI(lower penninsula),MN,MO,NE,SD,WI,WY

BLOOMING PRAIRIE NATUAL FOODS - 510 Kasota Ave., SE, Minneapolis, MN 55414
612-378-9774 800-328-8241 (orders)
See delivery requirements above.
States served: (parts of)ND,MN,WI,MI(upper penninsula)

FEDERATION OF OHIO RIVER CO-OPS (FORC) - 320 Outer Belt St., Ste. E, Columbus OH 43213 614-861-2446 888-936-9648 (orders)
Minimum order: $600 delivered on-route, $200 drop-off.
States served: DC,GA,IN,KY,MD,MI,NC,OH,PA,SC,VA,WV

GENESEE FOODS - RD 2, Box 105, Genesee, PA 16923
814-228-3200 800-445-0094 (orders)
Minimum order: $300 delivered, but will also ship UPS with no minimum.
States served: DE,MD,NJ,NY,OH,PA

HUDSON VALLEY FOODS - 6 Noxon, Poughkeepsie, NY 12603
914-473-5400 Must order at least once per year.
Minimum order: $500 delivered, $25 pickup (not $250).
States served: NY,NJ,(western)CT,(northeast)PA

MOUNTAIN PEOPLE'S WAREHOUSE - 12745 Earhart Ave., Auburn, CA 95602
800-679-6733 800-679-6733 (orders)
Minimum order: $500 on-route delivery, $200 warehouse pickup.
States served: AK,AZ,CA,CO,HI,ID,MT,NM,NV,OR,UT,WA,WY and Mexico.

MOUNTAIN PEOPLE'S NORTHWEST - 4005 Sixth Ave. So., Seattle, WA 98108
800-336-8872 (orders)
Minimum order: $500 delivered, $150 pickup.
States served: AK,WA,(western)OR,(northern)ID,MT

NISHEMENY VALLEY NATURAL FOODS - 5 Louise Dr., Ivyland, PA 18974
215-443-5545 800-490-0044 (orders)
Minimum order: Rates vary depending on location, but range from $250-$450+.
States served: CT,DE,DC,NJ,NY,PA,VA(northern)
Also call to receive their retail catalog, "Good Eats".

NORTHEAST COOPERATIVES - 49 Bennett Dr., Brattleboro, VT 05304
802-257-5856 800-334-9939 (orders)
Minimum order: $500 for orders every 4 weeks, $700 one-time pickup.
States served: CT,MA,ME,NH,NY,RI,VT

NORTHFARM COOPERATIVE - 204 Regas Rd., Madison WI 53714
608-241-2667 800-236-5880 (orders)
Minimun order: $500 on-route delivery, $100 drop-off.
States served: IA,IL,IN,KY,MT,MI,MN,MO,MT,ND,OH,SD,WY

OZARK COOPERATIVE WAREHOUSE - P.O. Box 1528, Fayetteville, AR 72702
501-521-4920 800-967-2667 (orders)
Ask for Jennifer for information on buying clubs, and Martha for truck routes. Currently, they will ship a one-time order if you can wait until there is room on a truck, or if you pay for commercial shipping they will give you a 5% shipping allowance. Minimum order: on-route delivery - $300, order drop-off on existing route - $500.
States served: AR,AL,FL,GA,LA,KS,MO,MS,OK,TN,TX.

TUSCON CO-OP WAREHOUSE - 350 S. Toole, Tuscon, AZ 85701
520-884-9951 800-350-2667 (orders)
Minimum order: $250
States served: AZ,CA,CO,NM,NV,UT,TX

APPENDIX B
INTERNET LINKS

I recently saw some statistics stating that *currently, there are over a quarter of a million web-sites devoted to Year 2000 issues!* Obviously, I can list only a fraction of these below. But these are some that will take you to many others via their rich links pages, so you should be able to locate just about anything you desire, beginning here. I don't have the site titles in every case, so I'll just give the address under each heading. Sites come a go a lot, and I will periodically check these adresses, but if you find any that don't work, please let me know via mail, email, (on the Website at www.yourark.com) or by leaving a message at 888-240-9074.

I'll list what I call the "master sites" first, those with lots of pages about - and links to - all aspects of the Y2K. Order up a pizza, get comfy and happy surfing!

GENERAL Y2K INFORMATION

If you're new to the Y2K, start with these sites. They will lead you to all the rest...

www.garynorth.com - *Extensive information on Y2K.*
www.y2ktimebomb.com - *Westergaard's Webzine - many Y2K articles.*
www.prepare4y2k.com - *Just what it says...lots of info. and links.*
www.y2koncepts.com - *Includes the Millinneum Adventure Game, plus a great list of questions...*
www.y2kchaos.com - *One of the biggest and best.*
www.erols.com/steve451/impact.htm - *Dealing With the Y2k Problem.*
www.year2000.com/y2klinks.html - *Lotsa links!*
www.csis.org/html/y2ktran.html - *Center for Strategic and International Studies - transcript of talks on June 2, 1998 by Ed Yardini, Senator Bennett, etc.*

BOOKS

Where to order online for many books mentioned in the text.

www.amazon.com
www.y2knews.com/library.htm

BUSINESS

www.webring.org/cgi-bin/webring?ring=y2kring&list - *A source for many Y2K business sites.*
www.y2k.com - *Legal and management information about Y2K.*
www.year2000.com - *Peter deJager's site - many biz links.*

ENERGY AND UTILITIES

www.euy2k.com - *Extensive links to utility and general subjects - run by a*

veteran in the electric utility industry.
www.chinadiesel.com - *Info about alternative energy and products - generators, diesel motors, etc.*
www.northern-online.com - *The catalog with lots of good generators and other tools.*
www.y2ksurvival.com - *Twisted Oak Energy Systems - extensive alternative energy ideas.*
www./ext.vt.edu/pubs/disaster/490-303490-303.html - *Information on how to select electric generators.*

FINANCE AND ECONOMICS

www.yardeni.com - *Ed Yardeni's page - one of world's top economists.*
www.buycoin.com - *Swiss America coin dealers.*

FIRST AID AND HEALTH

www.redcross.org/disaster/safety/tips.html - *Red Cross disaster planning.*
www.redcross.com - *Red Cross general info.*
millenia-bcs.com/prep.htm#fa - *List of First Aid supplies.*
www.millinneum_ark.net/News_Files/LTAH_First_Aid(8).html - *Another supplies list.*
www.peaceofmindessentials.com - *Online source for homeopathics and herbs.*

FOOD SUPPLIES AND STORAGE

Webpages of some of the food storage companies mentioned in the catalogs:

1.icserv.net/D100001/X100043/fscalc.html - *Working calculator for amount of basic foods to store for your family for one year.*
www.revelar.com/fsp.html - *Food storage software.*
www.millennium-ark.net/News_Files/LTAH_Food_Store(5).html - *Food Storage information and info. on software.*
www.millennium-ark.net/News_Files/Disasters/storable_food.html - *Links to most sites listed below.*
www.arkinstitute.com - *Read "6 June, 98" article on Terminator Gene...*
www.alpine aire.com - *Alpine Aire Foods.*
web2.airmail.net/foodstr2/ - *Best Prices Storable Food.*
www.beprepared.com - *Provident Pantry Foods (also Mountain House).*
www.hrvst.com - *Harvest Foods.*
www.shopsite.com/millennium/aisle5.html - *Millennium Foods.*
www.ofd.com/mh/index.html - *Mountain House Foods.*
www.nitro-pak.com - *Nitro-Pak Foods (including Mountain House).*
www.cococo.net/rmr - *Ready Made Resources Foods.*
www.thecornucopia.com/rrf.home.html - *Ready Reserve Foods.*

www.waltonfeed.com - *Walton Feed Food Storage.*
www.prepare4y2k.com/980726.htm - *Good forum for general Y2K information.*

GARDENING

www.garden.org - *The National Gardening Association's site.*
//communitygarden.org - *A nonprofit site for those without their own land who can do community gardens.*
//gardening.com - *A searchable directory on all gardening subjects.*
www.tpoint.net/neighbor - *Over 2,000 links to home-gardening web sites, in 60 categories.*
//classifieds.yahoo.com/gardening.html - *Gardening classifieds.*
www.gardenguides.com - *Beautiful site with searchable categories on all gardening subjects.*

HOMESCHOOLING

www.y2kchaos.com/s35p309.htm

NEWS UPDATES, PRESS CLIPPINGS, ARTICLES

Check these every day or two and keep up with the latest thinking on the Y2K...they are usually updated daily and contain news and articles from worldwide media.

www.y2klinks.com/garynorth/latest.htm - *Gary North's latest Y2K news, updated daily.*
ourworld.compuserve.com/homepages/roleigh_martin/w9798idx.htm - *Index to Late-Breaking Year 2000 News Items.*
www.techweb.com/wire/technews/year2000.html - *Tech info.*
www.year2000.com/y2karticles.html - *Up-to-date news articles.*
www.y2knews.com
www.y2k.net.com/Headlines

PREPAREDNESS

This list includes many sites with varied information, all related to preparedness, including some of the catalogs mentioned in the book.

www.Millennium-ark.net/News_Files/Disasters/Pet_Links.html - *Lots of info. about our furry and feathered friends and their needs...*
www.Millennium-ark.net/News_Files/Disasters/Prep_Products.html - *This link will lead you to most of those merchants listed below and more!*
millinnia-bcs.com -*The Cassandra Project, well-respected site for all aspects of preparedness.*
www.baproducts.com - *Site for B&A Products catalog.*
www.dnet.net/~basics - *Back to Basics site, good self-reliance links.*
www.campmor.com - *Site for the Campmor catalog.*

www.beprepared.com/Home.html - *Site for Emergency Essentials.*
www.fema.gov/emi/crslist.htm - *FEMA disaster preparedness site.*
www.fema.gov/fema/wnlsft.htm - *FEMA winter preparedness site.*
www.wwmagic.com/haphov - *Site for Happy Hovel products.*
www.smallfarm.com/kanswind - *Site for Kansas Wind products.*
www.lehmans.com - *Site for Lehman's non-electric catalog.*
www.majorsurplusnsurvival.com - *Site for Major Surplus catalog.*
www.mapleleafinc.com - *Site for Maple Leaf Inc. products.*
www.nitro-pak.com - *Site for Nitro-Pak catalog.*
www.northern-online.com - *Site for Northern catalog.*
www.enol.com~preplus - *Site for Preparedness Plus products.*
www.cococo.net/rmr/ - *Site for Ready Made Resources.*
www.realgoods.com - *Site for Real Goods products.*
www.zyz.com/survivalcenter - *Site for Survival Center catalog.*
www.teleport.com/~dany/mill/index.htm - *Online y2k products, not found in a printed catalog.*
www.avillagesquare.com/market/emprep.html - *Preparedness supplies.*

APPENDIX C
PREPARING FOR PETS

If you have pets or other animals, don't forget your furry and feathered friends in your storage program! Determine how much food they eat each week, and be sure to store enough food for least a year. If this seems like a lot, realize that *it's not likely the manufacture and distribution of pet foods will be considered a national priority in case of a severe crisis.* And most of our domesticated pets simply can't forage for themselves anymore. You will have to provide it.

Canned food will last longer than most dry packaged food, but you could extend the storage life of the various kibbles by putting it (still in the store packages) in metal garbage cans with the oxygen absorbers (OAPs) described in Chapter 5 - Food Preservation. Then only open them as needed, so they don't spoil as quickly. Most are laced with a lot of preservatives, anyway. You'll have to be even more careful if you buy petfood without such additives. Only one catalog that I found offered prepacked storage pet food:

CATALOG CODE	ITEM
SU	1) Dog food packed in 6-gallon poly buckets, contains no chemicals or preservatives, in two flavors, Chicken & Rice, and Lamb & Rice - $26.
	2) ***FLINT RIVER RANCH PET FOODS*** - A source for breeder-preferred, highest quality all natural, whole foods for your dog or cat - no animal "parts" or fillers, artificial colors, flavors, or chemical preservatives - not prepacked. Call for information packet and free samples - 888-240-9074 (leave message).

You can stretch your food stores by feeding pets mostly dry food and occasionally adding some canned petfood meat for flavor and nutrition. Add sprouts and greens to their food, as they will need vitamins and enzymes, also. If you run out of stored food, there are recipes in several of the pet books listed below, that use standard household ingredients, such as grain flours, oils, eggs, etc. This probably wouldn't suffice for long for a cat because cats need much more meat and fat in their diet than dogs. However, they are more willing to go out and catch it, if they can! If they can't, it's up to you to supply it. If you live in a rural area and can fish, hunt or if you have chickens for eggs, you can supply your pets with these foods.

I buy inexpensive canned mackerel and salmon for my own table and for my cats as an occasional treat; they love it, the bones supply lots of minerals, and we can both eat it! And if you have birds, remember, in a pinch, depending on the species, they can also eat your stored peanut butter, millet and sunflower seeds...they're good for both of you.

And, don't forget to store water for your pets, if you live where they can't get their own outside. The amounts to store would depend largely on the size and activity level of your pet, but it's been suggested that you aside two quarts to one gallon per day for dogs, and about a pint to one quart for cats. If you obtain water from outside your home that you suspect is badly contaminated, especially with chemicals, filter it for your pets, also. If your pet is outside, check regularly to be sure that their water is unfrozen and drinkable. They can't go very long without water, either.

If your cats must stay inside, you'll also have to store enough litter to provide for their needs, although if you save old newspapers and shred them fine enough, they can be persuaded to use that in a pinch! If you have a composting toilet that uses sawdust or peatmoss, (*see Chapter 8 - Sanitation And Cleaning*), you can use either for the cats if you run out of litter. Dispose of the litter the same way that you dispose of other waste - seal it in plastic bags until sanitation pickups resume, or bury it in the yard. Don't add it to a compost pile, as it can contain unhealthy organisms. Since it will be winter in most locations, be sure your pet has a warm place to sleep or shelter from the weather. They get cold, too.

CATALOG CODE	BOOKS ABOUT PETS
SU	***"Cat First Aid"*** - A guide to emergency treatment and health care - $10.
SU	***"Complete Herbal Handbook for Dogs and Cats"*** - Alternative foods and treatments for your pets - $13.
SU	***"Dr. Pitcairn's Complete Guide to Natural Health For Dogs and Cats"*** - Includes natural remedies and home-made healthy recipes for dog and cat food - highly recommended! - $17.

You might want to prepare a first aid kit for your pet because they can get sick and have accidents too. Ask your veterinarian for his/her suggestions. Homeopathic remedies, *(mentioned in Chapter 10, First Aid and Health)* work great on pets, too, and are totally harmless. They could be a lifesaver if your vet is unavailable.

Many people feel as strongly about their pets as about any other members of their family, so don't forget to include them in your Y2K preparations!

If you have larger stock animals, you will have to begin early to stock up on feed and other necessities. Be sure to lay in a sufficient store of hay and other cold weather foods for your animals. If their water comes from a well, be sure there is a way to pump it if the electricity goes out. If your barns or other animal housing are heated with propane or natural gas, be sure that your tanks are full before winter.

APPENDIX D
SUPPLY CATALOGS / OTHER RESOURCES

The following list of catalogs and resources is not presented as being complete. These are the ones that sent me their material on request, but there are probably others out there that I don't know about. If you find a good one, please mail or email me their information (via the form on the Order Page at our Website: www.yourark.com), and I'll include it in future updates. In each case, I've given all the information I have about the catalogs and the companies behind them. Most have an 800 number that you can call to order the catalog or products. Expect to pay a few dollars for some of the catalogs - they're worth it. Call to get the current price and availability of any catalog, as they are subject to change.***The reference code for each catalog - that links it to the products listed in the text - is on the left margin; for example, the in first entry below: "BA" just to the left of the catalog name - " B & A Products".*** (The publications without a catalog code are not keyed to any particular products in the text.)

Please note that several of the catalogs have a distinctly religious/philosophical tone; I am not promoting any personal belief system, and include them only because of the products that they carry. Several catalogs are not well organized, but carry a lot of useful products, and some are very helpful to read (NP), contain product information, and many good hints. If a new edition of a catalog no longer offers a product reviewed in this book, there can be several reasons: one, many suppliers rotate their inventories in their catalogs, and they still may carry the item. Two, since demand is expected to exceed supply as we draw nearer to the Y2K deadline, some items may have been deleted from catalogs because they are no longer available. Check with the supplier before you place an order.

Be aware that prices on certain products can vary widely, sometimes as much as double; so if you're on a budget, you may want to get most of these catalogs and do some comparison shopping. Unfortunately, no one catalog seems to be consistently less expensive on everything.

NOTE: Catalogs are listed twice: first by category (below), and then alphabetically (beginning on page 217), for quick reference, and no special recommendation is implied. Also check Appendix B - Internet Links, for Website information on many of these companies.

CATALOGS LISTED BY SUBJECT

GENERAL PREPAREDNESS PRODUCTS

With the exception of several unique items in other brochures and catalogs, these catalogs offer the best general collection of appropriate products for the Y2K crisis that I've seen:

BA ***B&A PRODUCTS*** - Rt.1, Box 100, Bunch, OK 74931-9705
918-696-5998 (office), 918-696-5999 (fax), Byron@baproducts.com (email)
http://www.baproducts.com (Website)

Emergency preparedness and first aid kits, food, solar products, water filters, stoves, books, and more.

CF ***CHRISTIAN FAMILY RESOURCES*** - P.O. Box 405, Kit Carson, CO 80825
719-962-3228 (phone-fax) Hours 1-5 p.m MST, Mon.-Fri.

A small, family-owned business that carries storage food, water and food preparation supplies, electronic equipment, books, home schooling materials, and more. Ask for their food storage bro chure when you order this catalog.

EE ***EMERGENCY ESSENTIALS*** - 165 S. Mountain Way Dr., Orem, UT 84058-5119
800-999-1863 (order phone) Mon.-Fri. 9-6, Sat. 9-5 MT,
http://www.beprepared.com (Website) (*Also see Provident Pantry catalog*)

This small catalog focuses on survival products, including food, water and water filters, sanitation, first aid, stoves, etc.

MA ***MAJOR ARMY/NAVY SURPLUS*** - 435 Alondra Bl., Gardena, CA 90248
800-441-8855(order phone), Mon.-Fri. 9-6, Sat. 9-5, Sun 11-5, PT,
310-324-8855(office phone), 310-324-6909 (fax) *Ask for their new Disaster Preparedness catalog.*

Storage food, stoves, lanterns, water containers, water filters, first aid, sanitation supplies, generators, survival gear. Good prices.

NP ***NITRO-PAK PREPAREDNESS CENTER*** - 151 N. Main St., Heber, UT 84032-1647
800-866-4876 (order phone) Mon.-Fri. 8-6, Sat. 9-3 MT,
888-648-7672 (24-hour order fax) or http://www.nitro-pak.com (Website)

Probably the most informative catalog available, well-organized, good prices. Carries wide selection of emergency and survival supplies, including food.

PP ***PROVIDENT PANTRY*** - (from Emergency Essentials - see above)
165 S. Mountain Way, Orem, UT 84058-5119
800-999-1863 (order phone) Mon.-Fri. 9-6, Sat. 9-5 MT

This small food storage catalog also carries some interesting food preparation and storage utensils - order with the EE catalog above).

RM ***READY-MADE RESOURCES*** - 125 County Rd. 585, Englewood, TN 37329
800-627-3809 (order phone), Mon.-Fri. 9-9 ET, 423-746-9814 (fax),
robert@avicom.net(email)

A catalog for the serious survivor. Large first aid, medical supplies, storage food, and book section, plus major equipment for large groups, in addition to most other survival supplies. They also deal in coins and precious metals.

SC ***SAFETY CENTRAL*** - 1100 W. El Camino Real, Mountain View, CA 94040
800-782-5396 (order phone) 650-965-3509 (customer service), Mon.-Fri. 10-7, Sat.-Sun. 10-6 PT, 800-552-8004 (24-hour order fax)

A very complete catalog of emergency survival supplies. They have many unique products for lighting, heating, cooking, first aid, and a few things that can't be found elsewhere.

SA ***SAM ANDY EMERGENCY SUPPLIES*** - P.O. Box 141741, Irving, TX 75014
800-331-0358 (order phone) 24-hours/7 days.

Another small but very focused catalog, with supplies similar to EE above, and specializing in their own storage food items and books.

SU ***SURVIVAL CENTER*** - P.O. Box 234, McKenna, WA 98558
800-321-2900 (order phone), Mon.-Fri. 10-6 PT, 360-458-6778 (office phone), 360-458-6868 (fax), sales@survivalcenter.com (email)
http://www.zyz.com/survivalcenter (Website)

The basics of survival, water filters, food storage, first aid kits, solar products, and lots of helpful how-to books.

SS ***SURVIVAL SUPPLY CO.*** - P.O. Box 4582, Couer d'Alene, ID 83815
208-765-6201 (phone), 208-765-4295 (fax), SURSUPCO@Nidlink.Com (email)
http://www.nidlink.com/~sursupco (Website)

Small catalog containing emergency food, stoves, lanterns, water carriers, first aid kits, books, and most other necessities. Good prices.

CAMPING SUPPLIES

CM ***CAMPMOR, INC.*** - P.O. Box 700-Q, Saddle River, NJ 07458-0700
800-525-4784 (customer service) Mon.-Fri. 8 am-9:30 pm, Sat. 8-6,ET
800-226-7667 (order phone) Mon.-Fri. 8am.-midnight, Sat. 8-6 ET,
800-230-2153 (24-hour order fax), info@campmor.com (email),
http://www.campmor.com (Website)

Just about everything for the serious camper. For Y2K, lots of sleeping bags, heaters, lanterns, cookstoves, water filters, sanitation, personal care.

GENERAL MERCHANDISE

These catalogs serve the Amish and similar communities, and are becoming very popular with the general public, as well. They have many old-timey products that serve a non-electric lifestyle, and provide fascinating reading, as well as some supplies not available elsewhere. Don't miss these!

CG ***CUMBERLAND GENERAL STORE*** - #1 Highway 68, Crossville, TN 38555
800-334-4640 (order phone) Mon.-Sat. 8:30-4:40 CT,
615-456-1211 (24-hour order fax).

Supplies for the simple life - everything from woodstoves to well pumps, oil lamps to oak water barrels. It'll take you back to another century. Many old-timey and useful items.

LE ***LEHMAN'S NON-ELECTRIC CATALOG*** - P.O. Box 321, Kidron, OH 44636
330-857-5757 (order phone) Mon-Sat. 7am-10pm ET, 330-857-5785
(24-hour order fax), GetLehmans@aol.com (email),
http://www.lehmans.com (Website)

The classic catalog for folks living the simple life! A large inventory of woodstoves, lamps, well supplies and water storage, composting toilets, clothes washers, and other fascinating products.

MISCELLANEOUS CATALOGS

These catalogs contain many products not applicable to the Y2K, but they also offer a couple of items not found in the above catalogs that you might want to consider.

HM ***HARMONY*** (Formerly known as Seventh Generation) - 360 Interlocken Blvd.
Suite 300, Broomfield, CO 80021
800-869-3448 (customer service) Mon.-Fri. 9-5 ET
800-869-3446 (order phone) 9am-10pm, Sat. 10-5, Sun. 12-5 ET,
800-456-1139 (order fax)

Rechargable Nicad batteries, sanitary wipes, environmentally friendly cleaning products and papers, hand-crank clothes washer, a nifty Rainsaver (covered water cistern), and lots more.

IM ***IMPROVEMENTS*** - Hanover, PA 17333-0084
800-642-2112 (order phone) 800-757-9997 (fax)
www.improvementscatalog.com (Website)

Packed full of interesting and helpful gadgets to make life easier - health, personal care, cooking, household, fireplace accessories etc. Several handy items for Y2K.

LF ***LIFESTYLE FASCINATION*** - P.O. Box 3023, Lakewood, NJ 08701-8123
800-669-0987 (order phone), 732-364-4448 (fax) both 24-hours/7 days,
732-364-5777 (office phone), http://www.lifestylefascination.com (Website)

This catalog carries the Starlight no-battery flashlight, and the Myotron for self-defense, among many other fascinating products.

NL ***NATURAL LIFESTYLE*** - 16 Lookout Dr., Asheville, NC 28804-3330
800-752-2775 (order phone Mon.-Fri. 8:30-6:00 ET,
828-252-3386 (24-hour fax), naturally@mindspring.com (email)
www.natural-lifestyle.com (Website)

A catalog devoted to the natural and Macrobiotic lifestyle and diet. Many unusual and healthful foods, cooking utensils, personal care items, clothes and books.

NO ***NORTHERN*** - P.O. Box 1499, Burnsville, MN 55337-0499
800-533-5545 (order phone), 612-894-0083 (fax) both 24-hours/7 days,

Specializes in a large selection of tools, camping equipment, also good selection of generators, solar chargers, chainsaws, cookstoves, etc.

RG ***REAL GOODS*** - 555 Leslie St., Ukiah, CA 95482-5576
800-762-7325 (order phone), 800-508-2342 (order fax) Mon.-Fri. 6am-8pm,
Sat. 8-6 PT, realgood@realgoods.com (email),
http://www.realgoods.com (Website) 707-468-9292 x2160 (overseas orders)

Solar oven, solar shower, rechargable batteries, and a host of other neat, non-survival items for ecological living.

SPECIALTY CATALOGS/BROCHURES/RESOURCES

BW ***BACKWOODS SOLAR ELECTRIC SYSTEMS*** - 8530 Rapid Lightening Creek Rd.
Sandpoint, ID 83864 208-263-4290 (phone), 8-5 PT 208-265-4788 (fax)
swilley@nidlink.com (email)

Many items for non-electric living, including solar panels, propane wall furnaces and heaters, and composting toilets.

KW ***KANSAS WIND POWER*** - 13569 214th Rd. Holton, KS 66436-8138
785-364-4407 (phone)

Small catalog devoted to the serious alternative energy user. Contains radios, heaters, composting toilets, books, and more.

NW ***NATURE'S WONDERLAND*** - Penn Herb Co., Ltd., 10601 Decatur Rd., Suite #2,
Philadelphia, PA 19154-3293
800-523-9971 (order phone), Mon.-Fri. 8:30-5 ET, 215-632-6100 (phone),
215-632-7945 (24-hour/day fax) orders@pennherb.com (email)
www.pennherb.com (Website)

Natural herbal supplements and products for internal and external use.

RS ***ROCKY GROVE SUN CO.*** - HC65, Box 280, Kingston, AR 72742
501-665-2457, info@rockygrove.com (email), www.rockygrove.com

(Website)

Complete catalog for solar and off-the-grid living - include "Y2K" solar electric system packages, well pumps, wind generators, composting toilets, refrigerators, and more.

CL ***STOREY'S HOW-TO BOOKS FOR COUNTRY LIVING*** - Schoolhouse Rd., Pownal, VT 05261. 800-441-5700 (order phone) 8am-10pm/7 days 413-664-4066 (fax)

Good prices on a fascinating array of self-sufficient-living books. Complete selection of the inexpensive "Country Wisdom" booklets.

VACU-DRY FOODS - 707-829-4600 - *Recommended low-moisture food packers (cans). Two outlets: Perma Pak - 800-594-8974 and 800-464-0094.*

MEDICAL SILVER

SV ***SILVER SOLUTIONS*** - P.O. Box 923, Forest Grove, OR 97116-0923 888-505-6005 (order phone), 503-359-5954 (office phone) 503-359-5518 (fax), www.silversolutions.com (Website)

Resource for obtaining supplies and equipment for making colloidal silver antibiotic solution. Free article available.

CS ***CS PRO SYSTEMS*** - Rt. 7, Box 510GG, San Antonio, TX 78264 888-710-2773 (order phone) www.csprosystems.com (Website)

Another resource for colloidal silver generators and AC Colloidal Silver Solution, plus steam distillers.

GARDENING SUPPLY

There are hundreds of seed catalogs available through any gardening magazine, but you may not have heard of the catalogs listed here:

ABUNDANT LIFE SEED FOUNDATION - P.O. Box 772, Port Townsend, WA 98368 360-385-7192 (order phone), 360-385-7455 (fax)

A non-profit organization dedicated to the preservation of genetic diversity. Services include an apprenticeship program, and a catalog of non-hybrid, "heirloom" seeds, plants, and books at good prices. Memberships available.

GARDENING FOR LIFE - P.O. Box 1001, Wixom, MI 48393 800-888-0010 (order phone)

Master Gardener Jerry Baker's catalog of his own and others' gardening products, tools, natural insecticides, fertilizers, pet products, etc.

GARDENS ALIVE! - 5100 Schenley Place, Lawrenceburg, IN 47025
812-537-8650 (order phone) 812-537-5108 (fax)

Wide variety of natural garden supplies - insecticides, fertilizers, biological pest control, lawn care, pet care, etc.

NITRON INDUSTRIES - P.O. Box 1447, Fayetteville, AR 72702
800-835-0123 (order phone) 501-587-0177 (fax) 8-5 Mon-Fri. CT

Internationally-known producer of a large line of high-quality organic garden products - fertilizers, soil amendments, etc. Call for catalog.

SEED SAVER'S EXCHANGE - 3076 North Winn Rd., Decorah, IA 52101
319-382-5990 (order phone), 319-382-5872 (fax)

A non-profit organization dedicated to the preservation of heirloom vegetables and fruits. Members receive three publications a year, which include many educational articles. Members may also purchase the Seed Savers Yearbook with access to over 11,000 varieties of seeds offered by members. SSE maintains a farm where over 18,000 heirloom vegetable varieties are being maintained and grown out.

PET PRODUCTS

THE NATURAL PET CARE CATALOG - 8050 Lake City Way, Seattle, WA 98115
800-962-8266 (order phone) 1-206-522-1667 (Canada & Int'l.)
206-522-1132 (fax) 10-5 Mon.-Fri. PST

Nice selection of natural pet remedies, supplements, foods, treats, bath aids, pest products, and more.

R. C. STEELE - 1989 Transit Way, Brockport, NY 14420-0910
800-872-3773 (order phone) (Wholesale - minimum order $50.)

A wholesale catalog with a wide selection of pet supplies - beds, travel cages, collars, toys, feeding bowls, fences, and things for the owner, too.

WHISKERS - 235 E. 9th St., New York, NY 10003
800-944-7537 (order phone) 718-423-3504 (fax) healthypet@msn.com (email) http//choicemall.com/whiskers (Website)

Fascinating supply of natural foods, supplements, herbs, homeopathic remedies, grooming aids, treats, pest products.

MAGAZINES

BACK HOME - 828-696-3838, (office), 800-992-2546 (orders), or backhome@ioa.com, (email) and www.BackHomeMagazine.com (Website).

Billed as "Your Hands-On Guide To Sustainable Living", with features on every aspect of downhome life, from alternative power and gardening, to cooking and animal care. Subscription is bimonthly for $18.97 per year.

BACKWOODS HOME - 800-835-2418 (subscriptions and orders), or www.backwoodshome.com (Website)

This little magazine packs a lot of information in its pages, and also offers compilations of their last five years' issues in several books. Subscription is six issues - $19.95/year.

COUNTRYSIDE - 800-551-5691 (subscriptions), or csymag@midway.tds.net (email) and www.countrysidemag.com (Website),

This one's been around since the sixties, and is filled with useful information for those serious about a self-sufficient lifestyle. With the July/Aug., 1998 issue, (Vol. 82, No.4), the publisher began a 10-month additional feature in the magazine about the implications of the Y2k which is packed with helpful suggestions. You can probably backorder issues. This is well worth the subscription! Six issues - $18/year.

THE MOTHER EARTH NEWS - 800-234-3368 (subscriptions), or 303-682-2438 (office), or MEarthNews@aol.com (email), or www.motherearthnews.com (Website).

This is the well-known back-to-the-land magazine that is full of helpful advice on every area of self-sufficient living. Subscription is 12 issues for $18.

ALPHEBETICAL CATALOG/SUPPLIES LIST

ABUNDANT LIFE SEED FOUNDATION - P.O. Box 772, Port Townsend, WA 98368 360-385-7192 (order phone), 360-385-7455 (fax)

BA ***B&A PRODUCTS*** - Rt.1, Box 100, Bunch, OK 74931-9705
918-696-5998 (office), 918-696-5999 (fax), Byron@baproducts.com (email)
http://www.baproducts.com (Website)

BACK HOME MAGAZINE - 828-696-3838, (office), 800-992-2546 (orders), or backhome@ioa.com (email) and www.BackHomeMagazine.com (Website).

BACKWOODS HOME MAGAZINE - 800-835-2418 (subscriptions and orders), or www.backwoodshome.com (Website

BW ***BACKWOODS SOLAR ELECTRIC SYSTEMS*** - 8530 Rapid Lightening Creek Rd.
Sandpoint, ID 83864 208-263-4290 (phone), 8-5 PT 208-265-4788 (fax)
swilley@nidlink.com (email)

CM ***CAMPMOR,INC.*** - P.O. Box 700-Q, Saddle River, NJ 07458-0700
800-525-4784 (customer service) Mon.-Fri. 8 am-9:30 pm, Sat. 8-6 ET
800-226-7667 (order phone) Mon.-Fri. 8am.-midnight, Sat. 8-6 ET,
800-230-2153 (24-hour order fax), info@campmor.com (email),
http://www.campmor.com (Website)

CF ***CHRISTIAN FAMILY RESOURCES*** - P.O. Box 405, Kit Carson, CO 80825
719-962-3228 (phone-fax) Hours 1-5 p.m MST, Mon.-Fri.

COUNTRYSIDE MAGAZINE - 800-551-5691 (subscriptions), or
www.countrysidemag.com (Website), or csymag@midway.tds.net, (email)

CS ***CS PRO SYSTEMS*** - Rt. 7, Box 510GG, San Antonio, TX 78264
888-710-2773 (order phone) www.csprosystems.com (Website)

CG ***CUMBERLAND GENERAL STORE*** - #1 Highway 68, Crossville, TN 38555
800-334-4640 (order phone) Mon.-Sat. 8:30-4:40 CT,
615-456-1211 (24-hour order fax).

EE ***EMERGENCY ESSENTIALS*** - 165 S. Mountain Way Dr., Orem, UT 84058-5119
800-999-1863 (order phone) Mon.-Fri. 9-6, Sat. 9-5 MT,
http://www.beprepared.com (Website) (*Also see Provident Pantry catalog*)

GARDENING FOR LIFE - P.O. Box 1001, Wixom, MI 48393
800-888-0010 (order phone)

GARDENS ALIVE! - 5100 Schenley Place, Lawrenceburg, IN 47025
812-537-8650 (order phone) 812-537-5108 (fax)

HM ***HARMONY*** (Formerly known as Seventh Generation) - 360 Interlocken Blvd.
Suite 300, Broomfield, CO 80021
800-869-3448 (customer service) Mon.-Fri. 9-5 ET,
800-869-3446 (order phone) 9am-10pm, Sat. 10-5, Sun. 12-5 ET,
800-456-1139 (order fax)

IM ***IMPROVEMENTS*** - Hanover, PA 17333-0084
800-642-2112 (order phone) 800-757-9997 (fax)
www.improvementscatalog.com (Website)

KW ***KANSAS WIND POWER*** - 13569 214th Rd. Holton, KS 66436-8138
785-364-4407 (phone)

LE ***LEHMAN'S NON-ELECTRIC CATALOG*** - P.O. Box 321, Kidron, OH 44636
330-857-5757 (order phone) Mon-Sat. 7am-10pm ET, 330-857-5785
(24-hour order fax), GetLehmans@aol.com (email),
http://www.lehmans.com (Website)

LF ***LIFESTYLE FASCINATION*** - P.O. Box 3023, Lakewood, NJ 08701-8123
800-669-0987 (order phone), 732-364-4448 (fax) both 24-hours/7 days,
732-364-5777 (office phone), http://www.lifestylefascination.com (Website)

MA ***MAJOR ARMY/NAVY SURPLUS*** - 435 Alondra Bl., Gardena, CA 90248
800-441-8855(order phone), Mon.-Fri. 9-6, Sat. 9-5, Sun 11-5, PT,
310-324-8855(office phone), 310-324-6909 (fax)

MOTHER EARTH NEWS - 800-234-3368 (subscriptions), or 303-682-2438
(office), or MEarthNews@aol.com (email), or www.motherearthnews.com
(Website).

NL ***NATURAL LIFESTYLE*** - 16 Lookout Dr., Asheville, NC 28804-3330
800-752-2775 (order phone Mon.-Fri. 8:30-6:00 ET,
828-252-3386 (24-hour fax), naturally@mindspring.com (email)
www.natural-lifestyle.com (Website)

NATURAL PET CARE CATALOG - 8050 Lake City Way, Seattle, WA 98115
800-962-8266 (order phone) 1-206-522-1667 (Canada & Int'l.)
206-522-1132 (fax) 10-5 Mon.-Fri. PST

NW ***NATURE'S WONDERLAND*** - Penn Herb Co., Ltd., 10601 Decatur Rd., Suite #2,
Philadelphia, PA 19154-3293
800-523-9971 (order phone), Mon.-Fri. 8:30-5 ET, 215-632-6100 (phone),
215-632-7945 (24-hour/day fax) orders@pennherb.com (email)
www.pennherb.com (Website)

NITRON INDUSTRIES - P.O. Box 1447, Fayetteville, AR 72702
800-835-0123 (order phone) 501-587-0177 (fax) 8-5 Mon-Fri. CT

NP ***NITRO-PAK PREPAREDNESS CENTER*** - 151 N. Main St., Heber, UT 84032-1647
800-866-4876 (order phone) Mon.-Fri. 8-6, Sat. 9-3 MT,
888-648-7672 (24-hour order fax) or http://www.nitro-pak.com (Website)

NO ***NORTHERN*** - P.O. Box 1499, Burnsville, MN 55337-0499
800-533-5545 (order phone), 612-894-0083 (fax) both 24-hours/7 days,

PP ***PROVIDENT PANTRY*** - (from Emergency Essentials - see above)
165 S. Mountain Way, Orem, UT 84058-5119
800-999-1863 (order phone) Mon.-Fri. 9-6, Sat. 9-5 MT

R. C. STEELE - 1989 Transit Way, Brockport, NY 14420-0910
800-872-3773 (order phone) (Wholesale - minimum order $50.)

RM ***READY-MADE RESOURCES*** - 125 County Rd. 585, Englewood, TN 37329
800-627-3809 (order phone), Mon.-Fri. 9-9 ET, 423-746-9814 (fax), robert@avicom.net(email)

RG ***REAL GOODS*** - 555 Leslie St., Ukiah, CA 95482-5576
800-762-7325 (order phone), 800-508-2342 (order fax) Mon.-Fri. 6am-8pm, Sat. 8-6 PT, realgood@realgoods.com (email), http://www.realgoods.com (Website) 707-468-9292 x2160 (overseas orders)

RS ***ROCKY GROVE SUN CO.*** - HC65, Box 280, Kingston, AR 72742
501-665-2457, info@rockygrove.com (email), www.rockygrove.com (Website)

SC ***SAFETY CENTRAL*** - 1100 W. El Camino Real, Mountain View, CA 94040
800-782-5396 (order phone) 650-965-3509 (customer service), Mon.-Fri. 10-7, Sat.-Sun. 10-6 PT, 800-552-8004 (24-hour order fax)

SA ***SAM ANDY EMERGENCY SUPPLIES*** - P.O. Box 141741, Irving, TX 75014
800-331-0358 (order phone) 24-hours/7 days.

SEED SAVER'S EXCHANGE - 3076 North Winn Rd., Decorah, IA 52101
319-382-5990 (order phone), 319-382-5872 (fax)

SV ***SILVER SOLUTIONS*** - P.O. Box 923, Forest Grove, OR 97116-0923
888-505-6005 (order phone), 503-359-5954 (office phone) 503-359-5518 (fax), www.silversolutions.com (Website)

CL ***STOREY'S HOW-TO BOOKS FOR COUNTRY LIVING*** - Schoolhouse Rd., Pownal, VT 05261. 800-441-5700 (order phone) 8am-10pm/7 days 413-664-4066 (fax)

SU ***SURVIVAL CENTER*** - P.O. Box 234, McKenna, WA 98558
800-321-2900 (order phone), Mon.-Fri. 10-6 PT, 360-458-6778 (office phone), 360-458-6868 (fax), sales@survivalcenter.com (email) www.zyz.com/survivalcenter (Website)

SS ***SURVIVAL SUPPLY CO.*** - P.O. Box 4582, Couer d'Alene, ID 83815
208-765-6201 (phone), 208-765-4295 (fax), SURSUPCO@Nidlink.Com (email) http://www.nidlink.com/~sursupco (Website)

WHISKERS - 235 E. 9th St., New York, NY 10003
800-944-7537 (order phone) 718-423-3504 (fax) healthypet@msn.com (email) http//choicemall.com/whiskers (Website)

THE ACTION CHECKLIST

for

"BUILDING YOUR ARK"

HOW TO USE THE *ACTION CHECKLIST*

Please read these instructions before you begin using the *ACTION CHECKLIST*. A few suggestions can make your efforts much easier:

1) The first page is a blank template to print out or copy for any other lists that you wish to make. For example, you can use this template when making lists of barter goods, or food shopping and preparation lists, if you do your own food storage plan.

2) The next page is the Catalog Order Form. Use this form immediately to order your chosen catalogs from the Catalog Appendix. (Hint: The more catalogs you order, the wider your selection of products and prices as you go through the Checklist.)

3) Note that the Checklist sections are arranged in the same order as, and keyed to the chapters in the book. This key is in the upper right hand corner of each page. The Checklist *pages* are not numbered, so you can rearrange them in any order that you wish. Some sections each have several pages, which are numbered next to the section title. For convenience, you may wish to print out, or in the hard copy, tear out or copy the Checklist and keep it in a three-ring binder or on a clipboard.

4) As you read through the book, note any items you want to obtain on the appropriate Checklist. Working in pencil allows you to erase any mistakes or changes, and you may wish to use a colored see-through marker to highlight the areas or items that you want to emphasize.

5) The basic headings are as follows:

   a) **ITEM:** This is the name of the product or supplies you wish to purchase or obtain before the Y2K.
   b) **SOURCE:** This is the name of the catalog or local supplier for that item.
   c) **AMOUNT TO GET:** This indicates the number or amount of any item that you wish to obtain.
   d) **COST:** These figures will allow you to develop a budget to know how much you will be spending, either in each category or in total.
   e) **HAVE BY DATE:** This is the latest date that you feel will be safe to obtain this item. This column may have to be changed from time to time, but it will help you stay on course.
   f) **DATE(S) OBTAINED:** This lets you know how much of any category you have completed.

6) There are several extra charts included:

a) For those who wish to collect their own First Aid kit, I've included a list of suggested supplies compiled from several sources. It is probably not complete, so feel free to add anything that you deem necessary. Keep the everyday medicines in your bathroom, and store the specialized supplies (emergency, surgery, burns, dental, etc.) along with an illustrated how-to First Aid book or two in a closed container or barrel that is easy to get to when needed.

b) Under the Finance heading, there is a Vital Records chart. During the Y2K, it will be crucial that you keep good records of any important information that could be lost due to computer malfunction. A safe method of storage is to put these records in plastic sleeves in a three-ring binder, and then store the binder in a poly bucket with a dessicant to repel moisture and protect the papers.

c) Also, there is a Personal Information page where you can record all pertinent information about your family. Print out as many copies of this page as you need in order to include everyone in your family. When you have finished this page, check off box #XV on the Vital Records form to indicate that you have completed this chart.

d) There is a chart for your pets and livestock, and one that includes many useful household tools and equipment. These crucial items should be stocked well before the Y2K, while supplies are readily available, as they may be hard to get afterwards. Include any other useful items that you can think of on this list.

7) I've starred (*) any items that should be part of everyone's preparations, such as water filters, heaters, and so on. If an entire section is essential, I've starred the title.

8) Finally, if you think of anything that I've left out, please mail *(see address on page 2),* or email me *(go to www.yourark.com and go to the order page for the email form),* with your suggestions. With your input, these charts can be continually updated and made even more useful for everyone.

ACTION CHECKLIST

____

ITEM AND/OR BRAND NAME	SOURCE (CATALOG/LOCAL)	AMT. TO GET	COST EA.	COST TOTAL	HAVE BY (DATE)	DATE(S) OBTAINED

ACTION CHECKLIST

(Appendix D, page 206)

CATALOG ORDER FORM

CATALOG	ORDER PHONE	DATE ORDERED	DATE RECEIVED

ACTION CHECKLIST

(Chapter 2, page 29)

HEATING #1

ITEM AND/OR BRAND NAME	SOURCE (CATALOG/LOCAL)	AMT. TO GET	COST EA.	COST TOTAL	HAVE BY (DATE)	DATE(S) OBTAINED
I. KEEPING WARM DRAPES (for sleeping area)						
*THERMAL UNDERWEAR Name						
Name						
Name						
Name						
Name						
Name						
*WARM ACCESSORIES (hats, gloves, socks etc.) Name						
Name						
Name						
Name						
Name						
Name						
*BLANKETS AND COVERS Name						
Name						
Name						
Name						
Name						
Name						
*SLEEPING BAGS Name						
Name						
Name						
Name						
Name						
Name						
II. SPACE HEATING *HEATER(S)/STOVE(S)						
*FUEL (liquid)						
*FUEL (solid)						
*FUEL (wood)						
*FUEL STORAGE CANS						

ACTION CHECKLIST

(Chapter 2, page 29)

HEATING #2

ITEM AND/OR BRAND NAME	SOURCE (CATALOG/LOCAL)	AMT. TO GET	COST EA.	TOTAL	HAVE BY (DATE)	DATE(S) OBTAINED
WOOD HEAT EQPT. CHAINSAW						
Oil						
Gasoline						
Extra Chain						
Other						
CHIMNEY FIRE RETARDANTS						
FIRE STARTERS						
ACCESSORIES						
*SMOKE (& CO_2) DETECTORS						
MISCELLANEOUS						
BOOKS						

ACTION CHECKLIST

WATER

(Chapter 3, page 45)

ITEM AND/OR BRAND NAME	SOURCE (CATALOG/LOCAL)	AMT. TO GET	COST EA.	TOTAL	HAVE BY (DATE)	DATE(S) OBTAINED
*I. FILTER/PURIFIER						
* EXTRA CARTRIDGE(S)						
COFFEE FILTERS						
MISC.						
SOLAR DISTILLER (or plans)						
*II. CHEMICAL PURIFIERS						
*III. CONTAINERS (barrels, bottles, etc.)						(Date Filled)
CISTERN (and supplies)						
IV. ACCESSORIES (misc)						
V. WELL SUPPLIES						
VI. BOOKS						

ACTION CHECKLIST

FOOD STORAGE #1

(Chapter 4, page 62)

CALORIC AND STORAGE REQUIREMENTS
I. CALORIC REQUIREMENTS Amount/Person/Day
Name
Name
Name
Name
Name
Name
Name
Name

II. AMTS. TO STORE	GRAINS	BEANS/LEG	DAIRY/EGGS	MEATS/SUB	FRUITS/VEG	OILS	SWEETS	SPTG. SEED	MISC.
Name									
Name									
Name									
Name									
Name									
Name									
Name									
Name									
TOTALS									

ACTION CHECKLIST

(Chapter 4, page 62)

FOOD STORAGE #2

ITEM AND/OR BRAND NAME	SOURCE (CATALOG/LOCAL)	AMT. TO GET	COST EA.	 TOTAL	HAVE BY (DATE)	DATE(S) OBTAINED
I. LOW OXYGEN PACKAGING PREPACK UNITS						
*INDIVIDUAL FOODS Grains						
Beans/Legumes						
Pastas						
Dairy & Eggs						

ACTION CHECKLIST

FOOD STORAGE #3

(Chapter 4, page 62)

ITEM AND/OR BRAND NAME	SOURCE (CATALOG/LOCAL)	AMT. TO GET	COST EA.	COST TOTAL	HAVE BY (DATE)	DATE(S) OBTAINED
INDIVIDUAL FOODS (cont.)						
Sweeteners						
Fats & Oils						
Vegetables						
Fruits						
TVP/Meat Substitutes						
Soups/Mixes						
Cooking Aids (yeast, etc.)						
Misc.						

ACTION CHECKLIST

FOOD STORAGE #4

(Chapter 4, page 62)

ITEM AND/OR BRAND NAME	SOURCE (CATALOG/LOCAL)	AMT. TO GET	COST EA.	COST TOTAL	HAVE BY (DATE)	DATE(S) OBTAINED
II. FREEZE-DRIED FOODS						
PREPACKAGES						
INDIVIDUAL ITEMS Meats						
Entrees						
Soups						
Vegetables						
Fruits						
Desserts						

ACTION CHECKLIST

(Chapter 4, page 62)

FOOD STORAGE #5

ITEM AND/OR BRAND NAME	SOURCE (CATALOG/LOCAL)	AMT. TO GET	COST EA.	TOTAL	HAVE BY (DATE)	DATE(S) OBTAINED
II. FREEZE DRIED (cont.) Snacks						
Beverages						
Misc.						
III. MREs						

ACTION CHECKLIST

FOOD PRESERVATION #1

(Chapter 5, page 83)

ITEM AND/OR BRAND NAME	SOURCE (CATALOG/LOCAL)	AMT. TO GET	COST EA.	COST TOTAL	HAVE BY (DATE)	DATE(S) OBTAINED
I. BOOKS						
II. DEHYDRATORS ELECTRIC						
NON-ELEC.						
MISC. EQPT.						
III. CANNING BOOKS						
CANNER(S)						
CANNING EQUIPMENT Alum						
Cans						
Can Sealer						
Jars						
Jar Lifter						
Lids						
Rings						
Pectin						
Salt						
Sugar/Honey						
Wax						
Other						
IV. MISC. EQUIPMENT						

ACTION CHECKLIST

FOOD PRESERVATION #2

(Chapter 5, page 83)

ITEM AND/OR BRAND NAME	SOURCE (CATALOG/LOCAL)	AMT. TO GET	COST EA.	COST TOTAL	HAVE BY (DATE)	DATE(S) OBTAINED
V. LOW-OXYGEN PACKING						
BUCKET LINERS						
BUCKET OPENER/WRENCH						
DESSICANTS						
DIATOMACEOUS EARTH (DE)						
GAMMA BUCKET SEALS						
HEATSEALER						
OAPs						
POLY BUCKETS						
OTHER						
Misc.						
VI. VACUUM PACKING						
ELECTRIC VACUUM PACKER						
PLASTIC BAGS						
PUMP 'N SEAL						
Other						
VII. NITROGEN PACKING						
INSTRUCTIONS						
EQUIPMENT						

ACTION CHECKLIST

FOOD PRODUCTION #1

(Chapter 6, page 94)

ITEM AND/OR BRAND NAME	SOURCE (CATALOG/LOCAL)	AMT. TO GET	COST EA.	COST TOTAL	HAVE BY (DATE)	DATE(S) OBTAINED
I. SPROUTING BOOKS						
SPROUTERS/KITS						
II. WHEATGRASS BOOKS						
JUICER						
OTHER GREENS (See Food Appendix)						
II. GARDENING BOOKS						
SUPPLIES						
Potting Soil						
Soil Amendments						
Fertilizers						
Containers						
Tools - (See Misc. Household Supplies)						
Other						
IV. SEED SAVING BOOKS						
SEEDS (See Food Prod. #2)						

ACTION CHECKLIST

FOOD PRODUCTION #2

(Chapter 6, page 94)

ITEM AND/OR BRAND NAME	SOURCE (CATALOG/LOCAL)	AMT. TO GET	COST EA.	COST TOTAL	HAVE BY (DATE)	DATE(S) OBTAINED
* OPEN-POLLINATED SEEDS						

ACTION CHECKLIST

(Chapter 7, page 103)

FOOD PREPARATION/COOKSTOVES

ITEM AND/OR BRAND NAME	SOURCE (CATALOG/LOCAL)	AMT. TO GET	COST EA.	 TOTAL	HAVE BY (DATE)	DATE(S) OBTAINED
*I. STOVES						
*FUEL						
*FUEL CONTAINERS						
II. SOLAR COOKING BOOKS						
OVEN						
OTHER						
III. WOOD COOKSTOVE BOOKS						
STOVE						
MISC.						
IV. COOKBOOKS						
*V. APPLIANCES/UTENSILS GRAIN GRINDERS						
ACCESS.						
CAST IRON COOKWARE BOOK						
PRESSURE COOKERS BOOK						
VI. OPTIONAL ACCES. OVEN						
OUTDOOR ACCESSORIES						
OTHER						

ACTION CHECKLIST

(Chapter 8, page 121)

SANITATION AND CLEANING #1

ITEM AND/OR BRAND NAME	SOURCE (CATALOG/LOCAL)	AMT. TO GET	COST EA.	TOTAL	HAVE BY (DATE)	DATE(S) OBTAINED
*I. PORTABLE OR COMPOSTING TOILETS						
Disinfectants						
Sawdust, Peat Moss, etc.						
Scoop						
6-Gallon Buckets						
Toilet Liners						
Toilet Paper						
Toilet Seat						
Waste Bags						
Other						
II. MFG. COMPOST TOILET						
*III. CLEANING SUPPLIES						
Ammonia						
Baking Soda						
Carpet Sweeper						
Cleanser						
Dish Detergent						
Disinfectant Cleaner						
Rubber Gloves						
Scrubbing Pads						
Sponges & Cloths						
Vinegar						
Other						
*IV. LAUNDRY SUPPLIES						
Bluing						
Clothesline						
Clothes Pins						
Detergent						
Fabric Softener						
Iron						
Starch						
Washboard						
Wash Tubs						
Washer/Plunger						
Wringer						
Other						

ACTION CHECKLIST

SANITATION AND CLEANING #2

(Chapter 8, page 121)

ITEM AND/OR BRAND NAME	SOURCE (CATALOG/LOCAL)	AMT. TO GET	COST EA.	COST TOTAL	HAVE BY (DATE)	DATE(S) OBTAINED
V. WASHING MACHINE						
*VI. PERSONAL CARE						
Bath Soap						
Body Powder						
Cleansing Towels						
Waterless Washing Prod.						
Deodorant						
Hair Rinse						
Hand Lotion						
Razors						
Shampoo						
Sharpeners (razor)						
Shavers						
Toothbrushes						
Toothpaste						
Other						
*VII. SOLAR SHOWER(S)						
VIII. HOT SHOWER(S)						
IX. BOOKS						

ACTION CHECKLIST

LIGHTING #1

(Chapter 9, page 131)

ITEM AND/OR BRAND NAME	SOURCE (CATALOG/LOCAL)	AMT. TO GET	COST EA.	COST TOTAL	HAVE BY (DATE)	DATE(S) OBTAINED
*I. LIGHTING WITH FUEL CANDLES						
CANDLE LANTERNS						
OIL LAMPS						
KEROSENE LAMPS						
LAMP ACCESSORIES Mantles						
Wicks						
Chimneys						
OUTDOOR LANTERNS						
DUAL FUEL LANTERNS						
LIGHTING ACCESS. Matches						
Elec. Match						
FUEL						
FUEL CONTAINERS						

ACTION CHECKLIST

(Chapter 9, page 131)

LIGHTING #2

ITEM AND/OR BRAND NAME	SOURCE (CATALOG/LOCAL)	AMT. TO GET	COST EA.	COST TOTAL	HAVE BY (DATE)	DATE(S) OBTAINED
*II. BATTERY LIGHTING BATTERY RECHARGERS						
BATTERIES Battery Adaptor						
BAT.LAMPS/LANTERNS						
FLASHLIGHTS						
SOLAR LIGHTING						
MISC. LIGHTING Salt-Water Battery						
Lightsticks						
Other						
III. GENERATORS						
FUEL CONTAINERS						
FUEL						
OIL						
MISC.						

ACTION CHECKLIST

(Chapter 10, page 145)

FIRST AID AND HEALTH #1

ITEM AND/OR BRAND NAME	SOURCE (CATALOG/LOCAL)	AMT. TO GET	COST EA.	COST TOTAL	HAVE BY (DATE)	DATE(S) OBTAINED
I. FIRST AID TRAINING						
* II BOOKS ON FIRST AID						
*III. FIRST AID KITS (general)						
IV. FIRST AID KITS (professional)						
V. FIRST AID KITS (specialty)						
VI. MISC. F/A SUPPLIES						

ACTION CHECKLIST

FIRST AID AND HEALTH #2

(Chapter 10, page 145)

ITEM AND/OR BRAND NAME	SOURCE (CATALOG/LOCAL)	AMT. TO GET	COST EA.	COST TOTAL	HAVE BY (DATE)	DATE(S) OBTAINED
VII. BOOKS ON NAT. HEALTH						
VIII. NATURAL PRODUCTS COLLOIDAL SILVER						
BOOKS/INFO.						
GENERATOR						
SILVER SOLUTION						
GRAPEFRUIT EXTRACT						
ESSENTIAL OILS						
IX. MISC. HEALTH PRODUCTS						

ACTION CHECKLIST

(Chapter 10, page 145)

* FIRST AID AND HEALTH #3

ITEM AND/OR BRAND NAME	APPOINTMENT DATE	APPOINTMENT KEPT	RESULTS OF EXAMINATION	MEDICATIONS PRESCRIBED	DATE(S) OBTAINED
I. MEDICAL CHECKUPS					
Name					
Name					
Name					
Name					
Name					
Name					
II. DENTAL CHECKUPS					
Name					
Name					
Name					
Name					
Name					
Name					
Name					
III. VISION CHECKUPS					
Name					
Name					
Name					
Name					
Name					
Name					
IV. HEARING CHECKUPS					
Name					
Name					
Name					
Name					
Name					
Name					
V. MISC. CHECKUPS					

ACTION CHECKLIST

FIRST AID SUPPLIES #1

(Chapter 10, page 145)

ITEM	SOURCE (CATALOG/LOCAL)	AMT. TO GET	COST EA.	COST TOTAL	HAVE BY (DATE)	DATE(S) OBTAINED
NOTE: You will have to determine the amounts of each item to purchase, depending on the size of your family or group.						
I. EMERGENCY EQUIPMENT						
Ammonia Inhalant						
Antiseptic Swabs						
Bandages (see below)						
Disp.Recusicitator Bag						
Headlamp						
Inflatable Air Splints						
I.V. Set/Glucose						
Medications (see below)						
Mouth-to-Mouth Forms						
Nasal/Oral Airway Kits						
Splints						
Sterile Water Packs						
Sterile Gloves						
Tourniquet Hose						
Traction Splint						
Trauma Pants						
Velcro Tourniquet						
Other						
II. SURGICAL EQUIPMENT						
Butterfly sutures						
Drape Sheets						
Face Masks						
Gloves (latex surgical)						
Glue (surgical)						
Kelly Hemostats (straight 5.5")						
Razors (single edge)						
Ring Cutter						
Saw (surgical)						
Scalpels (Dispos.#10,11,15)						
Scissors (surg. blunt & pointed)						
Silver Nitrate						
Skin Stapler (& remover)						
Steri-Strips						
Thread (black silk/nylon)						
Other						

ACTION CHECKLIST
FIRST AID SUPPLIES #2

(Chapter 10, page 145)

ITEM AND/OR BRAND NAME	SOURCE (CATALOG/LOCAL)	AMT. TO GET	COST EA.	COST TOTAL	HAVE BY (DATE)	DATE(S) OBTAINED
III. DIAGNOSTIC EQPT.						
Blood Pressure Cuff						
Flashlight (small, very bright)						
Magnifying Glass						
Stethoscope						
Thermometers (digital)						
Tongue Depressors						
Other						
IV. POISON CONTROL						
Cutter Snakebite Kit						
Liquid Charcoal						
Syrup of Ipecac						
Other						
V. BURNS						
Aloe Vera Gel						
Burn Gel						
Burn Sheets						
Green Clay						
"Second Skin"						
Sterile Water Packs						
Other						
VI. BANDAGES						
Ace Elastic (2",4",6")						
Band Aids (assorted)						
Cotton (Sterile)						
Eyepads (sterile)						
Gauze Pads 2"x2"						
Gauze Pads 3"x3"						
Gauze Pads 4"x4"						
Gauze Pad 18"x36"						
J & J Plaster Rolls						
NuDerm Wound Dressing						
Sanitary Pads (heavy)						
Trauma Pads 5"x9"						
Triangle Bandage						
Other						

ACTION CHECKLIST

(Chapter 10, page 145)

FIRST AID SUPPLIES #3

ITEM AND/OR BRAND NAME	SOURCE (CATALOG/LOCAL)	AMT. TO GET	COST EA.	COST TOTAL	HAVE BY (DATE)	DATE(S) OBTAINED
VII. DISINFECTANTS						
Alcohol (rubbing)						
Antibacterial Soaps						
Antiseptic Ointments						
Colloidal Silver						
Iodine/Iodine Pads						
Oxygen Solutions						
Saline Solutions						
Other						
VIII. DENTAL						
Cavit						
Cotton Rolls						
Eugenol						
Floss						
Mirror						
Pick						
Wax						
Other						
IX. TREATMENT SUPPLIES						
Amber Dropper Bottles						
Cervical collar						
Cotton Swabs						
Douche & Enema Bag						
Hot Water Bottle						
Hot/Cold Packs (reusable)						
Hypodermic Syringes						
Reusable (5cc glass)						
Needles #22 (1.5")						
Dispos. (variety)						
Medicine Droppers						
Moistened Towelettes						
Safety Pins						
Syringes						
Tweezers (pointed)						
Other						

ACTION CHECKLIST

FIRST AID SUPPLIES #4

(Chapter 10, page 145)

ITEM AND/OR BRAND NAME	SOURCE (CATALOG/LOCAL)	AMT. TO GET	COST EA.	COST TOTAL	HAVE BY (DATE)	DATE(S) OBTAINED
X. OVER-THE COUNTER MEDICINES						
Antacid						
Anti-Diarrheal						
Anti-fungal						
Bicarbonate of Soda						
Antihistamines						
Cold/Flu Tabs						
Constipation						
Cough Syrups						
Decongestant						
Eye Drops						
Hemorrhoid Relief						
Inhalant Medication						
Hydrogen Peroxide						
Itching/Rash Cream						
Lip Balm						
Lubricants						
Nausea/Motion Sickness						
Non-aspirin Pain Relief						
Petroleum Jelly (Bag Balm)						
Pain/Fever Relief						
Powders (medicated)						
Yeast Infection						
Other						
XI. Prescription Med.						
ANESTHETIC						
Xylocaine (Ointment)						
Lidocaine (1%injectable)						
ANTIBIOTIC (long-date)						
Cephalexin						
Erythromycin						
ALLERGIC REACTIONS						
Isuprel (sublingual)						
Prednisolone (5mg. tabs)						
(Cont.)						

ACTION CHECKLIST

(Chapter 10, page 145)

FIRST AID SUPPLIES #5

ITEM AND/OR BRAND NAME	SOURCE (CATALOG/LOCAL)	AMT. TO GET	COST EA.	COST TOTAL	HAVE BY (DATE)	DATE(S) OBTAINED
XI. PRESCRIPTION MED. (CONT.) BURNS Silvadene Cream						
DIARRHEA Lomotil Tabs						
PAIN Tylenol Codeine #3						
OTHER PERSONAL Rx						

ACTION CHECKLIST
FOR PARENTS #1

Chapter 11, page 160)

ITEM AND/OR BRAND NAME	SOURCE (CATALOG/LOCAL)	AMT. TO GET	COST EA.	COST TOTAL	HAVE BY (DATE)	DATE(S) OBTAINED
I. PREGNANCY CHILDBIRTH KIT						
CHILDBIRTH SUPPLIES Nursing Bras						
Nursing Pads						
Delivery Eqpt.						
BOOKS						
II. INFANTS FORMULA						
SPECIAL FOOD						
FOOD MILL						
BOTTLES						
OTHER EQPT.						
DIAPERS						
DIAPER PAIL						
CLOTHES/BLANKETS						
MISC. SUPPLIES Bath Soap						
Body Powder						
Diaper Rash Ointment						
Lotion						
Pacifiers						
Q-Tips						
Shampoo						
Teething Ring						
Teething Medicine						
Toys						

ACTION CHECKLIST
FOR PARENTS #2

(Chapter 11, page 160)

ITEM AND/OR BRAND NAME	SOURCE (CATALOG/LOCAL)	AMT. TO GET	COST EA.	COST TOTAL	HAVE BY (DATE)	DATE(S) OBTAINED
III. CHILDREN CLOTHING Name						
Name						
Name						
Name						
Name						
Name						
SHOES Name						
Name						
Name						
Name						
Name						
Name						
PLAY SUPPLIES						
HOME SCHOOLING						

ACTION CHECKLIST

(Chapter 12, page 168)

FINANCIAL

ITEM AND/OR BRAND NAME	SOURCE (CATALOG/LOCAL)	AMT. TO GET	COST EA.	COST TOTAL	HAVE BY (DATE)	DATE(S) OBTAINED
I. HARD CURRENCY						
GOLD						
SILVER						
OTHER						
SAFEBOX						
*II. BARTER ITEMS						
III. BOOKS						

ACTION CHECKLIST

(Chapter 12, page 168)

*VITAL RECORDS #1

DOCUMENTS / ITEMS	OBTAIN BY (DATE)	SECURED (DATE)	INFORMATION (Location, Account #, etc.)
I. ABSTRACT OF TITLE FOR PROPERTIES			
II. ACCOUNTS RECEIVABLE RECORDS			
III. CANCELED CHECKS/BANK STMTS.			
Acct. #			
Acct. #			
Acct. #			
Acct. #			
IV. DEBTS (ACCOUNTS PAYABLE)			
Credit Card #			
Credit Card #			
Credit Card #			
Credit Card #			
OTHER ACCOUNTS			
V. GUARANTEES/WARRANTIES			
ELECTRONIC EQPT.			
HOUSEHOLD APPL.			
OUTDOOR EQPT.			
MISC.			
VI. HOME IMPROVEMENT RECORDS			

ACTION CHECKLIST

(Chapter 12, page 165)

VITAL RECORDS #2

DOCUMENTS / ITEMS	OBTAIN BY (DATE)	SECURED (DATE)	INFORMATION (Location, Account. #, etc.)
VII. HOUSEHOLD EXPENSES RECORDS (monthly bills, utilities, etc.- with account numbers)			
ELECTRICITY			
GAS			
WATER			
TELEPHONE(S)			
VIII. HOUSEHOLD INVENTORY			
WRITTEN			
PHOTOS			
VIDEO			
IX. INCOME PROPERTY RECORDS			
ADDRESS			
ADDRESS			
ADDRESS			
ADDRESS			
X. INSURANCE POLICIES (incl. policy #s)			
WHOLE LIFE			
TERM			
PENSION PLAN			
DISABILITY			
HEALTH			
OTHER			
XI. INVESTMENTS			
STOCKS			
BONDS			
MUTUAL FUNDS			
OTHER			
XII. KEYS (Extra)			
FOR PROPERTIES			
SAFE DEPOSIT BOX(ES)			
STORAGE FACILITY			
OTHER			

ACTION CHECKLIST

(Chapter 12, page 165)

VITAL RECORDS #3

DOCUMENTS / ITEMS	OBTAIN BY (DATE)	SECURED (DATE)	INFORMATION (Location, Account. #, etc.)
XIII. MORTGAGE DOCUMENTS			
XIV. PEDIGREES & PET RECORDS			
XV. PERSONAL INFO. PACKET - Family (See Personal Information Checklist)			
XVI. PROPERTY DEEDS			
XVII. SAFE DEPOSIT BOX(ES) INVENTORY			
XVIII. SAVINGS ACCOUNTS (passbooks)			
XIX. TAX RECORDS / INFO.			
19			
19			
19			
19			
19			
19			
19			
Other			
XX. TRUSTS - RECORDS/INFO.			

ACTION CHECKLIST

VITAL RECORDS #4

(Chapter 12, page 165)

DOCUMENTS / ITEMS	OBTAIN BY (DATE)	SECURED (DATE)	INFORMATION (Location, Account #, etc.)
XXI. VEHICLE TITLES/REGISTRATIONS			
XXII. OTHER VITAL RECORDS			

ACTION CHECKLIST

(Chapter 12, page 168)

PERSONAL INFORMATION

NOTE: Fill out this chart for every family member and then check off on Vital Records List under # XV. To add more family members, make extra copies of the chart.

RECORDS	NAME	NAME	NAME	NAME	NAME
VITAL STATISTICS					
Adoption Papers					
Birth Certificate					
Church Records					
Citizenship Papers					
Divorce Papers					
Driver's License Copy					
Marriage Records					
Military Records					
Passport/Visa					
Social Security Records					
Will					
EDUCATION / AWARDS					
Academic Records					
Awards/Prizes					
Diplomas					
Education Certificates					
Other					
EMPLOYMENT RECORDS					
Company Benefits					
Employment Contracts					
Retirement Plans					
Settlements					
Unemployment Benefits					
Other					
HEALTH RECORDS					
Dental					
Immunization					
Medical					
Misc. Health Records					
Optical					
Prescriptions					
Other					
MISC. RECORDS					

ACTION CHECKLIST

PERSONAL SAFETY

(Chapter 13, page 175)

ITEM AND/OR BRAND NAME	SOURCE (CATALOG/LOCAL)	AMT. TO GET	COST EA.	COST TOTAL	HAVE BY (DATE)	DATE(S) OBTAINED
I. BOOKS						
II. SELF DEFENSE COURSE						
Name						
Name						
Name						
III. ELECTRONIC ALARMS						
IV. PEPPER SPRAYS						
V. STUN GUNS						
VI. AIR TASER						
VII. MISC. PRODUCTS						
*VIII. FIRE SAFETY						
GAS SHUT-OFF TOOL						
FIRE EXTINGUISHERS						
SMOKE HOODS						
ESCAPE LADDER(S)						
FIRE BLANKET						
IX. RADIATION EQUIPMENT						

ACTION CHECKLIST

TRANSPORTATION

(Chapter 14, page 181)

ITEM AND/OR BRAND NAME	SOURCE (CATALOG/LOCAL)	AMT. TO GET	COST EA.	COST TOTAL	HAVE BY (DATE)	DATE(S) OBTAINED
* I. VEHICLE(S)						
* II. FUEL & OIL						
OIL						
FUEL						
FUEL CONTAINERS						
PUMP						
GAS SAVER						
MISC. ADDITIVES						
* III. ACCESSORIES						
BATTERY CHARGERS						
OTHER						
TOOLS & SUPPLIES						
Antifreeze						
Brake Fluid						
Extra Battery						
Extra Hoses, Belts						
Extra Tires/Patches						
Extra Wipers						
Flares						
Hand Tire Pump						
Hand Winch & Cable						
Jack(s)						
Power Steering Fluid						
Ramps						
Repair Manuals						
Socket Sets						
Sparkplugs						
Stands						
Tire Removal Bar						
Tire Traction (sand, etc.)						
Transmission Fluid						
Winch & Cable						
Windshield Wiper Fluid						
Other						

ACTION CHECKLIST
COMMUNICATIONS

(Chapter 15, page 186)

ITEM AND/OR BRAND NAME	SOURCE (CATALOG/LOCAL)	AMT. TO GET	COST EA.	COST TOTAL	HAVE BY (DATE)	DATE(S) OBTAINED
*I. RADIOS HAND OPERATED						
MULTI-POWER						
MULTI-USE						
SHORTWAVE						
ANTENNAS						
BATTERIES (see lighting)						
II. WEATHER RECEIVERS						
III. TWO-WAY RADIOS						
IV. CB RADIOS						
V. OTHER						
VI. MISC. EQUIPMENT						
VII. BOOKS						

ACTION CHECKLIST

PETS / LIVESTOCK

(Appendix C, page 208)

ITEM AND/OR BRAND NAME	SOURCE (CATALOG/LOCAL)	AMT. TO GET	COST EA.	COST TOTAL	HAVE BY (DATE)	DATE(S) OBTAINED
I. FOOD Cats						
Dogs						
Other						
STORAGE CONTAINERS Cans						
Bags & Ties						
II. WATER Cats						
Dogs						
Other						
STORAGE CONTAINERS						
III. MISC. EQUIPMENT						
VITAMINS, SUPPLEMENTS Cats						
Dogs						
Other						
LEASHES/COLLARS						
LITTERBOX						
LITTER						
GROOMING AIDS Shampoo						
Other						
MEDICATIONS Cats						
Dogs						
Other						
IMMUNIZATIONS Cats						
Dogs						
Other						
IV. LIVESTOCK FEED						
WATER						
VET. SUPPLIES						
MISC. EQUIPMENT						

ACTION CHECKLIST

* HOUSEHOLD TOOLS & SUPPLIES #1

ITEM AND/OR BRAND NAME	SOURCE (CATALOG/LOCAL)	AMT. TO GET	COST EA.	COST TOTAL	HAVE BY (DATE)	DATE(S) OBTAINED
I. SEWING						
Buttons						
Fabric						
Patterns						
Pins, Needles						
Tapes						
Thread						
Scissors						
Zippers						
Other						
II. HOUSEHOLD						
Bungee Cords						
Extra Toilet Parts						
Extra Faucet Parts						
Extra Window Screen						
Extra Window Glass						
Glues, Fixatives						
Insect Repellants						
Mop, Broom, Rags						
Paper & Plastic Bags						
Rodent Traps						
Rubber Gloves						
Spray Bottles						
Other						
III. TOOLS						
Bolt & Wire Cutters						
Caulking Gun & Caulks						
Duct and Other Tapes						
Electrical & Pipe Tape						
Extra Lumber, Pipe						
Goggles/Eye Protection						
Hammers, Nails						
Hand Drill						
Handsaws,						
Hinges, Door Locks						
Nuts, Bolts, Wrenches						
Padlocks, Fasteners						
Paints, Removers, Brushes						
Plastic Sheeting (rolls)						
Pliers, Vise Grips						
Oils & Lubricants						
Ropes, Chains						
Sandpaper, Scrapers						
Screwdrivers, Screws						
Sharpening Files, Stone						
Staple Gun, Staples						
Tarps						
Tin Snips, Scissors						
Other						

ACTION CHECKLIST

HOUSEHOLD TOOLS & SUPPLIES #2

ITEM AND/OR BRAND NAME	SOURCE (CATALOG/LOCAL)	AMT. TO GET	COST EA.	COST TOTAL	HAVE BY (DATE)	DATE(S) OBTAINED
IV. OUTDOOR TOOLS						
Axe, Hatchet						
Cement, Morter						
Fencing						
Garden Cart, Extra Parts						
Hand Clippers, Pruners						
Hand Mower, Repair Parts						
Hoses, Repair Parts						
Hoes, Froes						
Ladders						
Pitchforks						
Post Hole Diggers						
Rakes						
Sawhorses						
Shovels & Spades						
Sledgehammer						
Small Hand Garden Tools						
Splitting Maul, Wedge						
Tree Trimmers						
Watering Cans, Buckets						
Wheelbarrow, Extra Parts						
Wire(s)						
Work Gloves						
Other						
V. Hunting & Fishing Gear						
VI. OFFICE SUPPLIES						
Envelopes, Stamps						
Highlighters, Markers						
Household String(s)						
Paper & Other Clips						
Pens, Pencils						
Rubber Bands						
Rulers, Compass						
Tacks, Pushpins						
Tapes-Packing, Strapping						
Wrapping Paper, Tape						
Writing Paper						
Other						
VII. MISC. SUPPLIES						
Battery or Windup Clocks						
Extra Watch Batteries						
Shoelaces, Polishes						
Cameras, Films						

To order "BUILDING YOUR ARK"

To order "a printed copy of Building Your Ark" send payment (in U.S. funds only - check, Money Order, or Credit Card information) along with the order form below. *(Orders paid for by personal check must wait for bank clearance.)*

_______ **PRINTED COPY OF "Building Your Ark" for $29.97 (taxes included), plus $3.98 S&H (U.S. only)**
(Shipping outside U.S.- via air freight - and for multiple-copy orders will vary.)

NOTE: "Building Your Ark is also available in an online, downloadable version from our website at: **www.yourark.com.** Please visit our site and go to the Order Page, or send your order information with this sheet and we will email you your download codes.

_______ **DOWNLOADABLE ADOBE ACROBAT COPY OF "Building Your Ark" for $ 19.97 (taxes included)**

(PLEASE PRINT CLEARLY)

NAME____

ADDRESS____

CITY______________________________ **STATE**______ **ZIP**________

EMAIL ADDRESS__________________________(For online Member Updates)

TELEPHONE____

PAYMENT METHOD:

MONEY ORDER__________

CHECK________________ (Make checks out to DAL Enterprises)

CREDIT CARD (Note: We take Master Card, Visa, Am. Express, and Discover/Novus)

TYPE OF CREDIT CARD ____________________**EXP. DATE**________

CREDIT CARD NUMBER_____________________________________

SIGNATURE____

(If cardholder is different from person listed above as purchaser, please give name and address of cardholder)

CARDHOLDER NAME______________________________________
CARDHOLDER ADDRESS___________________________________
CITY ______________________________STATE_______ZIP________
CARDHOLDER PHONE NUMBER_____________________________

MAIL TO: DAL Enterprises, P.O. Box 17, West Fork, AR 72774
CREDIT CARD ORDERS ONLY - fax order to: 501-839-8396
or call to order: 888-240-9074
(see other side for dealer and bulk order prices)

"BUILDING YOUR ARK"

Building Your Ark, 250+ pages, including the *Action Checklist,* is available at dealer prices as follows:

# of Copies	Discount	Cost
1- 5	Retail	$29.97
6-11	10%	$26.97
12-24	15%	$25.47
25-49	25%	$22.47
50-99	30%	$20.97
100+	40%	$17.97

Shipping via UPS ground unless otherwise specified. Books weigh approx. 1 lb. each. For more info. call DAL Enterprises: 888-240-9074